Shakespeare in Performance

General Editors: J. R. MULRYNE
and J. C. BULMAN
Associate Editor: Margaret Shewring

King Lear

Published in our
centenary year
~ **2004** ~
MANCHESTER
UNIVERSITY
PRESS

Already published in the series

Of related interest

Kate Chedgzoy *Shakespeare's queer children:
sexual politics and contemporary culture*

Jonathan Dollimore and Alan Sinfield, eds *Political Shakespeare:
new essays in cultural materialism, 2nd edn*

Alison Findlay *Illegitimate power: bastards in Renaissance drama*

John J. Joughin *Shakespeare and national culture*

Michele Marrapodi, A. J. Hoenselaars, Marcello Cappuzzo
and L. Falzon Santucci, eds *Shakespeare's Italy*

Ann Thompson and Sasha Roberts *Women reading Shakespeare
1660–1900: an anthology*

King Lear

Second edition

ALEXANDER LEGGATT

Manchester
University Press

Manchester and New York

Distributed exclusively in the USA by Palgrave

First edition published 1991 by Manchester University Press

This edition published 2004 by
Manchester University Press
Oxford Road, Manchester M13 9NR, UK
and Room 400, 175 Fifth Avenue,
New York, NY 10010, USA
www.manchesteruniversitypress.co.uk

Distributed exclusively in the USA by
Palgrave, 175 Fifth Avenue,
New York, NY 10010, USA

Distributed exclusively in Canada by
UBC Press, University of British Columbia,
2029 West Mall, Vancouver, BC
Canada V6T 1Z2

British Library Cataloguing-in-Publication Data
A catalogue record for this book is available
from the British Library

Library of Congress Cataloging-in-Publication Data
applied for

ISBN 0 7190 6224 1 *hardback*
EAN 978 0 7190 6224 7
ISBN 0 7190 6225 X *paperback*
EAN 978 0 7190 6225 4

This edition first published 2004

13 12 11 10 09 08 07 06 05 04   10 9 8 7 6 5 4 3 2 1

Typeset in New Aster
by Koinonia, Manchester
Printed in Great Britain
Biddles Limited, King's Lynn

CONTENTS

LIST OF ILLUSTRATIONS

Every effort has been made to obtain permission to reproduce
copyright material in this book. If any proper acknowledgement has
not been made, copyright-holders are invited to contact the
publisher.

SERIES EDITORS' PREFACE

Recently, the study of Shakespeare's plays as scripts for performance in the theatre has grown to rival the reading of Shakespeare as literature among university, college, and secondary-school teachers and their students. The aim of the present series is to assist this study by describing how certain of Shakespeare's texts have been realized in production.

The series is not concerned to provide theatre history in the traditional sense. Rather, it employs the more contemporary discourses of performance criticism to explore how a multitude of factors work together to determine how a play achieves meaning for a particular audience. Each contributor to the series has selected a number of productions of a given play and analysed them comparatively. These productions – drawn from different periods, countries and media – were chosen not only because they are culturally significant in their own right but also because they represent something of the range and variety of the possible interpretations of the play in hand. They illustrate how the convergence of various material conditions helps to shape a performance: the medium for which the text is adapted; stage-design and theatrical tradition; the acting company itself; the body and abilities of the individual actor; and the historical, political, and social contexts which condition audience reception of the play.

We hope that theatregoers, by reading these accounts of Shakespeare in performance, may enlarge their understanding of what a play-text is and begin, too, to appreciate the complex ways in which performance is a collaborative effort. Any study of a Shakespeare text will, of course, reveal only a small proportion of the play's potential meaning; but by engaging issues of how a text is translated in performance, our series encourages a kind of reading that is receptive to the contingencies that make theatre a living art.

J. R. Mulryne and J. C. Bulman, General Editors
Margaret Shewring, Associate Editor

PREFATORY NOTE

I am grateful, first of all, to the General Editors for inviting me to undertake this project, and for their advice and encouragement throughout. My thanks also to the Shakespeare Centre Library, Stratford-upon-Avon, and its staff, and to the Stratford Festival Archive at Stratford, Ontario, and its archivists Dan Ladell and Lisa Brant for letting me use their collection; to the University of Toronto for financial support; to the Media Committee of the Department of English for making possible a screening of the Kozintsev *King Lear*; and to Richard Paul Knowles for sharing his expertise on the work of Robin Phillips. Henry Auster, William Blissett, Martha Kurtz, Jill Levenson, G. B. Shand and J. A. B. Somerset provided help and encouragement of various kinds. The students of ENG 220Y and ENG 2650Y allowed me to use them as a sample audience, and responded beyond the call of duty. In the writing of the first edition, my wife Anna and my daughters Judith and Helen helped me join the ranks of the computer semi-literate. My wife Anna and Andrew Osyany provided further technical help on the second edition. My thanks to them all; and to the Folger Shakespeare Library for permission to quote from Hallam Fordham's 'Player in Action' and the Shakespeare Centre Library for permission to quote from promptbooks in their collection.

A.L.

For
Alan and Felicity Somerset

CHAPTER I

Problems and choices

Lear must leave this first scene as he entered it, more a magnificent portent than a man.

No, Lear is easy. He's like all of us, really: he's just a stupid old fart.

These statements are both by theatre professionals whose work on *King Lear* will figure in later chapters. The first is Harley Granville-Barker, in his Preface to the play (Granville-Barker, p. 285); the second is Laurence Olivier, in his book *On Acting* (Olivier, p. 137). In their radical opposition they establish the basic problems and choices that have shaped *King Lear* in performance. Granville-Barker gives us the titanic Lear, the almost impossible challenge for the actor, a carryover from the Romantic view of the play as having a scale and grandeur impossible for the theatre to compass. Granville-Barker insisted that the theatre could compass it, and demonstrated his point in practice, though as we shall see he sometimes resorted to trickery to make Lear a titanic figure. Reviewing John Gielgud's 1931 attempt at the part, James Agate specified 'The actor ... should present Lear to the eye as though he were one of Blake's ruined giants' (Agate, pp. 194–5). Even in Restoration and eighteenth-century performances, using Nahum Tate's drastic re-writing of the play – which turned it towards moralizing sentiment, introducing a happy ending and a love story for Edgar and Cordelia – the tradition established by Betterton and others was to play Lear as 'a character of tremendous vitality and power' (Carlisle, p. 295). This tradition resurfaced in the twentieth century with Donald Wolfit's grand but erratic performance in his own touring production, and continued with (for example) Michael Gambon at Stratford-upon-Avon in 1982 (discussed in Chapter V) and Christopher Plummer at Stratford, Ontario in 2002.

It was David Garrick, a short actor whose gift was not for massive passion but for lightning changes of mood, who made

Lear a feeble old man, moving the audience to pity his distress. Actors who look as though Blake could have drawn them are in short supply, and while critics have continued to talk of the ruined titan actors have more often than not played Lear on a human scale – in Olivier's phrase, 'like all of us, really'. It is natural that this should be so; the theatre is the most immediately human of the arts: its essential medium is the actor, its fundamental dynamic the relation between actor and audience. Hazlitt's insistence that Lear's curse on Goneril 'should not be *scolded*, but recited as a Hymn to the Penates' (*London Magazine*, June 1820) is typical of the Romantic view which by insisting on the grand scale draws us away from the human reality of the scene; and, however much stylization it may use, human reality is what the theatre finally deals in. Even in the Romantic period, the German actor Ludwig Max Devrient went for frailty and pathos rather than grandeur; he made his first entrance leaning on a crutch (Rosenberg, p. 25). Henry Irving, the leading English actor of the late Victorian period, stressed the pathos of senility. His first entrance was a barbaric spectacle, but 'He used his sword as a walking-stick, plucked at his beard and toyed with his hair' (Hughes, p. 53). His running exit, 'without a shred of dignity, ... a scared, eccentric, lunatic shamble' (Rosenberg, p. 281) was perhaps his greatest moment. Reviewing the first major London production of the twentieth century, A. B. Walkley praised Norman McKinnell for aiming at 'nothing colossal, nothing Michelangelesque'; playing a weak, child-like Lear, he was 'content to feel the part, and thus to make the audience to feel it in their turn' (*The Times*, 4 September 1909).

And yet the human scale entails its risks. Laurence Olivier, an actor who could scale the heights – and, according to some reviewers, did so in the later scenes – began his 1946 Lear at the Old Vic by entering from the side, sharing a whispered private joke with Cordelia, pausing for a quick inspection of one of his soldiers, and generally working against the imposing impression of his physical appearance by establishing Lear as fussy, whimsical and unpredictable. In his extended review of the performance G. Wilson Knight complained that this 'wilful, almost naughty old man' could not 'grow into the Lear of the Storm scenes; the stuff is not there' (Knight, pp. 190–1). Even the first scene loses something if the scale is too small. Lear not only asks his daughters how much they love him; he carves up a map of his kingdom – a map which, unlike that used by the rebels to divide the England of *Henry IV Part 1*, has no particular geography and therefore seems a grand abstraction, so that 'Lear marking the map with his finger might be marking the land itself, so Olympian should he appear' (Granville-Barker, p. 284.) Lear, in short, is both father and king. In their attempts to make him more accessible, actors have frequently preferred to stress the father. The *Aberdeen Free Press* reported of Henry Irving, 'It is a father's agony, rather than a king's humiliation, which we see' (Hughes, p. 158). At Stratford-upon-Avon in 1959, Charles Laughton presented 'A bulky, genial, rosy-cheeked, hale and hearty old man ... the very picture of the complacent paterfamilias' (Byrne, p. 190). This is from a sympathetic review; but while the performance moved some to tears with its humanity, it also drew boos – very much against Stratford tradition – from part of the audience on opening night. It was 'Mr Macready's representation of the father at the end' that moved Charles Dickens to call his performance 'the only perfect picture that we have had of Lear since the age of Betterton' (Salgādo 1975, pp. 286–7). But Henry Morley, a few years later, was to complain that Samuel Phelps was too weak and infirm, too merely pathetic, so that 'The king is utterly lost in the father' (Salgādo 1975, p. 292.) The domestic scale may come naturally and draw the readiest response from the audience, but *King Lear* is not just a family drama.

I have suggested that the lack of detail on Lear's map creates a sense of abstraction, of universality; this has often been noted in the characterization of the play. Objecting to Peter Brook's attempt to motivate the evil of Goneril and Regan by having Lear and his knights behave badly, Maynard Mack calls the sisters 'paradigms of evil rather than (or as well as) exasperated spoiled children' (Mack, p. 32). The reservation, we may think, comes just in time; actors are always highly individual presences (this can be true even of actors in masks) and Mack, who refers elsewhere to the play's 'archetypal characters', in calling for walking paradigms is calling for something theatrically bloodless. Goneril and Regan, as we shall see, have often been sharply individualized in performance. And yet his sense that there is something universal and archetypal in the drama is part of the common response to *King Lear*, and surely a legitimate one: in its radical opposition of good and evil characters, in the extremity of its action, *King Lear* is as close to the methods of the morality play as anything in

Shakespeare. How can this be translated into the language of theatre? Esther Merle Jackson has suggested that the play has worked better in the non-English-speaking world, given the European tradition of expressionism, 'a plastic theater-symbol, an ambiguous structural image composed of word, gesture, song, dance, light, color, shape, design, and suggestion' (Jackson, p. 31). Robert Speaight wrote of Theodore Komisarjevsky's 1927 production at Oxford: 'he gave us the true cosmic *Lear*. A bare geometric set of steps and levels – but as satisfying to the eye as a Cubist or Vorticist drawing – suggested the world of the play. No detail pointed you to time or place' (Speaight 1962, p. 51). Even within an abstract set, however, there will be particular actors. By an essential paradox of theatre, they can use the particular to establish the universal. *The Times* called Charles Laughton's Lear 'the representative of the common man' (*The Times*, 19 August 1959), and Harold Hobson summarized the impact the performance made on him: 'That the universe should single out so small a figure for its wrath gives a lurid splendour to the performance: it is as if an ordinary man were called to crucifixion' (*Sunday Times*, 23 August 1959). No one would think of Charles Laughton as an abstraction; he was one of the most strikingly individual actors of the twentieth century, and his performance appears to have been not just individual but in many respects eccentric. Yet what Hobson describes is an impression as universal, as cosmic as the Komisarjevsky set. The play worked at this level for him not because Laughton was abstract but because he was recognizable. For others, the individuality was a problem, killing the full effect of the tragedy: to David Wainwright, Laughton, 'tubby in a long white nightgown', looked like 'a benevolent Druid plodding up Primrose Hill on Midsummer morning' (*Manchester Evening Chronicle*, 19 August 1959). Not exactly representative humanity.

The mixed reaction to Laughton shows it is not just the artist's work that creates the sense of universality; it is also the viewer's response. Critics frequently register their displeasure with a production by declaring that they did not see themselves reflected in it. Complaining of what he saw as the Marxist slanting of Kozintsev's film, Stanley Kaufmann concludes, '*Lear* is not an anti-aristocratic play about the troubles of, and caused by, a remote breed of beings called kings. If *Lear* isn't about me, it's not about anything' (*New Republic*, 6 September 1975). Jay Carr's objection to Peter Ustinov's performance is strikingly similar: 'I felt this "Lear" was only about the Lear on stage and not about me, and I can't think of it as having enough reach' (*Detroit News*, 9 October 1979). The recurrence of this complaint reflects not just the egocentricity of reviewers but an expectation that tragedy – this tragedy in particular – ought to be somehow representative. As Clifford Leech puts it: 'We dare not equate ourselves with Lear ... But his death has been an emblem of our deaths, his madness of the frenzy that we too, from time to time, know, his rejection of Cordelia of the rejections that we have made' (Leech, pp. 50–1).

This recognition, if it comes, will depend not on the production alone or the audience alone but on whether the individuality of each manages to interlock with the other. And each will be individual, particular. The abstraction of Komisarjevsky, which Speaight describes as timeless, now seems to belong very much to a particular phase of modern design; if we saw it now it would look dated. We shall return to the audience, here and in later chapters. In the final chapter, on Kurosawa's *Ran*, we shall also see that *King Lear* can be transported even into a non-Western culture, not just because of its universality but because the particulars of its story interact with the particulars of the culture that receives it. Individuality, again, is the key. Our present concern is with the choices that create the individuality of particular productions in the English-speaking world. One of these is the period in which the play is set. From a contemporary drawing of the first scene of *Titus Andronicus*, which shows a mixture of Elizabethan costumes and classical dress, with Tamora in a flowing robe that could belong to any period, we may infer that in Shakespeare's theatre the costuming of *King Lear* would have been eclectic, suggestions of an earlier period blending with frankly Jacobean dress. In *Julius Caesar* the conspirators wear hats; Cleopatra has a dress with laces. In our time productions have experimented with eclectic costuming: Julie Taymor's film *Titus* (1999) is a good example, mixing modern and Roman conventions as, the surviving drawing indicates, Shakespeare's theatre did with the original play. Yet when this happens now it is a conscious artistic decision, specific to a particular production. It is not (or not yet) an agreed convention followed unselfconsciously, and this means we cannot quite reproduce the effect it had in Shakespeare's time. Nor can we reproduce the neutrality of the Globe Theatre stage. Our knowledge of the visual taste of the time suggests that it was not a bare stage in the sense of being austere and undecorated, though we can only speculate about the nature and extent of the decoration; but it was neutral in that it was the same stage not only for every scene but for every production, occasionally augmented by scenic elements (a bed, a tree, a throne) but making no statement in itself. In our time every production has its own distinctive set, which the audience sees as soon as it enters the theatre, and which is therefore the first statement the production makes. There was no such moment of decision in Shakespeare's theatre.

In matters of costume and setting we have no prevailing convention we can take for granted; every production must make a choice. What guidance does the text offer? Shakespeare has in one sense been stricter than he usually is about period, creating a remote, pre-Christian world with no obvious anachronisms – unlike *The Winter's Tale*, which combines references to the Delphic Oracle and Whitsun pastorals, or *Hamlet*, in which the Danes have recently invaded Britain and boy actors have driven adult companies on to the road. And yet, primitive and close to nature though the world of *Lear* is, there is a sophisticated Renaissance feeling in its evocation of the social covering that hides the naked animal. Granville-Barker, having called in his Preface for costumes of 'a splendid barbaric temper' (Granville-Barker, p. 327), set his own production in the Renaissance. For Peter Brook, 'all periods are inappropriate', the Renaissance particularly so (Berry, p. 125). Yet timelessness, when it becomes a license for the designer to invent a fantastic world of his own, can be distracting in its own way: this appears to have happened in Komisarjevsky's 1936 Stratford-upon-Avon production, and in the elaborately symbolic designs of Isamu Noguchi for John Gielgud's 1955 performance. In both cases what was designed to free the play tied it down (Jackson, pp. 35–7).

A precise historical period at least makes the characters more recognizable, or so we might think. Charles Kean, a nineteenth-century pioneer of historically 'accurate' productions, was firm about his period: 800 AD. Henry Irving created a society of barbaric Britons camping out in the ruins left by the Roman occupation. The knights were long-haired Vikings and the king entered to a 'wild march'; but the general effect was of worn, decayed grandeur. In 1838 Macready created a more generalized, picturesquely remote world: 'The castles are heavy, sombre, solid; their halls adorned with trophies of the chase and instruments of war; druid circles rise in spectral loneliness out of the heath' (O'Dell, II, 210). Scenic elaboration of this sort belongs to the nineteenth century, and later reviewers become testy if they are distracted in this way: there were complaints about the distant panorama of red roofs in the 1946 Old Vic production, which seemed to belong to dolls' houses and created a fairy-tale atmosphere. Robert Speaight called it 'too clever by half' (Speaight 1962, p. 52). The long waits for shifting scenes, which the nineteenth century took for granted, were by 1946 no longer acceptable (Williamson, p. 194). Moreover, the primitive setting, though on the surface the most logical one for the play, creates its own problems. As Maynard Mack points out, it distances the play's cruelties 'as the errors of a barbarous age with no compelling relation to oneself' (Mack, p. 24). William Poel complained that the Dark Age costumes in the productions of his time blurred social roles: 'In vain do we seek among these sexless creatures for our familiar characters, to know who is who' (Poel, p. 180). The later and more familiar the period, the more closely social roles can be defined; the Fool and Oswald, in particular, belong in the Renaissance. Yet Peter Brook is not just being literal-minded when he objects to post-Norman-conquest settings: 'ninety per cent of our audiences know that sandwiched between Henry VI and somebody else there didn't happen to be a King Lear' (Brook 1987, p. 88). Behind this superficial objection there are deeper ones: in a late setting the play's religion, with its persistent references to the gods, not God, seems strange. When Garrick in his final run of the play exchanged contemporary costumes for 'Old English' dress, his audience approved (Burnim, p. 151), evidently finding the play made better sense in an older setting. In the chapters that follow we shall see a variety of choices being made, and we shall see that every choice involves both loss and definition.

Among the play's staging problems the most notorious is the storm. In his prologue to *Every Man in his Humour* Ben Jonson pours a neoclassicist's scorn on the simple methods that were evidently used in Shakespeare's theatre; his list of promises about what his audience will not be subjected to includes

> nor roll'd bullet heard
> To say, it thunders, nor tempestuous drum
> Rumbles, to tell you when the storm doth come ...

The nineteenth century, the great age of scenic elaboration, had the resources for a full-scale storm; but reviewers of Charles Kean's production complained that the shifting lights, rustling leaves (the threads that operated them were unfortunately visible) and general hubbub were a distraction that drowned out the efforts of the actors. *The Times* concluded, 'He should have recollected that it is the bending of Lear's mind under his wrongs that is the object of interest, and not that of a forest beneath the hurricane. The machinery may be transferred to the next new pantomime' (O'Dell, II, 165; see also Bratton, p. 28). The dangers of a 'realistic' storm whose fakery will at some point be obvious, and whose principal effect will be to drown out the actors, are plain enough. Yet in toning down the storm to something he could cope with Macready incurred the criticism that the effect was tame, and the grandeur of the scene was replaced by mere distress (Bratton, p. 135). The responsibility for the scene's effect is shared by the technicians and the leading actor. John Gielgud wrote of his 1931 performance, 'I was wholly inadequate in the storm scenes, having neither the voice nor the physique for them. Lear has to *be* the storm, but I could do no more than shout against the thundersheet' (Gielgud 1953, pp. 157–8). Gielgud's view that Lear himself has to be the storm has been widely echoed; but it is a rare production that puts all the weight on the actor. This was tried in Glen Byam Shaw's 1959 production with Charles Laughton: there were visual effects of rain and cloud, but (accounts vary, and there seem to have been changes during the run) either no sound at all, or only minimal thunder and 'a distant hiss of rain' (*Daily Mail*, 19 August 1959). The experiment, like everything else about the production, divided the house; some appreciated the chance to listen to the speeches, others found the impact of the scene diminished. Peter Brook put his finger on the problem: 'there is a conflict. An actor can't make the energy and the dynamics of the storm scene any more than you can make a sculpture on water. It's like shadow-boxing. So there has to be an element that says "storm"' (Labeille, p. 224). The dialogue between Lear and the storm needs to be just that – a dialogue; not a competition in decibel levels. The answer finally lies not in the technology, which can be anything from a beaten drum to a Moog synthesizer, but in the intelligence with which the technology is used.

If the storm is the obvious problem of the play, there are other peculiarities that have to be coped with, that demand choices. The battle is the most perfunctory in Shakespeare. It is represented only by offstage sound, and the fact that Gloucester is on stage throughout implies that Shakespeare wanted the sound-battle to be brief. Kurosawa's *Ran*, as we shall see, goes to the opposite extreme: most of the film's vision of chaos is conveyed by images of war. In our war-obsessed age there is always a temptation to do more with the battle than Shakespeare asks for; it is for us an inevitable image of cruelty and violence. In the Byam Shaw production, generally praised for its visual simplicity, primitive war-machines were dragged on stage and fired arrows into the wings. More recently, directors have gone in the direction of stylization: in Trevor Nunn's 1968 Royal Shakespeare Company production the battle was a slow-motion ballet freezing occasionally into tableaux, with Gloucester sitting in front, his head thrown back in a silent scream (Bratton, p. 197). Like the storm, the battle is a test of how far, and to what purpose, a production is prepared to elaborate on the text.

In the text itself the most appalling image of violence is not the battle but the blinding of Gloucester. Here the test is different: what will the production expect an audience to take? Recently, audiences have been made to face the full horror of it. But throughout the eighteenth and nineteenth centuries the scene was partially or entirely cut (Bratton, p. 157). When it was restored in the twentieth century, audiences found it hard to take. Hallam Fordham reported of the scene in Granville Barker's 1940 production, 'the effect was sufficient to cause some (and especially men!) to grope towards the exits with unbecoming haste' (Fordham, III.7). In 1950 at Stratford-upon-Avon 'a few people had to be taken to the first aid department' (*Western Daily Press*, 21 July 1950). At the Old Vic between the wars, Lilian Baylis insisted that the blinding of Gloucester should come immediately after the interval, so that audience members who weren't up to it could wait it out in the lobby (Trewin 1971, p. 128). This custom was observed in the Gielgud productions of 1940 and 1950. Byam Shaw in 1959 and Peter Brook in 1962 shifted the interval to just after the blinding of Gloucester, thus making the atrocity the climactic event of the production's first act. This decision about the interval, no less than the return of the full text, shows a change from a theatre that was prepared to spare its audience the more painful aspects of the play to a theatre that insisted on them – and a corresponding shift in the reading of the play itself.

Horror and revulsion are now seen, as they were not in earlier ages, as legitimate responses to draw from the audience. Care still needs to be taken to ensure that the horror is moral, not just physical, and we shall see how different directors have managed that. But throughout the production history of *King Lear* the main test has been, surprisingly, whether the audience can be made to cry. Tyrone Guthrie once wrote, 'The performance of a tragedy must aim higher than at an audience's susceptibility to pathos. An audience will cry readily; the death of Little Willie or a pretty girl singing the sorriest rubbish will melt to tender tears the hardest-bitten men and the hardest biting women. The emotion aroused by even a half-decent performance of a great tragedy cannot be measured in terms of chewed hankies and misted specs' (Davies *et al.*, p. 137). The force of this seems obvious; yet in reading newspaper reviews of *King Lear* from the 1950s and early 1960s in particular I was struck by the number of times journalists (not on the whole a sentimental lot) measured the success of a production by whether or not it made them cry. The 1959 production at Stratford (Laughton) was praised for drawing tears, the 1962 production (Peter Brook) condemned for failing – indeed, refusing– to do so. Several of my own students, jotting down their reactions to a screening of the Kozintsev film, applied the same test. Shortly after Olivier's death, some of my colleagues paid tribute by recalling how his television production had moved them to tears. By this test, David Garrick must have been the supreme Lear. Some audience members reported they took literally days to recover from the emotions he roused in them; when he was at his height, even the actresses playing Goneril and Regan broke down and sobbed (Burnim, pp. 141–2, 151; O'Dell, I, 454). According to George Winchester Stone, Jr, 'Garrick saw in *King Lear* a Shakespearean play which could surpass competition from all writers of pathetic tragedy and could command the emotional pleasure of tears more successfully than sentimental comedy' (Stone, p. 91). The key probably lies in Stone's reference to the pleasure of tears, which applies beyond the age of sentiment in which Garrick played. Tears, like laughter, are a release, a way of coping with pain by letting it out. Faced with an experience like that of *King Lear* (even in the modified Tate version that Garrick used) some audiences seem to need that relief, and to become resentful if it is denied them.

Tate of course went further in compensating for the play's

horror by producing a happy ending in which Cordelia survives to marry Edgar and Lear goes off to a comfortable retirement with Kent and Gloucester. Tate made *King Lear* acceptable by the simple expedient of writing a new play, and his version served the theatre for generations. What kind of affirmation can be found in Shakespeare's play is an essential debating point in criticism, and productions have reflected different sides of the debate. One crucial question is what Lear sees on Cordelia's lips as he dies. Gielgud followed Bradley's speculation that he sees returning life and dies in unbearable joy; Morris Carnovsky saw only death, and died in shock and horror (Rosenberg, p. 319). Cutting can slant a production one way or another. Peter Brook was accused of unfairly darkening the play by cutting the servants who comfort the blinded Gloucester and Edmund's attempt to reprieve Cordelia. Gloucester's 'As flies to wanton boys are we to the gods, / They kill us for their sport' was cut by Macready, Irving and Charles Kean, presumably to remove the despair as Brook had removed the comfort (Bratton, p. 161). Shakespeare's company ended their production with a dead march and the bodies carried off. Later productions, ending with a dropped curtain or a blackout, make some final statement, often in a visual tableau, that sums up their view of the play. Sometimes it is a formal gesture, which by its sheer formality implies order and completeness, working against the play's vision of chaos: Irving's soldiers lowered their spears and bowed their heads around the dead king; Komisarjevsky in his 1936 production ended as he began, with a row of upraised trumpets (Sprague 1944, p. 297; Bratton, p. 213). Affirmative readings have depended on the view that Lear can be seen as educated, even redeemed, by the end. Since the text shows both his capacity for new insight and his stubborn resistance to it, it leaves the actor with important choices, moment by moment, as to whether Lear develops or resists.

Here we return to the individuality of the performer, the personality he brings to the role and the choices he makes. The range of Lears, as we have seen, goes from frail to titanic. The possibilities for other characters are not so varied – with the exception of the Fool. Of the secondary characters he is the one to whom we shall return most often, since he has left the strongest and most varied impression in the production records. Tate cut him altogether. Macready restored him, but thinking of him as a 'fragile, hectic, beautiful-faced, half-idiot-looking boy' had him played by a woman (O'Dell, II, 195). Phelps returned him to his true sex. Yet the tradition of fragility persisted in the early years of the twentieth century: the Fool to Gielgud's 1931 Lear was Leslie French, 'a most delicate actor ... and very touchingly he handled it' (Speaight 1962, p. 49). Alec Guinness's Fool, with Olivier in 1946, was 'wry, quiet, and with a dog's devotion' (Trewin 1964, p. 203). But the Fool can have a harder edge than this. As befits an Elizabethan clown, he can be disruptive, chaotic, obscene; and the history of the part in our time has been a turning away from pathos and a recovery of comedy – whether the pointed intellectual wit of Alec McCowen (1962) or the inventive anarchy of Antony Sher (1982). Like the return of the blinding of Gloucester, the hardening of the Fool has been part of a general toughening of the play in recent productions.

If the Fool leaves strong, concrete impressions in the record, Cordelia – so essential to the play – has a disconcerting tendency to disappear. (There is a notable exception, to be considered in Chapter X.) For the most part the Cordelias who stick in memory are the bad ones: strident, weepy, or artificial. Is this because the key to the part is simplicity, and simplicity leaves fewer traces in the memory? Reviewers disagree about the Cordelias they have seen, more often and more radically than can be accounted for by the sort of natural disagreement one takes for granted. Jessica Tandy, John Gielgud's Cordelia in 1940, was variously described as 'ineffectual – empty' (*New Statesman and Nation*, 20 April 1940) and possessed of 'a delicate and wistful grace' (Williamson, p. 137). As Lady Bracknell would say, it is obviously the same person: elusive, hard to pin down, leading different viewers to disagree about what – if anything – they have seen. Goneril and Regan give actresses, and reviewers, much more to chew on. The principal choice here is whether they are Maynard Mack's paradigms of evil or recognizable human beings with a viewpoint of their own. Peter Brook's decision to show Lear and his knights as boisterous, impossible house guests allowed us to see them as Goneril does, and to realize that she had a case. This was praised as a stunning new insight and damned as a distortion of the text. Yet there were many precedents for it. The essence of Brook's interpretation can be found in Granville-Barker's Preface (Granville-Barker, p. 286). Irving and his knights were also an unruly lot, the difference being that the shrewishness of his Goneril drew away any sympathy the audience might have felt for her housekeeping problems (Hughes, pp. 54–5). Charles Kean's knights looked at each other 'with intense surprise' on being told they were a disordered rabble, yet gave some credence to Goneril's complaints when they protested against her by striking their spears on the stage (Sprague 1944, p. 284). Lear calls his knights men of choice and rarest parts, Goneril calls them disordered, neither is a reliable witness, and the production must decide. This decision will help tilt the balance on the question of whether the evil of Goneril and Regan is arbitrary and therefore monstrous, or springs from a recognizable grievance. We are back to the tension between abstraction and humanity that affects virtually all interpretations of this play.

In the chapters that follow, the focus will be mostly on the main plot of Lear and his daughters, with little discussion of the Gloucester subplot as a separate entity. This is partly for reasons of space, but it is also worth noting that the Gloucester story does not seem quite so separate in the theatre as criticism can make it sound. Apart from I.ii, where Edmund begins the plot against his father and brother, the sequence in act IV in which Edgar leads his blind father, and the final duel between the brothers, the principal figures of the subplot are kept mostly separate from each other, and in some of their most important scenes they are involved with the Lear plot: Edgar's impersonation of Tom in the storm sequence, Gloucester's blinding and his later role as Lear's interlocutor; Edmund's growing relationship with Goneril and Regan. Yet the Gloucester subplot raises the same questions as the main plot, questions of domesticity versus universality, of a clear-cut division of good and evil versus a more open judgement.

It seems at first glance more fully committed to the domestic scale than the Lear story, and in certain ways the production history bears this out. There is a persistent tradition that Gloucester dons spectacles to read the forged letter, though in a production that has committed itself to a primitive setting this detail looks odd. The blinding of Gloucester, as we shall see, gains in horror from the use of ordinary domestic implements (a long pin, a spoon, a letter-opener) and its use of an ordinary setting (a study, a room with a hearth). The least effective staging of this scene I remember had Cornwall, in a kinky leather outfit, open a chest full of instruments of torture. The point to make is that the props needed for this scene can be found in the average kitchen; the membrane that separates ordinary life from horror is that thin. Yet in its own way the Gloucester story, domestic though it may be, contributes to the play's universality, simply by the number of parallels it sets up to the story of Lear, parallels emphasized by Gloucester's speech on the eclipses in I.ii. The Gloucester plot also contains some of the play's most striking challenges to realism. Edgar's multiple disguises, which produce so much head-scratching in criticism, are less problematic than one might expect in the theatre, perhaps because the impulse to role-playing finds a natural home there. Gloucester's attempt to leap off Dover Cliff has sometimes caused greater difficulties, depending on the idiom of the production. Nahum Tate, following the dictates of reasonableness and decorum prevalent in his own time, simply cut it. Grigori Kozintsev, filming the play in a largely realistic idiom, did the same. Yet in a more stylized production, such as the stage and screen versions directed by Peter Brook, it too has seemed natural.

To challenge the play's moral divisions by getting sympathy for Goneril and Regan requires, as we have seen, a special effort of interpretation. It takes less effort for Edmund to win the audience's sympathy: the character as written has wit, energy and magnetism, and actors have exploited these qualities. There is a danger of going too far and making him a lightweight rogue: John Gielgud told Robert Speaight, who played Edmund in the 1931 Old Vic production, that he had made 'a reasonably good shot at Joseph Surface' (Speaight 1962, p. 49). Edmund also has a chance to bring out the sexuality of Goneril and Regan, letting them show themselves 'vamps as well as vampires' (Venezky, p. 76), though whether this adds to their humanity or makes them more grotesque involves another set of choices. The duel between the brothers, like the battle, can be simple or elaborate. It can also be a chance for the director to make a final distinction between the characters, as in Kozintsev's film, where their fighting styles are significantly different; or to refuse such a distinction, as Peter Brook did in his stage and screen versions, where the two armoured figures were identical. Richard David, commenting on the eclecticism of the 1976 Royal Shakespeare Company production, reported that 'Edmund and Edgar, for their first brotherly colloquy, lounged in basket-chairs like two undergraduates in an early Forster novel, but for their final duel, a rough, scuffling affair with the duellists at opposite ends of a rope held in their free hands, they could have been Norman and Saxon' (David, p. 96). The Gloucester plot, in short, is not necessarily a chance for the production to relax into a more domestic manner. Like the Lear plot, it offers a wide range of choices and challenges.

It is striking how often the business of interpreting *King Lear* has been compared to mountain-climbing. J. C. Trewin complained that Norman McKinnell 'stayed in the foothills of the part, refusing nearly every call to climb' (Trewin 1964, p. 46). James Agate, reviewing Donald Wolfit, noted, 'Mountaineers who attempt Everest are assessed not by that which they achieve but by the amount by which they fail' (Agate, p. 204). This discouraging thought was echoed and elaborated by Peter Brook as he prepared his own production in 1962: 'Brook spoke of the play as a mountain whose summit had never been reached. On the way up one found the scattered bodies of other climbers strewn on every side. "Olivier here, Laughton there; it's frightening"' (Marowitz, p. 22). Yet this metaphor, though it speaks eloquently of the play's challenges, misleads us by presenting it as a fixed, solid entity, massive and inhuman. *King Lear* has never been fixed. The prevailing view of the text in our time is that the Quarto and Folio versions represent not damaged versions of a lost, perfect original but different stages in the play's development, though how much of the Folio revision is Shakespeare's work is a matter of debate. The text continues to change in different productions, and the play as a whole presents different faces to different times. M. St. Clare Byrne described Laughton's 1959 performance as 'a Lear for our time and of our time' (Byrne, p. 190). A scant three years later, in the same theatre, all the assumptions behind that production – scenic, psychological, emotional – were blown away by Peter Brook's version, which quickly became a *Lear* for *its* time. The play has an unusual capacity to touch contemporary nerves directly. It was withdrawn from the stage during George III's derangement, and the BBC cancelled a radio production during the crisis brought on by the abdication of Edward VIII. With Queen Victoria in his audience, Macready pointed Lear's speech about royal indifference to 'poor naked wretches' directly at her, much to her discomfort (Bratton, p. 143). In ways less local and specific than this, *King Lear* has always held up a mirror to its time, and has changed as the times have changed. It is what we make it. This is true, to one degree or another, of all of Shakespeare's plays; but it seems particularly true of *Lear*, which can make newspaper reviewers insist it is about them, and one of the most extraordinary actors in English history declare, 'He's like all of us, really'.

As the play changes, so the productions vanish. Reviewers disagree; promptbooks are silent on the things we most want to know; archive videotapes show tiny figures moving in a badly lit space with nothing like the effect of a live performance; production photos show posed shots and give close-ups of makeup that was never designed for a camera. Memory cheats: I have seen all the productions described in the following chapters except those involving Gielgud, and in researching this book I have been astonished by how often my memory is at odds with the evidence – much of which depends on other people's memories. The film and television versions are more fixed, but only in that the sounds and images do not change. (Even when a film exists in different cuts, each cut is fixed within itself.) What changes, continually, is the impression they make not only on different viewers but also on subsequent encounters by the same viewer. In the chapters that follow, I hope *King Lear* will emerge not as a forbidding mountain that has to be scaled but as a living organism whose vitality lies in its capacity for constant growth and change. The final chapter will show that vitality operating in an independent work by another artist in a culture far removed from Shakespeare's own.

1 Opening scene of Peter Brook's 1962 production

2 Peter Ustinov as Lear in the opening scene of
the 1979 Stratford Ontario production

3 Michael Gambon as Lear and Anthony Sher as the Fool from
Adrian Noble's 1982 RSC production, Act III, scene ii

facing 4 Yuri Yarvet as Lear and Valentina Shendrikova as Cordelia
in Grigori Kozintsev's *King Lear* (1970)

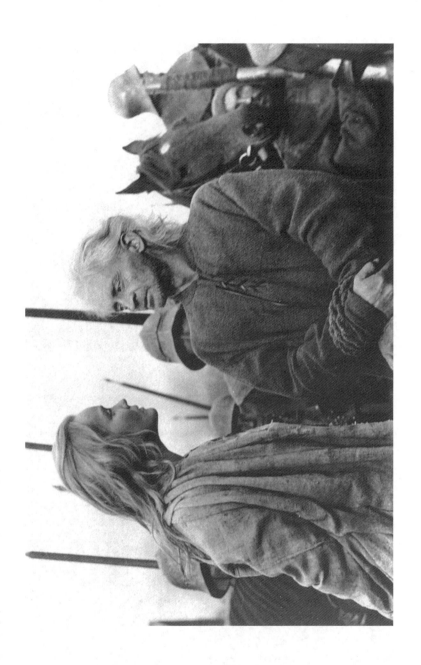

[20]

facing 5 John Gielgud as Lear and Jessica Tandy as Cordelia in the
1940 Old Vic production
6 Lear (Paul Scofield), and his people, in Peter Brook's 1971 film

7 Michael Hordern as Lear in the 1982 BBC Shakespeare Series
production

8 Laurence Olivier as Lear and Anna Calder-Marshall as Cordelia in the 1983 Granada Television production

9 Ian Holm as Lear and Victoria Hamilton as Cordelia in the 1998 BBC Television production

10 Peter as Kyoami and Tatsuya Nakadi as Hidetora
in Akira Kurosawa's *Ran* (1985)

11 Jiro (Jinpachi Nezu) and his troops in Akira Kurosawa's
Ran (1985)

CHAPTER II

John Gielgud and Harley Granville Barker

When John Gielgud first played Lear at the Old Vic in 1931 he was twenty-six. The production photos show a figure in long mediaeval robes, his dramatically flowing hair only emphasizing the slimness of the young actor beneath. James Agate complained that Lear seemed to get younger as the evening wore on and the actor's pretence of age faded: 'the pathos of [the] death-scene had less to do with Lear than with a talented young actor's comments upon an old man's passing' (Agate, p. 196). Yet there were powerful moments. Many years later Harcourt Williams, who directed the production, was to recall Lear's first entrance, 'stepping majestically down a steep slope between a forest of tall, scarlet spears ... and that odd twist to the neck, as if the head were too heavy for it, which gave at once a sense of mental danger' (Williams, p. 197). If there was a clash between the demands of the part and the resources of the actor, this clash could be exploited to create tension between the grandeur of the royal occasion and the human reality beneath. In searching for that human reality, Gielgud was less concerned with the traits of age than with the king's 'disastrous, indomitable will-power' (Speaight 1962, p. 49). His makeup was based on a seventeenth-century print of Anger (Hayman, p. 70).

When Gielgud returned to the part in 1940, he was not only more experienced, though still relatively young; he had the guidance of one of the major figures of the early modern theatre, Harley Granville Barker. Barker's Shakespeare productions at the Savoy theatre in 1912–14 were revolutionary, freeing the plays from the weight of elaborate scenery and throwing the emphasis back on the text. His *Prefaces to Shakespeare* were searching explorations by an artist with a strong theatrical imagination who had done his homework as a scholar. He had long retired from the theatre, and those who had worked with him felt the loss. Some blamed the influence of his second wife, but Barker's own plays are full of characters who give up the struggles they are engaged in; the hero of *Waste* is a reforming politician who commits suicide; the title character of *His Majesty*, Barker's last play, abdicates. (It was after his withdrawal that he hyphenated his last name, a convention I observe when citing his *Prefaces to Shakespeare*, or quoting sources that use that form, but not elsewhere.) But he agreed to come over from France to take ten days of *King Lear* rehearsals at the Old Vic. The programme's statement, 'The production by Lewis Casson, based on Harley Granville-Barker's "Preface to King Lear", and his personal advice besides', reflected Barker's desire that his contribution should be minimized. He left London before it opened and never saw it before an audience. But the evidence suggests that the production was essentially his (Dymkowski, pp. 139–41). Gielgud described Barker's ten days of rehearsals as 'the fullest in experience that I have ever had in all my years upon the stage' (Gielgud 1963, p. 52) and this has been echoed by other actors in the production. Barker gave Gielgud extra, private coaching, and Gielgud reproduced some of Barker's notes in an appendix to his *Stage Directions* (1963). There is also an invaluable account of Gielgud's performance by Hallam Fordham in 'Player in Action', an unpublished manuscript now in the Folger Library. It is based on observation of rehearsals and performances, and includes comments by Gielgud himself. Fordham's main interest, as his title implies, is in the leading actor; his comments on other performers, and on scenes in which Lear is absent, are very thin. This reflects not only Fordham's own interest but the condition of Shakespeare production at that time, when star performers dominated far more than they do now. Accordingly, the focus of this chapter, more than that of other chapters, will be on what the leading actor did.

It was Gielgud himself who posed the most significant problem. As Barker put it: 'Lear is an oak. You are an ash. We must see how this will serve you' (Gielgud 1963, p. 51). The last statement is a little enigmatic but suggests that Barker's intention was not to make Gielgud an oak, but to use the qualities he had, even to exploit the difference between the monumental Lear of his imagination and the slender actor with the light baritone voice he had to work with. In fact some technical devices were used to make Gielgud *look* like an oak. The hair and beard were carefully moulded to give his head a square, chunky look. A cloak hanging in diagonal folds gave a thicker appearance to his body. By means of a hidden sling, Lear carried the dead Cordelia in one arm, creating an impression of great physical strength while leaving the other arm free for gestures. Some observers found the effect of the one-arm sling artificial and distracting, and Gielgud's generally imposing appearance led Fordham to note 'a momentary surprise when the voice is heard, since it lacks by nature the full depth and rugged power which the actor's outward aspect gives us to expect'. He adds, 'this disparity is quickly accepted' (Fordham, I.i), but the initial disturbance suggests the danger of building up Lear's grandeur by externals alone. Barker's notes to Gielgud for the first scene suggest more subtle ways of establishing Lear's authority without going beyond the actor's range. As he mounts the throne he is 'Pleased. Happy'. When he announces his scheme of going everywhere with a hundred knights, 'He thinks this disposes of the whole thing, lean back, happy as at opening' (Gielgud 1963, pp. 121–2). At moments like this the authority comes not from a majestic voice or stature but from a feeling of security and confidence. Fordham notes that Gielgud's upright bearing and firm tread show 'a man who takes his absolute authority for granted' (Fordham, I.i). There is still, he adds, a certain tension in the pace of his walk. But the dangerous twist of the neck Gielgud adopted in 1931 is gone.

Barker's notes suggest at times a more obvious playing for power: 'Grind. Intimidation ... Big Ben striking' and on 'Who put my man i' the stocks?' simply 'King' (Gielgud 1963, pp. 122, 125). But the key to Gielgud's performance lay finally in his nervous energy, his intelligence, and the swift, volatile quality that allowed him to change moods with lightning speed. These are gifts he appears to have shared with David Garrick; contemporary accounts of Garrick's Lear cursing Goneril describe savage rage ending in sudden tears (Stone, pp. 92–3). Gielgud later praised Barker's 'understanding of every mood and nuance in the part of Lear' (Gielgud 1963, p. 121), and his own advice about Shakespearian acting emphasizes the importance of speed and flexibility: 'An actor who begins a speech in heroic style must be able to swiftly change (as Shakespeare's words so often do) to a sudden appearance of simplicity. There must be constant variety of pace and tone, stillness in repose, liveliness in attack' (Gielgud 1963, p. 25). Barker's notes show him constantly urging Gielgud in this direction: 'The curse sudden, surprise the audience. Speak nicely to

Albany … Burst into tears. Not too much. Not repeat the curse … Recover, then hysteria again … Entirely new voice … Horror. Then drop it … Rash mood suddenly back. Afterward slow, still, stare vacantly' (Gielgud 1963, pp. 123, 124–7). Fordham records a startling change of manner as Lear makes a final break with his daughters and goes out to confront the storm: 'he suddenly leaps up, with clenched fists above his head, and with a final exertion of tremendous vindictive power curses his enemies … But the effort can be sustained no longer. With a sudden, complete change of tone, helpless and pitiful, he calls to the Fool, who darts across to his feet' (Fordham, II.ii). A quick embrace, and the incongruous pair rushes out into the storm. The playing of the scene with Gloucester was equally volatile: he bent over the blind man as though hearing a whispered confession, then gave a great roar on 'let copulation thrive', swinging his staff over his head; the dignified acceptance of 'none does offend' was followed by a shriek of pain as his boots suddenly hurt and he demanded to have them pulled off.

This emphasis on variety gave light and shade to scenes in which Lear exerts his authority. His anger at Cordelia in the first scene was varied by sulkiness, including a childish refusal to look at her on his exit. After the banishment of Kent there was a 'complete change – smooth, courtly, charming, anger vanished'. Offering Cordelia to Burgundy he was 'smooth, cruel about Cordelia, … very ironic, schoolmaster showing up a dunce' (Gielgud 1963, p. 122). Fordham notes that on '*this* shall not be revoked' Barker called out 'Humour, humour', and Gielgud adds, 'He thought that the King should show a childlike, but often savage, sense of humour throughout' (Fordham, I.i). The authority was also varied by flashes of weakness; the frail, pathetic old man who for some actors was the whole of Lear was part (but only part) of Gielgud's. Though he had not made much effort to act old age in 1931, he noted of his 1940 performance that the final confrontation with Goneril and Regan demands fear, anger and 'the task of miming old age in movement, pose and gesture' (Fordham, II.ii). His eyes, Fordham noted, were those of an old man, and in the mad scenes his lower jaw hung loosely (Fordham, II.i, III.iv). Barker's notes on Lear's refusal to weep include 'Human, broken old man, futile … Wipe eyes', and on the escape of Goneril in the mad trial, 'Tiny, trembling, old man, childlike, tottering about' (Gielgud 1963, pp. 125, 129). On his reluctant decision to return to Goneril he approached her hiding his face in his cloak for shame. When the imaginary dogs barked at him he wept hysterically.

Too much of this would have reduced the effect to sentimental pathos, and the mad scenes in particular were controlled by a pervasive irony. In early rehearsals Gielgud had fallen back on convention: a doddering, twitching lunatic with staring eyes. Barker told him, 'The prevailing note must be kingly dignity; always, when in doubt, return to that' (Fordham, IV.vi). His detailed instructions included grandeur and courtesy in Lear's dealings with Poor Tom (Gielgud 1963, p. 127). Surrendering to Cordelia's doctor, Lear handed over his staff like a prisoner of state. A strange dignity was one key to the mad scenes; an equally strange happiness was another. In the scene with Gloucester, which Paul Scofield was to play with a dry, acerbic manner that suggested Beckett to many observers, Gielgud entered on Barker's instructions as 'Happy King of Nature. No troubles. Tremendously dignified. Branch in hand, like staff in opening scene, walk with it' (Gielgud 1963, p. 128). Fordham reports 'an unnatural spring in his step and a gleam in his eyes' and notes that the playing of the whole scene was distinguished by fluidity and spontaneity (Fordham, IV.vi). Though Gielgud was at first intimidated by this scene, the consensus was that it became the high point of his performance. The reunion with Cordelia likewise gained from dignity and control. Barker, who had specified in his Preface that Lear should not be 'mothered – please!' by Cordelia (Granville-Barker, p. 298), had him discovered sitting in profile, clothed in scarlet, in a dignified pose; his exit with Cordelia was equally digni-fied, and the scene as a whole had for Fordham 'an atmosphere of pulsating stillness, of gentleness and yet of pain. The joy of the scene's climax is carefully controlled, and raised to a plane of spiritual serenity' (Fordham, IV.vii). The dignity and happiness that were strange in the mad scenes were now simply and beautifully right. Lear's happiness continued in 'Come, let's away to prison', which drew one of Barker's most brilliant notes: 'Delighted. Really happy. Dance the whole speech like a polka. Music up and down. Variety' (Gielgud 1963, p. 129); 'but lightly, like a boy of nine telling a story to a child of six' (Fordham, V.iii). Gielgud even risked a swaying, dancelike movement as he walked down the stage with Cordelia. But there must have been, as in the mad scenes, something strange and unreal in this happiness, and it led to the last of the performance's sharp contrasts, with the 'lost and echoing anguish' of 'Howl, howl, howl, howl', heard first as 'a crescendo of sound off-stage'. The words are those of Audrey Williamson, who goes on to note that in the last scene Gielgud 'had a waxen immateriality, as if death had already touched him with a feathered wing' (Williamson, p. 136). Cathleen Nesbitt, the production's Goneril, recalls 'the sense of grief too deep for tears one had on all those "Never, Never's" like the tolling of a funeral bell' (Nesbitt, p. 195). Even here there was variety: Lear briefly recalled his anger at banishing Kent, then absent-mindedly shook hands with him. Then he totally lost touch and wandered aimlessly around the back of the stage until, his memory jogged by the sight of a soldier carrying the hangman's noose, he found Cordelia again. Barker's note on his last words, 'Look on her', reads simply, 'Joy' (Gielgud 1963, p. 129).

The notes we have from Gielgud, Barker and Fordham show Gielgud's great virtuosity as an actor and the care he and Barker took to provide musical variety in the performance. But they also imply something they do not state, perhaps because all concerned took it for granted: the constant variety of the performance shows a Lear capable of growth and change, of new insights and new experiences. In 1940 this view of Lear would have been simply taken as given, and it is still the common one. But later Lears, as we shall see, have been more intractable, more of one piece. There is also something in the Gielgud–Barker approach of the nineteenth-century assumption that a performance was a series of 'points', striking effects to capture the audience's attention. The point-making of older actors was more crudely self-conscious than anything these two artists would have wanted. But they did fix, quite carefully, on key moments of discovery, growth and change. Lear reacted to Kent's rebellion in the first scene: 'Dead quiet. Turn. Stare at him'; to the fear of madness: 'Now afraid *inside*. Simple'; and, most important, to his first sight of Poor Tom: 'The Fool's scream turns him off his head. Leans back on knees. Look through cage – fingers in front of face' (Gielgud 1963, pp. 122, 124, 126). This last moment was especially important for Barker – 'the precise moment at which Lear goes off his head' (Gielgud 1963, p. 132). The desire to mark a 'precise moment' is characteristic; so is the desire to find a cause for Lear's behaviour. The curse on Goneril, for example, did not just happen. It was triggered by a contemptuous laugh she gave, just as he was about to leave the stage. Lear can be seen as mad all the way through, or proud and foolish all the way through, but Barker wanted to show him changing; he wanted the changes to be clear to the audience, and properly motivated. Following a standard line in criticism at this time, Fordham sees the prayer to the 'poor naked wretches' as a similar point of change. 'The old pride and anger still flicker in his mind, but are gradually becoming assuaged by the dawning of patience and compassion.' Lear refuses to take shelter 'until the spiritual process is completed'. At the end of the prayer he radiates 'a new beauty of soul' (Fordham, III.iv). But of course it is just at this point that Tom enters, and sends Lear mad. Lear backtracks as well as advancing, and at certain points Barker and Gielgud marked this too. The reunion with Cordelia is arguably Lear's greatest spiritual advance; but in Barker's notes the beauty and serenity that are achieved in the scene as a whole are varied by touches that work the other way: 'A bit sulky ... Puzzled ... A bit cross' (Gielgud 1963, pp. 128–9). The commitment of both artists to variety of effect ensured that Lear's progress was not easy or glib. But this progress was for many observers the most important effect of Gielgud's performance. *The Times* praised him for tracing 'with a brilliant exactness Lear's progress from worldly to spiritual authority' (*The Times*, 16 April 1940). For Audrey Williamson the advance was steady: 'the gentleness that comes to him after the tumult of the storm stays with him now as an integral part of his character, and the anger at moments in the mad scene is an anger based on pity' (Williamson, p. 135).

We know far fewer details about the other performances, but enough to show the care that was taken even with the smallest parts. In his notes to the Fordham manuscript, Gielgud pays tribute to the way Charles Staite, as the doctor, contributed to the orchestration of Lear's reunion with Cordelia: 'Practical and kindly, he acted apart from the emotion of the scene, and thus contributed valuable change and contrast whenever he spoke' (Fordham, IV.vii). Cathleen Nesbitt recalls a moment Barker spent with the actor who confirms Lear's report that he has killed Cordelia's hangman: 'You must let the audience *feel* you have seen a miracle – you *have* – you are not accustomed to miracles – you are a rough soldier ... your heart must beat faster when you say, "'Tis true, my lord, he did"' (Nesbitt, p. 193). Barker's attention to detail included an emphasis on the informal, intimate side of the drama, which deals not just with kings and subjects but with parents and children, hosts and guests. The formality of the first court scene was set off by the realistic informality of the opening conversation of Kent and Gloucester, who entered as though they were already speaking, the audience picking them up as they came within earshot; and by the closing dialogue of Goneril and Regan, who paced to and fro in a natural, businesslike manner. In the second scene Gloucester donned spectacles and Edgar appeared with a book in his hand. The scene at Goneril's house showed this aspect of the production at its fullest. Barker instructed Gielgud to show Lear returning from the hunt: 'Sing, genial, throw things about (gloves, whip, etc.). Boots off, shoes on, nuisance. Suddenly checked by the insolence of the knight, continue gloves, etc., mechanically, sudden stop' (Gielgud 1963, p. 122). Lear beat on the table with his riding-whip, fed the Fool scraps as though he were a dog, and flung down his napkin in a fit of anger. Throughout the confrontation Goneril, maddeningly, went on with her needlework, dropping it only when Lear pronounced the curse on her. To Fordham even the domestic detail reflected Lear's kingliness: 'The little ceremony of the King's ablutions … is beautifully designed; the natural ease and fastidiousness with which he washes his hands and touches his brow and mouth with the water is eloquent of his station' (Fordham, I.iv). But Gielgud noted something else, that Lear never actually got his dinner and had to leave Goneril's house without it. It is an observation worthy of one of Gielgud's other favourite playwrights: all through act II of Chekhov's *Three Sisters* Vershinin declares he is dying for a cup of tea, and he leaves without getting one. Barker also allowed, even insisted on, the comedy of the play – for example, in Lear's exchange with Kent in the stocks ('By Jupiter, I swear no'; 'By Juno, I swear ay'). Gielgud at first resented the notion of comedy, and played this scene (against Barker's instructions) at a conventionally fast cross-talk pace; later in the run, when he tried playing it seriously, it was funnier than ever. Some broad comedy was allowed in the relations between Edmund and the sisters. Edmund was played with cheerful sexual magnetism – too much to the gallery, Williamson thought (Williamson, p. 136) – by Jack Hawkins. Goneril's reaction to his passionate kiss, 'Oh, the difference of man and man!' got an enormous laugh. Desmond MacCarthy was offended – 'This should not be' (*New Statesman*, 20 April 1940), but Cathleen Nesbitt as Goneril found it useful in creating 'a wave of tolerance for her' (Nesbitt, p. 194), part of a general effort to make the sisters human and understandable. (Tapes and reviews of other productions, by the way, show that this laugh is a standard one.) The sexual comedy took a grimmer turn when Regan, in widow's weeds, was seen at a mirror putting on her makeup.

The use of domestic detail fitted naturally with Barker's decision – contrary to his Preface – to use Renaissance costumes. (When Gloucester donned spectacles in Peter Brook's production, set in an undefined but much earlier period, the effect was odd.) The impression was of colour, splendour and jewelled pomp against a dark background (Williamson, p. 133) – appropriate for 'Europe in the age of absolute monarchy' (Salgādo 1984, p. 48). Such a setting also puts the play, against the effect of its language, in the Christian era. In the BBC TV version, also set in the Renaissance, the sign of the cross is freely used; Barker instructed Gielgud to cross himself at the start of Lear's prayer, but some audience members objected to the use of this sign in a play they still thought of as pagan and Gielgud reluctantly dropped the business. Fordham thought the sight of Lear feeding the Fool was appropriate to 'the picture of semi-barbaric court life' (Fordham, I.iv). Though Barker had departed from his own idea of barbaric dress for the play, many in his audience were still thinking along those lines.

More consistent with the principles of Barker's Preface was the use of a single flexible set rather than a series of detailed and realistic stage pictures for each scene. The permanent features included a raised platform with steps at the back, arched entrances at the sides half-way down, two permanent raised seats near the front of the apron, and stairs at the front by which the apron could be reached from below. These entrances from the depths were used most interestingly for Gloucester's appearance in the hovel, when he confirmed Tom's view of him as 'the foul fiend Flibbertigibet' by coming on from below; and for Edgar when he entered for his scene with Albany just before the battle, setting up the duel with Edmund – this time a character from the *social* depths, coming to challenge the triumphant general. However, this was not really a production along bare-stage, Globe theatre lines. The forestage curtain could be closed altogether, or open only half-way, to vary the depth of the stage. It was used to conceal Kent in the stocks during Edgar's soliloquy, a concession to realistic staging principles. A number of scenic elements were included: a mound of stones for the Dover scene, blue hangings with gold fleur-de-lis for Cordelia's tent; and for the last scene the backcloth (which was changeable) showed a panorama of tents with waving banners. To the modern eye these banners, and the curlicues on the curtain, look fussy and inappropriate. They reflect the decorative taste of the period but not the spirit of the play, and Ashley Dukes found the decor 'weak in conception, effeminate in detail' (p. 468).

However, the combination of underlying formality with realistic detail is a fair reflection of Shakespeare's own dramatic idiom, and this combination seems to have been sustained not just in the design but in the staging and acting. Some of the realistic details have been noted. But Barker also 'encouraged grand entrances and exits centre-stage, a declamatory style, imposing gestures' (Gielgud 1963, pp. 53–4). Fordham noted his penchant for 'a simple, classical shape', with 'broad right-angled and diagonal crosses for the actors' and triangular groupings 'with the central character at the peak'. For key speeches the supporting characters were turned upstage to give the strongest position to the speaker (Fordham, II.ii). The casual opening dialogue was played before the closed forestage curtain; then trumpets signalled the king's entrance, and pages drew the curtain to reveal a centrally placed throne with a semicircle of seats on either side of it. The opening procession upstage to the throne may have been a less spectacular effect than Gielgud's 1931 entrance, Irving's 'wild march', or Komisarjevsky's row of uplifted trumpets; but what it sacrificed in spectacle it gained in formality and in natural dignity. At times, there was also a formality in Gielgud's performance. The contrast between the curse on Goneril, 'hands palms upwards, as if receiving the curse from heaven upon them' and the kneeling position with bowed head and clasped hands in the storm scene, suggests a contrast between good and evil prayers (Fordham, I.iv) as coded as anything in Eastern theatre.

The battle, after a brief procession of Lear, Cordelia and the French power, was a matter of symbolic sound effects alone: drums, trumpets and swordplay. This avoidance of a realistic battle was a matter of simply following the text. A more controversial use of formality was in the storm scene. Barker's notes to Gielgud for the storm include 'Oratorio. Every word impersonal' (Gielgud 1963, p. 125), and Fordham records a posed, stylized quality in his acting, a 'detached and unrealistic manner' that appears only at moments elsewhere: 'The postures are statuesque and broad, each change of attitude being made deliberately and held for a time according to the structure of the speech' (Fordham, III.iii, iv, vi). Here for once the production seems to have aimed at the universal, not the particular, to have tried for something like the stylization of expressionism. The figures were placed at the back of the stage, picked out in dim light; there was no visual realism. But the sound of wind and thunder was conventionally realistic and threatened to drown out the actors. The usually enthusiastic Fordham was bothered by the clash of conventions. Ashley Dukes found the conscious symmetry of the groupings inappropriate to the frenzied drama of the scene, and the upstage position ineffective (Dukes, p. 469). For *The Times* reviewer, on the other hand, the effect was to cast the weight of the storm where it belonged, on Lear's language: 'as a solitary silver figure in the dark loneliness, he speaks the storm, and his trust is never at any vital point betrayed' (*The Times*, 16 April 1940). But a majority of critics echoed the complaints about the positioning and the clash of idioms, and found Gielgud weak in the scene. When the play's range of reference was social, the production seems to have compassed this comfortably and effectively; but it did not find a theatre language for its metaphysical level.

The ending was also formal: Kent, Albany and Edgar hid the bodies of Lear and Cordelia with their cloaks as the curtain fell. This was a moment of order and dignity, like the bowed heads and lowered spears of Irving's soldiers. Barker wanted to extend the formality by having the bodies of Goneril and Regan brought on stage, as the text specifies; the result was an unwanted laugh from the audience, and later in the run the business was cut. But Barker's desire to try it shows his concern not just with small details but with the overall shape of the play, its end repeating its beginning, the wheel coming full circle. There was formality of another kind in his disinclination to talk about events that happened offstage, or before the beginning of the action. For him, such questions belonged to the modern realistic drama of Ibsen, not to Shakespeare; in that way the Shakespearian idiom was artificial. The actors had everything they needed in the lines themselves. (In his 1962 rehearsals Peter Brook had Cordelia and the Fool, who never meet in the play, improvise scenes together; an actress of the old school who was in the company and who saw no need for such tricks remarked to me, 'In my day, darling, we had something called natural talent'.)

The last consideration is the effect of this production on those who saw it. Gielgud played for, and largely achieved, the sympathy of the audience. The domesticity of his scene with Goneril had the effect of drawing the audience to him (Fordham, I.iv) at precisely the point where Brook took pains to alienate them. His forestage position for Goneril's entrance at Gloucester's house allowed him to appeal directly to the audience's sympathy (Dymkowski, p. 156). Edith Evans wrote to Gielgud that his performance had not just convinced her but drawn her in: 'I believed in your parenthood. I believed that you were a widower ... I wanted to come up and share your mood and sorrow, I wanted to be *in it* with you, not as an actress but as a woman' (Hayman, p. 128). We have seen, and Evans must have realized, how much art went into Gielgud's creation of Lear; yet this tribute from one professional to another speaks of a rapport between human beings, the one a stage invention, the other a woman in the audience. The general impact of the production was also bound up with its historical moment: 1940. For the second time in the lives of most of the audience, Europe was darkened by war. At the outbreak of hostilities Gielgud was rehearsing a stage version of Daphne du Maurier's *Rebecca*. He withdrew from it, explaining that while commercial work was all right for peacetime the war called for something classical (Gielgud 1981, p. 107) – this, against the conventional view that in war the public needs above all to be entertained. (In the First World War the musical *Chu Chin Chow* ran for years while *Heartbreak House* remained unstaged.) Cathleen Nesbitt reports that the Old Vic itself had suffered bomb damage, so that the principal actresses had to share a dressing room and queue for a single mirror; but this only increased the sense of excitement (Nesbitt, pp. 192–3). *The Times* review began, 'To be at the Old Vic last night, waiting in the somewhat dingy but much-liked auditorium for the curtain to rise, was to enjoy a sense of the first genuine theatrical occasion of the war. Occasions of the kind declare themselves not in the sheen of fresh paint, diamonds, and gardenias, but in the unmistakable stir of a common intellectual expectancy' (*The Times*, 16 April 1940). Gielgud's own belief that the war required the classics was justified by the event. He recalled in later years that audience members would come to his dressing room to thank him for the pride and courage the production gave them amid the horrors of war (Funke and Booth, p. 34; Gielgud 1981, p. 112).

[35]

There were plans for a tour of France, which came to nothing when the French government capitulated to the Nazis. The Old Vic went dark, and eleven months later was bombed and put out of action for years. The production went the way of all productions; but for Gielgud and others it remained a high point in their lives, and when Gielgud returned to the play in 1950, in a production directed by himself and Antony Quayle at the Shakespeare Memorial Theatre, Stratford-upon-Avon, the programme note included an acknowledgement to Granville-Barker, who had died in 1946. In his curtain speech on opening night Gielgud thanked 'the spirit of Harley Granville-Barker who taught me all I know about this play' (Trewin 1964, p. 216). Yet the 1950 production, in more than one respect, is a test case for the play's capacity to change. *The Times* reviewer called Gielgud's Lear 'in intention the same performance' as in 1940 (*The Times*, 20 July 1950). Many details were carried over: once again, Lear cut Cordelia dead on his exit from the first scene; his curse on Goneril was triggered by a contemptuous laugh from her; the details of his preparations for dinner were similar; Regan's hard heart was indicated (as in 1940) by Lear tapping the joint-stool; and Regan herself sat in her widow's weeds, applying her makeup. The prompt book shows that Gielgud restored Barker's original intention to have the bodies of Goneril and Regan brought back on stage, though they were not huddled on a single litter as in 1940 (this may have produced the laugh) but borne by six attendants each.

However, the prompt book also reveals important differences, notably in Lear himself. He came on with Cordelia in the first scene, a piece of business suggested by William Poel but rejected by Barker as anticipating their special relationship. When the Fool screamed at Tom's first entrance, Lear screamed too. In both cases Gielgud seems to have aimed at larger, broader effects than in 1940. On the other hand, his hair and beard were shorter and trimmer; there was no attempt, as in 1940, to conceal the natural shape of his thin pointed face. If anything, the makeup emphasized it: the lion had become a fox. The actor's slimness was not covered but exploited. In the storm he appeared 'tall and gaunt and incredibly elongated, like an El Greco Christ amidst the wreckage of a ruined universe' (*The Sunday Times*, 22 July 1950). In more than one review he was compared to Don Quixote. Gielgud, it seems, had gained the confidence to use his own features more directly than before. The thinner appearance may be bound up with a greater concentration on Lear as a creature of mind and spirit. We hear less of the changes and variety of Lear – perhaps because there was no Hallam Fordham to record them, but perhaps also because Gielgud was trying this time for a more sustained line of development. Fordham had noted that even in the scenes where the physical strain showed Gielgud was sustained by his intellectual grasp of the drama (Fordham, II.ii). In 1950 some reviewers complained that the effect was too intellectual: the scenes with Tom achieved pathos but it was 'the pathos of a keen mind dulled rather than of a proud heart broken' (*Birmingham Post*, 19 July 1950). *Time and Tide* concluded, 'I cannot imagine a more intelligent or more fastidious Lear. But that is not quite the whole story. In a wicked world, in the practice of the theatre, some wild Welsh bull might actually carry the play better' (*Time and Tide*, 29 July 1950).

In fact, not all the reviewers were describing the same performance. Anyone familiar with the theatre knows how a performance can change from night to night. Gielgud's 1950 Lear seems to have been a particularly striking example of this, a sign that the role offers an actor both extraordinary opportunities and extraordinary dangers, that the line between success and failure is alarmingly thin. At the dress rehearsal he 'gave a magnificent performance which had several of the other actors in tears, but on the first night he was tired and nervous' (Hayman, p. 174). The *Birmingham Post* found him 'strangely unmoving ... almost as if Mr. Gielgud had determined that emotion should remain on this side of the footlights' (*Birmingham Post*, 19 July 19 1950). The audience was too aware of the actor; his devices were too self-conscious. One vocal effect in Lear's last confrontation with his daughters, an uncontrolled shriek on 'the terrors of the earth', went so badly wrong that several reviewers commented on it. But from the second performance on the improvement was spectacular, and T. C. Worsley could write, 'I should not believe that anyone, however visually imaginative, could in his study bring the tears to his own eyes as Mr. Gielgud does to ours here' (*New Statesman*, 29 July 1950). We may wonder if this actually implies a diminution of effect; in 1940 audiences spoke not of crying but of being exalted and uplifted. Clifford Leech reports a deeper response. He saw the production with a colleague, with whom he usually walked after the theatre, discussing the performance. 'I suggested we should do it on this occasion. "Yes," he said, "a walk, but I don't want to talk".' They walked for several miles in the fields around Stratford, in silence, and bade each other a gruff goodnight. Leech reports his own feeling: 'this is what we have to face, and we do not know, and we cannot quarrel with the dramatist for not telling us, how to face it' (Leech, p. 50; supplemented by private conversation). We may speculate that while the fears of 1940 could be countered by courage, by 1950, with the opening of the death camps and the bombing of Hiroshima, the grimness of the world had become deeper and more pervasive, something that could not be countered but had to be endured.

Gielgud's performance, once he had recovered from the opening, could lift the audience to this level of tragic recognition; but there were problems on the physical side of the production that could not be so readily solved. Leslie Hurry's designs were more specific, detailed and limiting than those of Roger Furse in 1940. The set was dominated by an enormous oak tree, split in two, sometimes with a set piece in the middle, sometimes with the gap left empty. Gielgud must have recalled Barker's opening words to him: 'Lear is an oak.' Though the effect was symbolic, not realistic, there was no abstraction and the production photos show other scenic elements introduced to make clear in every case where we are: a throne room, a tent, open country. The backcloth for the Dover scene shows the sea with cliffs in the background, removing any ambiguity about the location as Gloucester and Edgar toil up the hill. Though some reviewers appreciated the symbolism of the riven oak, others found the scenery inappropriate in its evocation of Arthur Rackham and 'theatrically ... tiresome' (*Time and Tide*, 29 July 1950); '[it] dwarfs the players and breaks the action' (*Tribune*, 29 July 1950). The period, once again, was Elizabethan, with occasional mediaeval touches like the pointed arches of Lear's throne. The sense that the play cannot be confined to one period had now crept into the design. This seems to have drawn little or no comment from the reviewers, and we may conclude that it must have seemed natural. The most bothersome feature of the production was the storm, which was turned up too high on opening night: if the set dwarfed the actors, the storm drowned them out. The problem of volume was correctible, and a review published a month after the opening reported 'The first storm scene, one of the blots in the production, has been stripped of the superfluous sound effects, and Lear is himself again' (*Tribune*, 2 September 1950). But T. C. Worsley, in a generally favourable review, noted a confusion of conventions that recalls the problems of 1940: 'The drenching rain that comes over the loudspeakers is not a good realistic touch, in view of the all too dry and altogether too unruffled appearance of the figures on the stage' (*New Statesman*, 29 July 1950). The problem of the storm still awaited a solution.

Gielgud returned to the play in 1955, in a production directed by George Devine, under the aegis of Stratford but intended to tour. This time the problem of the decor was overwhelming. Gielgud, in a way more adventurous than in 1950, aimed not at the sort of poetic, classical acting that had always been associated with him but at psychological reality. *The Times* complained that he broke the verse 'into prose fragments' (*The Times*, 27 July 1955); instead of keeping Lear's age a matter of suggestion, as he had done earlier, 'By exaggerating Lear's senility he shatters the poetry, spluttering it out in little jagged lumps between the gasps and wheezes of a tottering old man' (*Punch*, 10 August 1955). In an interesting minority report, the reviewer of *Truth* found Gielgud's performance 'psychologically true' and of 'staggering coherence', a case a psychiatrist would recognize of a mad old man attempting 'to destroy with his hate the one he loves too much' (*Truth*, 5 August 1955). But what seems to have been a bold experiment by the leading actor attracted less attention than the more extravagant experiment of the designer, Isamu Noguchi. Instead of creating a particular time and place he went full out for abstraction and symbolism: 'Lear's world was encompassed by an arch and there was a black shape to represent doom. Noguchi intended his larger floating wall as a symbol of "time" or "history" while two smaller moving screens were meant to denote elements of evil human will, to be identified with Goneril and Regan. In the first scene there was a blue diamond shape which signified Lear's dominion, but the shade of blue was also intended to suggest a link with France and the distance to which Cordelia was banished' (Hayman, p. 190). Lear's deterioration was symbolized by costumes with larger and larger holes, leading the *Daily Sketch* to comment that he looked like a Gruyère cheese (*Daily Sketch*, 27 July 1955). The scorn and amusement of the reviewers can be imagined; but with the decor, as with the leading performance, there were minority reports. Alan Dent not only praised it but reported 'The huge audience received even its most eccentric phenomena with a breathless and unmistakable acclaim' (*News*

Chronicle, 27 July 1955). Some years later, I discussed the production with a woman who had seen it; she declared simply, 'It was beautiful.'

The intention of the designer had been to liberate the play from time and place; in the majority view, shared by Gielgud, the effect was simply distraction. And it may be that for its full effect *King Lear* needs time and place, a sense of people in a recognizable society. But this production cannot be dismissed as a dead end. Peter Brook called it an 'interesting but unfortunate … experiment', yet acknowledged that it prepared the ground for his own production (Brook 1987, p. 88; Hayman, p. 191). Brook was not to take Noguchi's way into elaborate symbolism and obtrusive stylization. But Noguchi, by exploding the established scenic conventions, had at least set a precedent for some of Brook's experiments. One detail may be noted: the 'black sausage thing' that descended from the flies during Noguchi's storm (*Liverpool Post*, 30 July 1955) may not have been a direct ancestor of the visible thundersheets that descended during Brook's; but it shows the same kind of thinking, and there is a clear family resemblance.

It would be wrong to end this chapter, however, with the reflection that Gielgud's last and possibly least successful stage Lear (he played the role one last time, on radio, in 1994, to mark his 90th birthday) simply paved the way for something better. Gielgud on his own terms was, for many viewers, the finest Lear they had ever seen; and this reaction comes from reports of all four stage productions. That the same actor should have found four different ways of scaling the heights is a tribute not only to his own resourcefulness but to the range and openness of the play.

CHAPTER III

Peter Brook and Paul Scofield

1962 was a transitional year for the Royal Shakespeare Company. In its repertoire at Stratford-upon-Avon its past and its future could be seen in the styles of different productions. Peter Hall's *A Midsummer Night's Dream*, revived from 1959, had an elaborate and beautiful set, an Elizabethan interior varied by realistic foliage for the forest sequence. John Barton's *The Taming of the Shrew*, revived from 1960, had a revolving set, a stylized but solidly detailed Elizabethan house. Both productions were firmly Elizabethan in look and atmosphere, and while they were free of the older convention that every new scene requires a new set, the pictorial thinking behind them was still that of the 1950s, and earlier. But the influence of Brecht, triggered by the Berliner Ensemble's visit to London in 1956, could be seen in William Gaskill's *Cymbeline*, set against a plain beige cyclorama, with sylized scenic elements frankly dropped in as needed, and a cool, ironic performing style that emphasized these were actors putting on a play. The set for Clifford Williams' *The Comedy of Errors* was a steeply raked platform, and the costumes, while vaguely Renaissance in outline, could not be located in any one period. Both productions were distinguished by bold, inventive stylization and by almost aggressive clarity. Against them *Dream* and *Shrew*, lively and engaging though they were, seemed stylistically old-fashioned. Over the proscenium arch was an elegant white swan, a tribute to the romantic tourist's view of Shakespeare. Its days were numbered. Each performance began (as was the custom then) with the playing of the national anthem, in a bouncy arrangement that restored an earlier form of the tune. Though it annoyed traditionalists, this too in its way was romantic, and like the swan it would shortly disappear.

I was a graduate student at the Shakespeare Institute at Stratford that year (which also marked the emergence of the Beatles – bliss was it in that dawn to be alive) and with a number of friends and colleagues I attended the opening of the last production of the season, *King Lear*, directed by Peter Brook, with Paul Scofield in the leading role. Stratford traditionalists, on the whole, were looking forward to it. Brook and Scofield had both worked at Stratford in that constantly shifting period known as the good old days, and had given much pleasure, though Brook had always had a tendency to stir controversy. Scofield was known as a sensitive and moving actor, Brook as an innovative director with a gift for spectacle. The audience was keyed up to expect something special, and that is what it got – though not quite on the terms it had imagined. The set declared itself as we walked in: three plain white walls, a bit of rough and simple furniture. Against one wall hung an oriental-looking shape, a capital H with the uprights curved inward; against another, a large metal rectangle that looked like (and, as it turned out, was) a rusted thundersheet. At starting time there was no national anthem. With the house lights still on, an actor (Tom Fleming, playing Kent) walked on to the stage, pulling on his gloves. He was dressed in a plain leather costume of jacket and trousers that could have belonged to a remote past or a science-fiction future. Four hours later, after what J. C. Trewin describes as 'the most blazing ovation in [the play's] modern history' (Trewin 1971, p. 126) and what I remember as a more sub-dued and tentative reception, we dispersed, and the arguments began. They continued for days. Some of us (myself included; my prejudices must be clear by now) were profoundly excited, feeling we had seen the play with unexpected clarity and depth. Others were unmoved, sceptical, even angry. For them the play had been not revealed but denied, suppressed, twisted out of shape. But it was an experience that left no one without an opinion, and in retrospect it seems that we had all been through a form of culture shock.

To begin with the designs, which were by Brook himself: we have already noted his view that the Renaissance (favoured in the 1940 and 1950 Gielgud productions) was inappropriate. But he did not see the play as timeless, either; he wanted a particular society and had a clear sense of what that society was like. For him, the play took place in 'big, violent and therefore very realistic circumstances, with flesh and blood actors in very harsh, cruel and realistic situations' (Brook 1987, p. 88). Accordingly, he created a primitive and violent society that could not be pinned down to a year or a century but seemed to J.C. Trewin 'a rusting Iron Age'

[42]

(*Birmingham Post*, 7 November 1962). The Russian film director Grigori Kozintsev, who was to set his own *Lear* in a similarly generalized though less primitive world, found the relations of the characters more convincing in the Brook setting than in a conventionally costumed production: 'This was not a copy of life but, if you will, its algebraic formula' (Kozinstev 1966, p. 31). In the costuming, Brook aimed at simplicity, commenting that 'when you have thirty or forty equally elaborate costumes, the eye is blurred and the plot becomes hard to follow. Here, we only gave important costumes to eight or nine central characters – the number one can normally focus on in a modern play' (Brook 1987, p. 90). This was also, one might add, the number of sharers (and therefore important actors) in an Elizabethan acting company. The minor characters, the hired men as Shakespeare would have called them, were in simple garments – smocks, trousers and boots – that had the effect of a uniform. This both reduced their individuality, highlighting the major characters as intended, and suggested something totalitarian about Lear's world. Lear was the only male character to wear a long robe. He wore it in the first scene, emphasizing his kingliness; in the middle scenes, when Lear loses his kingship and confronts his humanity, he was in jacket and trousers like the other men, though his costume was heavier and more imposing. In the later scenes with Cordelia he wore a robe again, but a simpler one, his kingship restored on new terms. The similarity in line between his robe and Cordelia's dress established a link between the two characters, setting them apart from the others. The aim was clarity and point, not period detail. But every production reflects its *own* period, and just as the waving banners of Granville Barker's production spoke of the year 1940, so a future historian trying to date the Brook *Lear* on photographs alone could fix it without difficulty at 1962–4 by the beehive hairstyles of the women. The adoption of a fashion as modish as the miniskirt suggests a conscious intention to link this primitive world with the world of the audience.

Props were few and economically used, and this meant that every prop stood out – notably the circular astrological chart used in the second scene to give point to Gloucester's speech about the eclipses and Edmund's scepticism about the stars. A large oval shape that was set behind Lear's throne in the first scene later doubled as the dinner table at Goneril's house. The props used for the mad trial, sacks and a tankard, were used again in the blinding of Gloucester, establishing that the play has not one mad trial but two. A twisted metal shape that reminded some reviewers of a broken auto part served as an uncomfortable-looking chair for Edmund in the later scenes, and as a rest for Lear to lean against as he died sitting on the floor. Brook had originally designed a very elaborate set, which he scrapped, leaving the three white walls, which could create larger or smaller spaces as the side walls were moved, and a rough fence that was occasionally brought in as needed. He commented: 'Why does one decorate a bad play? For that purpose – to decorate it. With *Lear*, on the contrary, one has to withdraw everything possible' (Brook 1987, p. 89). The most striking scenic element belonged to the storm sequence. Granville-Barker had said in his Preface to *King Lear*, 'In the storm-scenes the shaking of a thunder-sheet will not greatly stir us' (Granville-Barker, p. 266), but he was thinking of the sound alone. Brook, watching thundersheets backstage, had found the *sight* of these large, vibrating sheets of metal 'curiously disturbing' (Brook 1987, pp. 90–1) and accordingly decided to put the thunder on stage, visibly, in the form of three rusted thundersheets that descended from the flies at the front of the stage, their vibrations created by hidden motors. The effect was eerie, and Brook's assistant Charles Marowitz noted that their appearance accompanied a general change in the production to a more boldly stylized idiom (Marowitz, p. 27). Finally, the stage itself made its own statement. The Royal Shakespeare Theatre has a stage of considerable width and surprising depth; settings are frequently devised that create a new back wall, closer to the audience, making a smaller playing area and thrusting the action forward. Leslie Hurry's oak tree for the 1950 *Lear* had this effect. Brook, on the other hand, exploited the depth, particularly when the side walls moved back for the opening of the storm scene and the figure of Gloucester, left alone on stage (Alan Webb, a small actor) suggested tiny humanity dwarfed by a vast, bleak universe. Marvin Rosenberg summarizes the effect: 'The bareness of Brook's stage was metaphysical, as well as actual' and 'The fierce illumination banished any shadows of divinity, mystery, or superstition' (Rosenberg, p. 34). For Milton Shulman it was 'an eerie world somewhere between an antiseptic operating theatre and a concrete segment of nowhere' (*Evening Standard*, 7 November 1962). When the production later transferred to the smaller stage of the Aldwych Theatre in London, some of this effect was lost.

The visual shock of the production was so unexpected that some reviewers appear to have become confused about what they actually saw. One described the white set as 'bluey-grey' (*Coventry Evening Telegraph*, 7 November 1962). Another wrote, bewilderingly, 'The stage is warm with rich autumn tints of the kind which blazed from the Cotswold countryside as I drove to Stratford' (*Liverpool Post*, November 7, 1962). Others complained of the austerity and of the unfortunate associations some of the costumes had for them; a typical comment was that Lear's costume for the middle scenes was 'more suitable for an Edwardian motorist' (*Glasgow Herald*, 8 November 1962) than for a king. Others were bothered by what they saw as a clash of idioms in the general style of the production. T. C. Worsley complained of 'a fatal mixture of stylisation and realism', the latter represented by the knights running amok in Goneril's dining room and the former by the overtly symbolic, unrealistic storm (*Financial Times*, 7 November 1962). But we have seen in discussing Granville Barker's production that a mixture of the realistic and the formal was used there as well, and in fact reflects Shakespeare's style. For some, the mixture simply needed getting used to. Seeing the production for the second time on its transfer to London, Philip Hope-Wallace commented, 'The mixture of styles is more an illusion than it seemed at first' (*Guardian*, 13 December 1962).

One of the key devices involved the use of the house lights. As I have noted, they were on for Kent's entrance at the beginning of the production; the effect was repeated at the end of the interval when Edgar appeared and sat on stage for a few moments before the house lights dimmed and the play resumed. But the most important use of the device came at the ending of the first half. As the blinded Gloucester, a blanket thrown over his head, stumbled towards the back of the stage and off, the house lights gradually came on. The intention, according to Marowitz, was to 'remove all possibility of aesthetic shelter' (Marowitz, p. 29), or as Brook put it later, 'to make the audience take stock of the scene before being engulfed in automatic response' (Brook 1968, p. 73). The intention, in other words, was Brechtian: force the audience to a fresh examination of what it had seen. (Brook in rehearsal also used Brecht's device of having actors prefix their speeches with the formula 'he said' (Marowitz, p. 25).) But theatre habits die hard, and Brook observed with some chagrin that Gloucester always went off to conventional applause (Brook 1968, p. 74).

Within a year or so, the lights-on beginning had itself hardened into a Royal Shakespeare Company convention, and audiences began to take it for granted. But at least the device gave fair warning that the conventions of realistic theatre were not going to be observed. Night scenes were not indicated by a dimming of the stage lights. In the first storm scene Kent and the Gentleman took shelter under an imaginary tree. The most striking use of mime was in the Dover Cliff scene. Edgar held his staff in front of Gloucester as though to keep him from getting too close to the edge; Gloucester put out a foot, feeling sideways, lost his balance, and clung to the stick. In the neutral space that was the set we *could* have been at Dover Cliff; as the mime created it for us, we almost felt that we were. The effect was (I am certain) more powerful than that of the 1950 backcloth, which simply *told* us that was where we were. Then Gloucester threw himself forward and rolled across the floor. He was not at Dover, he was on a stage; or on level ground that could have been anywhere. The ambiguity that the scene would have had in the Globe Theatre was reproduced in the idiom of this production in a way that scenic realism would never have allowed. We got the *idea* of Gloucester's leap, undisturbed by the literal-minded worries that a realistic staging would create.

The storm, as we have seen, defeated the realistic scenic artists of the nineteenth century, and the mixture of realism and stylization in the 1940 and 1950 productions proved troublesome in its own way. In the widening of the set and the descent of the thundersheets, Brook established and maintained a stylized idiom that carried full conviction, and within it he produced something more than a competition between actor and sound effects. The Folio has the first direction for 'storm and tempest' near the end of II.iv, at Lear's 'You think I'll weep, / No, I'll not weep.' Earlier productions, from Kemble and Kean through to Komisarjevsky, had begun the storm at various points earlier in the scene, so that it could build slowly and realistically (Bratton, pp. 123, 129). In the 1962 promptbook the sound cue is where the Folio has it; but the impression left on my memory is that the storm was actually released by the words immediately before this cue, Lear's threat to unleash 'the terrors of the earth', a phrase Scofield isolated with grim intensity. The effect was that Lear's voice triggered the storm: it was a reply to his challenge and he was responsible for it. At their entrance in III.ii, Lear and the Fool created the wind. Lear did a steady diagonal cross from the back of the stage, bent forward into the wind, while the Fool, in the background, blew about in circles like a leaf. The thunder was not a continual noise, but marked in the promptbooks to hit at precise points, usually at the end of a clause or a sentence. In III.i the 1962 promptbook distinguishes between three, four, and five-second claps, each timed to Kent's movements on the stage. The promptbook for the 1964 tour distinguishes 'short', 'long' and 'longish' thunderclaps, and instructs the crew to time them to the words, gestures and movements of the actors. Not only are the instructions very specific, but in this case, though the characters may appear helpless, the actors are in control; the storm cues follow them. (The effect is like the stage trick of the reverse fight: Desdemona pulls Othello's hands towards her throat, while he tries to pull away; the impression is of a struggle, but the actor playing Desdemona is in control of it – as for reasons of safety she has to be.) The result was a clear sense of dialogue between Lear and the storm. The most dramatic moment came when Lear, with a shout of defiance, called himself 'a man more sinned against than SINNING!': there was a loud clap of thunder, and he reeled backwards. It was as though the storm had said, 'You're not getting away with that'. The storm scene worked not just because it abandoned the reaism that was bound to fail in any case, but because it treated Lear's encounter with the storm not as an exercise in special effects but as a dialogue.

The battle was more of a problem. Gloucester sat alone on stage – again, the smallness of Alan Webb contributed powerfully to the effect – while backstage sound created the clash of armies. But the sound effect, at first, was not far enough away from the realistic idiom of Barker's drums, trumpets and clashing swords. The 1962 promptbook calls for 'shields banged together'. The result sounded to various reviewers like 'the passing of a swarm of goods trains' (*Birmingham Post*, 7 November 1962) and 'a thousand servant girls dropping a thousand tin trays' (*Evening News*, 7 November 1962). The sound, whatever it was, brought an unwanted laugh from the audience. It was supplemented and later replaced by a single beaten drum, and by the end of the 1964 tour John Simon, in a generally scathing review, was able to list this as one of the production's good moments: 'a beautifully orchestrated but invisible battle majestically rages and wistfully dies away off-stage' (Simon, p. 427). One element of the scene was consistently effective: the small, blind Gloucester, alone on the empty stage, one of history's forgotten refugees. Here, as in the storm scene when the set opened to its fullest width around him, Alan Webb stood for vulnerable humanity in a vast and absurd cosmos. An equivalent simplicity and economy marked the staging of the duel between the brothers, which many directors have built up elaborately. Tall figures in identical helmets, Edmund and Edgar simply pressed their swords together in a brief contest of pure strength which Edgar won, forcing his brother to the ground. He then plunged his sword-point into Edmund's body as though skewering an insect; the moment of impact was marked by a wrenching cry from Goneril, 'Save him, save him' (Albany's line, transferred to her).

This economy and stylization created an air of conscious theatricality; one was aware of a director's decision to remove detail. At the same time the production, like Granville Barker's, had small natural touches: a certain amount of eating and drinking for Lear, and for Kent in the stocks; and some telling business for Edmund and Gloucester in the opening scene as the son gave his father his gloves, helped him on with his cloak, and brushed his shoes. (Later, Gloucester was to attend Lear in the same way, pulling off his boots.) The naturalness of the opening business made Harold Hobson think of guests at a weekend house party, helping themselves to bacon and eggs from a sideboard (*Sunday Times*, 16 December 1962). At the same time, low-key though it was, it suggested formal preparations for a public occasion. The formality deepened in Lear's love-test when, in the production's one piece of court ritual, Kent produced a large orb and gave it to each daughter in turn to hold while she made her speech. The convention recalled the conch in William Golding's *Lord of the Flies*, which Brook was to film in 1964. The orb weighed heavier in Cordelia's hands than in her sisters'.

We have seen an equivalent attention to detail in Gielgud's performance, but there the emphasis was on speed and variety of attack. Here, the pace was much more deliberate, each detail held up for inspection. Philip Hope-Wallace praised the 'Wagnerian deliberation of speed, which pays off in that the hieratic preliminaries and the whole curve of the play ... are wonderfully clear ... I have seldom noticed so many points intelligently taken' (*Guardian*, 7 November 1962). Such was the effect of fullness and care that some reviewers were fooled into thinking Brook had made no cuts in the text (*Warwick and Warwickshire Advertiser*, 10 November 1962). In fact there were significant cuts, as we shall see. At nearly four hours it was a full evening, but it was the style of playing, not the length of the text, that made it so. There was, it should be noted, nothing ponderous about it. The pointing was light and clear. As Lear determined 'that future strife may be prevented now' Albany and Cornwall glanced briefly at each other. As he cursed Cordelia the attendant who was holding up the map slowly lowered it, forgetting his job as he stared at the king. The light touch was especially evident in the playing of Cornwall, whom actors often make a conventional overbearing villain with a snarl in his voice. Tony Church, in Edmund Gardner's exact phrase, was 'lotion-smooth' (*Stratford-upon-Avon Herald*, 9 November 1962). On the day of the opening the actors were told to do an 'easy, underplayed' run-through to save their energies for the evening. According to Charles Marowitz, 'The result was astounding. Actors who had been belting out the verse since the first readings were suddenly giving scaled-down, unfussily true performances. Basic relationships, so long obscured during erratic rehearsals, suddenly became crystal clear' (Marowitz, p. 31). Describing the opening, *The Times* found similar qualities of 'freshness, lightness of touch, and ... lucidity' (*The Times*, 7 November 1962), and what Marowitz describes as characteristic of one special rehearsal corresponds to my memory of the performances I saw. The Fool and Tom often seem to be speaking gibberish; here, everything they said was clear. As the set and costumes had been stripped of extraneous detail, so music and sound were pared to the minimum – distant barking dogs for Edgar's escape, a short piece of soft horn music for Lear's waking – putting the concentration on the actors' voices.

Brook was determined to see the play not as one character's story but as 'a cluster of relationships' (Brook 1968, p. 91), with a greater focus than in previous productions on the secondary characters. He told the company in rehearsal that 'In verse which is properly spoken, each character plays his own rhythm – as personal as his own handwriting, but what often happens in Shakespeare is that everyone shares a generalised rhythm that passes impersonally from one to the other' (Marowitz, p. 23). The gain in clarity was particularly striking in the case of Alec McCowen's Fool – though, interestingly, McCowen was working somewhat against the director's intention. Brook wanted 'an inspired zany', brilliant and spontaneous; what he got was 'a bright, crisp, thoroughly professional reading of the Fool, but ... without that necessary daemonic touch' (Marowitz, p. 26). Other Fools had played for pathos with a touch of madness. In 1940 Stephen Haggard was 'a strange, frail creature with restless eyes' (Williamson, p. 137). Alan Badel, in 1950, was a 'haunting haunted fool, the very embodiment of pathos, loyal as a mongrel, frightened as a lost child' (*New Statesman*, 29 July 1950). If there was pathos in McCowen, it was not of a sentimental kind: he was a 'shivering monkey' (*Evening News*, 7 November 1962). His salient feature was intellectual sharpness. He pointed the key words of speeches: 'Have *more* than thou showest, / Speak *less* than thou knowest'. On 'Whoop, Jug, I love thee' he raised a jug to his lips, making the line logical, not crazy. He could be frightened, bitter, angry; his concern for Lear came out in the concentrated venom he directed at Goneril on 'A fox, when one has caught her, / And such a daughter, / Should to the slaughter ...' If there was anything disturbing about him (and there was) it lay in the fact that he was so alarmingly lucid.

Brook insisted on clear distinctions between characters, particularly Goneril and Regan. 'Goneril wears the boots and Regan wears the skirt. Goneril's masculinity continually fires Regan, whose squelchy softness of core is very opposed to the steely hardness of her sister ... Regan ... completely goes under and in the end creeps ignominiously off the stage poisoned in the stomach like a squashed spider, whereas Goneril takes her leave defiantly' (Brook 1987, p. 88). This contrast was caught exactly by the two actors, Irene Worth and Patience Collier. Brook also re-examined the conventional division of the characters into good and evil, which is as striking in this play as in any of Shakespeare's. As part of the attempt to make the audience see the text afresh, Goneril, Regan and Edmund were shown not as arbitrary monsters but as characters with their own point of view. Brook was later to write of Edmund as the most attractive character in the early scenes, affirming 'a life that the sclerosis of the older people seems to deny' (Brook 1968, pp. 91–2). This was not especially brought out in the production, though the condescending way Gloucester treated him in the opening conversation – including, in the 1964 promptbook, a playful slap – allowed us to see how galling that conversation must have been from Edmund's point of view. Regan, who in earlier productions had rejected the dying Cornwall's plea for help, ignoring his outstretched arm (*Punch*, 2 August 1950), helped him offstage here. She was a woman, not a monster. But the strongest and most controversial piece of re-thinking involved Goneril's housekeeping problems. As we have seen, Lear and his knights have traditionally been a noisy lot, but here their energy was turned up to the point of violence and the sequence was played to an unusual degree from Goneril's point of view. Lear's return from the hunt was preceded, according to the 1962 promptbook, by 'uproar off stage', and his calls for his fool and his dinner were taken up by the knights. When Kent attacked Oswald the knights crowded around them like playground bullies. They reacted loudly to the Fool's jokes, registering their disapproval of the more dangerous ones; when Lear ironically offered to kneel to Goneril they found this hugely funny. A large table was set in the middle of the stage, laid with plates and cups for Lear's dinner. On 'Woe, that too late repents' Lear, with the deliberateness of a naughty child, overturned the table. This was the signal for the knights to run amok, shouting, hurling and smashing. At one rehearsal the actors went right out of control, bringing down a large chandelier in the rehearsal hall, drawing a lecture on discipline from the stage manager and a Cheshire cat smile from the director. In production, the scene remained 'dangerously unpredictable' (Marowitz, p. 28).

Kent was of a piece with the knights. The blunt, honest, lovable old retainer of tradition turned into a bully who, not content with insulting Oswald on their second encounter, twisted his arm (1962 promptbook) and later seized his leg and upended him (1964 promptbook). Evoking Brecht, Kenneth Tynan called this 'the alienation effect in full operation: a beloved character seen from a strange and unlovely angle' (*Observer*, 11 November 1962). Albany, normally a weak character who grows stronger, stayed weak. Hearing of Gloucester's blinding, he threw up into his handkerchief (creating a certain confusion of conventions, since there was no ready way to dispose of the handkerchief afterwards). Telling Kent and Edgar, 'Friends of my soul, you twain / Rule in this realm' he emphasized 'you twain' with an outward push of the hands that conveyed not his respect for the other two but his own desperate anxiety to avoid responsibility. (The actor, Peter Jeffrey, went on to play the wishy-washy liberal headmaster in Lindsay Anderson's film *If* ...) Alan Webb's Gloucester, in his early scenes at least, was an almost comically fussy old man: on 'We have seen the best of our times' he sounded to me like Justice Shallow. For Gāmini Salgādo he was 'a self-satisfied Polonius-like busybody' (Salgādo 1984, p. 68); for Kenneth Tynan, 'a slippery old rake and something of a trimmer' (*Observer*, 11 November 1962). Traditional Gloucesters have also been fussy and pompous in their early scenes (Fordham, I.2) and the trimming is clear in the text; but Webb pointed these qualities in an unexpectedly vivid way. Brian Murray used lines like 'I cannot daub it further ... And yet I must' to show an Edgar torn and pained by what he was doing. Cordelia was not so much re-thought as re-styled. Diana Rigg played not for gentleness but for cool, self-contained strength. As usual the critics were divided, praising her 'reasoned and unreproachful firmness' (a first-night reaction: *South Wales Evening Argus*, 7 November 1962) or calling her 'a sort of New York career girl, brittle, lacquered, remote, more manikin than woman' (a reaction to the American tour: *Time*, 29 May 1964).

All this re-thinking did not reverse the moral poles of the play: the good were still good and the evil were still evil. Lear was still shut out in the storm and Gloucester had his eyes put out. But Brook was at some pains to block the easy emotional response that comes from a clear conflict of good and evil, the easy sympathy that comes to victims who do not deserve their suffering. While other productions have had Garrick's aim of drawing the audience's sympathy to Lear, this one aimed to disrupt, disturb and detach us. In the long run we could still react in the old way, but the reactions could not be triggered automatically; they had to be earned. In his film version Brook was to go further, using a freedom to re-arrange the text that he did not have in the stage production and almost flattening the distinction between good and evil. The strongest hint in this direction in the stage production was in the relationship between Edgar and Edmund. When they were both armed for the duel, in costumes of identical cut and helmets that hid their faces completely, it was hard to tell them apart. In the early scenes they signalled to each other with a whistled tune that was clearly a private code, suggesting a long-standing rapport between them. In the last scene Edmund was not carried out before Lear's entrance, to die offstage as the text specifies. He was on stage for the whole scene, and the final picture was not the traditional one of a group of mourners gathered around the bodies of Lear and Cordelia; it was Edgar, who had been left alone with his dead brother, slowly dragging him upstage, both facing the audience, Edmund still with the twisted smile that had been one of the hallmarks of James Booth's performance. Brook's concern with the play as a group tragedy led him to take the focus away from the leading character in the end. To a friend who saw the production with me the ending also suggested a reconciliation of the brothers, a marriage of good and evil. In the absurd and amoral universe the play had shown, the old moral oppositions seemed finally meaningless.

In any production that faces it honestly *King Lear* is a cruel play; but it has seldom been so cruel as it was here. Tony Church's Cornwall avoided the clichés of stage villainy, but the light, irregular taps he gave to Kent's cheek with his riding whip showed how much he knew about torture. For the blinding, Gloucester was bound to a kitchen chair and laid down on his back, his legs in the air, helpless and painfully undignified. Cornwall said, 'Upon those eyes of thine I'll set my foot' and the light caught his spurs. (One of my companions left at this point.) There have been more melodramatic stagings of this scene, but the cruelty of this staging was more shocking because it was so precise. The play shows equally striking images of kindness, but sometimes – not always – the kindness was played down. What could have been moments of contact became moments of distancing, even rejection. When Edgar led his blind father on to the stage they were not arm in arm but at either end of a long pole. Towards the end of the storm sequence the Fool drew apart from Lear and sat alone – not, I think, because Lear had treated him brutally (Styan, p. 221) but because he was jealous of the way Lear had turned to Poor Tom. Alec McCowen used the Fool's warning against trusting 'a boy's oath' very pointedly as a warning against Tom, and one could see his anger and distress mounting as Lear ignored him. In the last scene, where Gielgud's Lear had absently shaken hands with Kent and then wandered off, Scofield's Lear pushed Kent away. On 'Away, get thee away' Gloucester pushed off the old man who was trying to help him. (A cancelled note in the 1962 prompt-book shows that at one point the old man made several attempts to touch Gloucester, and each time Gloucester pushed him away.) Kent's 'Vex not his ghost; O, let him pass' had traditionally been a gentle requiem. Tom Fleming, standing not with a group of concerned friends around Lear, but on his own, well to the side, delivered it as a shout of anger. The opening night audience was palpably shocked; the production's detractors saw this as a characteristically perverse reading; but that Kent should be angry with Edgar for trying to keep Lear going after all he has suffered makes clear emotional sense.

More debatable were two cuts that Brook made, which had the effect of removing moments of consolation: the servants who comfort Gloucester after his blinding, and Edmund's attempt to reprieve Lear and Cordelia. The first is a Folio cut, but in the Globe Theatre, assuming performances there were continuous, its effect would be not so much to remove comfort as to put stronger emphasis on the meeting of Gloucester and Edgar which follows immediately after. In Brook's production the interval separated these two scenes, and in the opening of the second half a new quiet, exploratory manner suggested that the play was taking quite a different turn, increasing the separation. The effect of the cut, then, was more negative than in the Folio. This was underlined by the fact that Gloucester's servants remained on stage but were indifferent to his plight, casually pushing him off as they went about the business of tidying up. In the last scene, the cutting of Edmund's attempted reprieve of Lear and Cordelia was equally shocking. On opening night Lear's first offstage 'Howl', coming far earlier in the scene than expected, was as startling as the original scene must have been to the play's first audience, who knew the story only in versions with a happy ending. (A study of the 1962 promptbook, which shows small cuts followed by massive deletions and the note 'MORE CUTS COMING!' suggests that this cut was not planned from the beginning but that more and more of the sequence went during rehearsals until it was all gone.) In both cases the effect was to slant the interpretation in a manner that Bernard Levin called 'impermissibly cavalier' (*Daily Mail*, 7 November 1962). Brook himself was to object to the way Brecht's version of *Coriolanus*, in order to make Brecht's own ideological point, changed the reason for the hero's decision to spare Rome; he thought the play had been castrated (Brook 1968, p. 82). Though his own changes to *Lear* were cuts, not rewrites, and though they did not affect a moment of such central importance, here for once the 'healthy double attitude, with respect [for the text] on the one hand and disrespect on the other' (Brook 1987, p. 95) seems to have got out of balance. Interpretation became adaptation; the production made a strong, clear statement but at the cost of blocking some of the play's own signals. The production's final statement was also definite: as Edgar dragged his brother off, we heard muted thunder. For Marowitz, this avoided what he revealingly calls 'the threat of a reassuring catharsis' (Marowitz, p. 29). His own idea had been to have a tremendous storm break out at the end; Brook took up the notion but handled it more subtly. Here, however, the production decision did not limit the text but drew out something that is clearly there: a sense that the play ends not with order or reassurance but with profound unease. Irving and Granville Barker, by ending formally with gestures of mourning, had created a sense of order. Brook's ending was formal in its own way, and though it involved adding more to the text than the traditional endings had, it was arguably truer to its essential spirit. Though Brook had worked his own way to this moment, there was at least one precedent: the nineteenth-century American actor Edwin Forrest had ended his *King Lear* with the ominous sound of a gathering storm (Rosenberg, p. 323).

The production's bleak view of the play is frequently attributed to the influence of Samuel Beckett, via Jan Kott's essay '*King Lear*, or *Endgame*', which Brook read in French in 1962, and which was later published in English as part of Kott's *Shakespeare our Contemporary* (1964). This led J. L. Styan to call Brook's *Lear* a 'rare case of a major production directly inspired by the opinions of a literary critic' (Styan, p. 218). This view has frequently been parroted by journalists and academics (myself included) writing about the production. But while Marowitz reports 'In discussing the work of rehearsals, our frame of reference was always Beckettian' (Marowitz, p. 21), Scofield, while acknowledging the Beckettian quality of the Dover scene and the influence of the Beckett analogy (which he calls 'fun') on the visual style of the production, has declared that the actors were not much influenced by it, and that the play as a whole is much larger than Beckett (Carlisle, p. 291). In an interview given at the time of the production Brook called *King Lear* 'the prime example of the Theatre of the Absurd, from which everything good in modern drama has been drawn' (Brook 1987, p. 89); but in another interview some years later he took umbrage at the notion that he based his production on Kott's essay. He used the Beckett analogy, he claimed, as a kind of shorthand to make certain ideas clear in a quick and concrete way, just as in other rehearsals he and Scofield made reference to Charles de Gaulle (Labeille, pp. 219–21).

Given the way theatre normally works, the idea that the Beckett analogy was a practical rehearsal device is more plausible than the notion that the production was shaped by Brook's reading of a critic's interpretation. The view of the production as *Lear* seen through Beckett's eyes, having hardened into an orthodoxy, has also led to an over-simple account of its emotional effect as purely bleak. There were moments of gentleness and of human contact in it (as there are, by the way, in Beckett, who is also simplified by the conventional wisdom: think of Nagg's offer to share his biscuit with Nell). When Lear, staring into an abyss of fear, said quietly, 'O let me not be mad' the Fool took his hand; they were like two children admitting they were afraid of the dark. In the storm scene, on 'My wits begin to turn', the storm suddenly went quiet, the wind dropped, and the only sound became steady rain as Lear embraced the Fool: 'How dost, my boy? Art cold, my boy?' When Lear commanded Gloucester to pull off his boots Gloucester obeyed, clumsily, crying like a baby. If Brook added extra thunder at the end, he also added, on 'Alack, 'tis he', a brief passage of mime in which Cordelia and her attendants, standing at the front of the stage, watched in concern as Lear crossed in imagination through the back of the stalls. On 'Be your tears wet?' Lear touched Cordelia's face.

This brings us to Lear himself. Granville Barker was criticized for spoiling Gielgud's first entrance by bringing him on from the side, not the centre (Gielgud 1981, p. 110); but at least the entrance was part of a formal and dignified procession. At the opening of the court sequence in Brook's production there was no procession; characters came on promptly but informally, like members of a committee entering a meeting room at the appointed time. They formed a roughly triangular grouping, creating the expectation that the king would appear at the apex; instead he came on quickly and unexpectedly from the side. (Granted a certain difference in tone, the blocking was that of Groucho's first entrance in *Duck Soup*.) He was not conventionally regal: though a traditional mediaeval crown was set on a table beside his throne he actually wore a circlet of what looked like rough-cut stones. Nor was he a Blake-like ancient with floating white hair. Hair and beard were short, and dark hairs still mingled with the grey. This was a tough, wiry, still vigorous old man. If he had had a cane (which he didn't) he would have been more likely to beat someone with it than to lean on it. It was the voice that was most startling: a sound like grinding rocks, 'the voice of a man to be feared' (*Birmingham Post*, 7 November 1962). It would be capable of striking effects: the tremendous extended vowels of 'Blow, winds' and 'Howl' would have elemental force. Familiar lines would be re-punctuated. At the opening of Lear's curse on Goneril, most texts have 'Hear Nature, hear; dear goddess, hear'. Scofield gave us a rising tension: 'Hear, nature! Hear, dear goddess!' and a sudden grinding descent: '*Hear!*'

The sometimes alarming quality of the voice was carried over into Lear's behaviour. He impressed one reviewer as 'a malignant old man with a black canker in his heart' (*Evening News*, 7 November 1962). Where Gielgud struck Oswald in the face with a napkin, Scofield used a glove. On 'Kill, kill, kill' he drummed on the stage with his boots. The words were not enough; he needed a physical release for his violence. Gielgud's Lear had been frightened of Tom at first; in this production Tom, if anything, seemed frightened of Lear: one note in the 1962 promptbook has him backing away 'in terror and amazement'. While Fordham noted the fastidiousness of Gielgud's table manners, this Lear wolfed his food. Even in the mad scenes with Gloucester there was something alarming about his appearance: his head was decorated not with flowers or leaves but with burrs that suggested incipient horns. Searching for analogies, reviewers compared him to 'a general in Tzarist Russia' (*Nottingham Guardian Journal*, 7 November 1962), an 'old sea dog' (*Wolverhampton Express and Star*, 7 November 1962) and a countryman with a yokel accent (*Daily Mail*, 7 November 1962). An American student who saw and disliked the opening night thought Lear had been reduced to a Maine fisherman. In any case, he was a recognizable man, not an abstraction or a symbol. Harold Hobson summed up the effect: 'What walks the stage of the Stratford theatre is not an ancient Druidic myth, but a man, a man capable of tramping twenty miles a day over sodden fields, and arriving home at nightfall properly tired and in a filthy temper, insulting the servants and cursing his relations' (*Sunday Times*, 11 November 1962). He was unkingly only if one had conventional notions of kingly behaviour; if one recognized that kings can be human, stubborn, wilful and frequently undignified, he was every inch a king.

But for Charles Marowitz, and for other viewers, important areas of the character were missing: 'Lear the ruler is there, as is Lear the madman; but Lear the father and Lear in those supreme final moments where the play transcends itself, is only sketched in' (Marowitz, p. 32). For Edward Trostle Jones the absence of

Lear the father was connected with a general limitation in the production: 'All the characters ... were locked into their own existential isolation from the beginning, which ... affected the power and emotion of the drama's close' (Jones, p. 105). The society Brook created on stage was geared convincingly to hunting, fighting, torturing and killing; but it had no domestic life. Scofield's own intention, he later claimed, was that the play should emerge as a 'humanistic', affirmative tragedy (Carlisle, p. 291). He saw Lear's toughness as setting off by contrast the moments of tenderness with the Fool, Gloucester and Cordelia (Rosenberg, p. 24). By a circuitous route, then, Scofield intended to arrive at the traditional Lear, the Lear who learns and grows. For some viewers the effect worked as intended, and the moments of gentleness stood out movingly (Rosenberg, p. 288; *Evening Standard*, 7 November 1962). But growth certainly came less easily to Scofield's stubborn Lear than it had to Gielgud's volatile one. Where Gielgud used a variety of tones in reacting to his setbacks in the first scene, 'Scofield ground crisply on, seemingly as tough as ever' (Rosenberg, p. 74). Lear says to Cordelia, 'Nothing will come of nothing' and to the Fool, 'Nothing can be made out of nothing.' By using the same grinding rhythm on both lines Scofield not only alerted us to the echo but created a Lear whose mind worked in grooves. The moments of gentleness with the Fool and Gloucester were, I thought, clear and moving. What was much less clear was the massive transformation of Lear in the later scenes with Cordelia, the joy of their reunion and the anguish of her death. Marowitz's complaint that these scenes were only sketched in was echoed by Gāmini Salgādo, who found them 'drained' and 'bleakly formal' (Salgādo 1984, p. 66). Like so much else about the production, this was a matter of controversy: even some opening-night reviewers were moved by the later scenes (*Oxford Mail*, 7 November 1962; *New Statesman*, 16 November 1962). A friend who was in contact with the actors told me that at some of the later performances in London Scofield was profoundly moving, but these were performances when he 'broke free of the production'.

Reviewers who wanted a good cry were of course disappointed. Fergus Cashin found 'no tenderness, no sympathy, no tears' and added, 'The French woman journalist sitting next to me came out without wiping her eyes – the first time a King Lear had not moved her to tears' (*Daily Sketch*, 7 November 1962). Marowitz admitted the production was 'more cerebral than moving' but called this a necessary price to pay for the 'epic objectivity' that would make the tragedy 'not Lear's but ours' (Marowitz, p. 32) – again, a traditional end sought by an untraditional route. Others *were* moved, but not in a sentimental way: for Edmund Gardner, 'the effect is horribly moving. "Howl, howl, howl!" freezes the blood, while his sorrow over the dead Cordelia packs ice into the bones' (*Stage and Television Today*, 8 November 1962). Philip Hope-Wallace called the Stratford opening 'the most moving production of the play I have seen since the war' and noted that in the London transfer the scenes with the Fool, Gloucester and Cordelia 'were listened to with the kind of silence which accompanies only the deepest emotional response' (*Guardian*, 7 November 1962; 13 December 1962).

One note struck over and over in reviews is that the production caught the spirit of its time. For Roger Gellert, Brook and Scofield 'have demonstrated shatteringly how it can be acted for our generation' (*New Statesman*, 16 November 1962). Peter Lewis claimed he had not seen anything 'more starkly "modern"' than the blind Gloucester sitting on a bare stage, pulling off the boots of the mad Lear (*Daily Mail*, 13 December 1962). The likelihood that he would have seen exactly that on the stage of the Globe Theatre suggests that the production did not impose modernity on the play but drew out modernity that is already there. It also had a seminal effect on later Shakepeare productions, especially by the Royal Shakespeare Company itself. Like Brook's equally striking *A Midsummer Night's Dream* it was finally *sui generis* and dangerous to imitate. At Stratford in the following season another director did *Julius Caesar* with bare sets, leather costumes, and a slow, deliberate pace; the result was an evening of bottom-crushing tedium. But the clear intellectual pointing, the avoidance of easy emotion, the re-thinking of traditional sympathies, and to some degree the visual stylization, were to be features of the Royal Shakespeare Company style for years to come. The production belonged not just to a cultural period but to a historical one as well. It was rehearsed during the Cuba missile crisis of 1962, when the United States and the Soviet Union came frighteningly close to nuclear war. It was not Brook's way to use the topical background, as Adrian Noble was to use the Falklands war in his 1982 production. But Harold Hobson noted that one of the production's meanings for him was 'The meek shall inherit the earth only if an earth is left for them to inherit. Another Cuba will not end in a general handshake' (*Sunday Times*, 11 November 1962). The fear of nuclear destruction was more active and prominent than it is now. It was not necessary for Brook to work in a shot of a mushroom cloud at the end; actors and audience had this fear in their bones, and the refusal of comfort at the end was true both to the text and to the audience's perception of its own world.

As plays change in different productions, so productions change before different audiences, and what we might loosely call the political dimension of the Brook *Lear* was most strikingly revealed when it was revived in 1964 to tour Eastern Europe and the United States. The European tour was a triumph. On the last night in Bucharest hundreds of students pushed into the theatre, standing in the wings and hanging from the catwalks; in Warsaw the company mounted a free matinee for actors and directors who had not been able to get tickets. In Moscow an actress who had seen *Lear* the night before 'threw down her script in rehearsal and declared: "we can never act in this way again. The Royal Shakespeare Company has shown us a new freedom"' (*Stratford-upon-Avon Herald*, 3 April 1964; 10 April 1964). According to Brook, 'the best performances lay between Budapest and Moscow', where audiences with little understanding of English listened with 'silence and concentration ... that affected the actors as though a brilliant light were turned on their work' (Brook 1968, pp. 21–2). He attributed the production's impact to the contact it made with the lives of people who had been through a terrible period of history. They were moved not by 'the sentimental image of a poor old father howling' but by Lear as 'the figure of old Europe, tired, and feeling, as almost every country in Europe does, that after the events of the last fifty years people have borne enough' (Brook 1987, p. 93). As Tom Fleming put it, 'One feels that we have been playing great tragedy to people who have known greater sorrow, greater privation, than the people we play in "Lear". Now one cannot indulge oneself as an actor. You don't weep at the end of "Lear" any more because suddenly you have found yourself playing to people who know what it is to be beyond tears' (*Stratford-upon-Avon Herald*, 10 April 1964).

The reviewers I quoted in the first chapter who insisted that the play is 'about me' were North Americans looking for a personal, emotional experience; European audiences, more used to thinking collectively and politically, were excited to find that the play was 'about us'. On Brook's own principle that theatre must constantly renew itself, that 'Yesterday's performance is by now a failure' (Brook 1987, p. 56), the production that had worked so brilliantly in Europe went dead in the United States. Catching up with the company in Philadelphia, Brook found that 'the quality had gone from their acting' and the austerity 'which had seemed so right in Europe no longer made sense'. He blamed the change on an audience that cared nothing for the play but went to the theatre for social reasons. That may have been true; but it may be that the audience was looking for an emotional experience of a sort the production was not designed to offer. Worse was to follow. At the Lincoln Centre in New York, *Lear* opened in a new auditorium whose acoustics had never been properly tested and turned out to be terrible. To make anything register at all, the actors inevitably had to coarsen their work (Brook 1968, pp. 22–3). Some American reviews were favourable, but the complaint that the production was unmoving now became the dominant note. The pity of it is that many people who never saw the production have formed their impressions of it from reviews of the American tour. One could say that, like Lear himself, it had lived too long. Though for some years to come other productions were tested against its memory, the play itself, as it always does, broke free, and the production became history. But Shakespeare production, in England at least, was never the same again, and for some of us who experienced the shock and revelation of that Stratford opening, it became part of the history of our own imaginations.

CHAPTER IV

Robin Phillips and Peter Ustinov

For anyone who expects *King Lear* to be a titanic drama in a barbaric setting, the production directed by Robin Phillips at Stratford, Ontario in 1979, with Peter Ustinov as Lear, would have been doubly startling – first of all for its restraint, its avoidance of large effects. As a director, Phillips aims above all at clarity: 'I direct plays for a fourteen-year-old of either sex who's never been to the theatre before, and I want them to understand it' (Berry, p. 102). Maurice Good's account of rehearsals for this production, *Every Inch a Lear* (1982), quotes Phillips' advice to Rodger Barton, who was playing Edgar: 'Don't be too emotional ... Emotions are fine, but when I get too much of them I don't get the text' and a general note to the company, *'Cool and clear is very alarming'* (Good, pp. 187, 189). The clarity of Phillips' productions is not a matter of highlighting certain points, as was done in different ways in the Gielgud and Brook productions, but of close, steady concentration on the text. He rehearses with a copy of the complete *Oxford English Dictionary* at hand, not only to check the meanings of words but to explore their full range and resonance (Knowles 1993, p. 62). According to Richard Paul Knowles, who has made a close study of Phillips at work, he urges actors 'to relax, to remove the "muscle," the "acting," from a performance, to allow the thought and emotion to become clear. It is for this reason that people are so often lying or sitting on the floor in rehearsals, and even in performances, relaxed, still, but communicating absolute clarity of thought and emotion' (Knowles 1987, pp. 51–2). He told the *Lear* company after one run-through, 'still too fast and with too much energy' (Good, p. 124). The insistence on relaxation leading to clarity recalls Marowitz's account of the final scaled-down run-through of Brook's *Lear*, but the quiet of a Phillips production goes further than this, becoming an intense stillness. Watching an acting exercise performed by schoolchildren, he particularly admired one little boy who crawled under a piano and just crouched quietly, on his own. He was being a beetle (Good, p. 101). In scenes that appear to demand big emotion the emotion is there, but intensified by being reined in. In the final confrontation between Lear and his daughters, 'though voices get raised sometimes, they are as instantly lowered, pulled back, increasing the intensity of the frustration, the venom, the failure on both sides' (Good, p. 19). A 'sedate, measured' delivery of Regan's scene with Oswald (IV.v) achieved 'a quite chilling ... menace. A barely throttled-back hysteria lurks in every syllable' (Good, p. 35).

Like Brook, Phillips looked at the text freshly, but with less in the way of a deliberate agenda. He cut more heavily than Brook (especially in the Fool's part) but the cuts did not have the effect of slanting the interpretation. For example, he omitted the Fool's rhyme beginning 'Have more than thou showest', the sort of cut that saves time and removes obscurity but (unlike some of Brook's cuts) does not change the essential meaning of the scene. He began rehearsals with an exercise in which each actor gave his name and said what he thought the play was about; the exercise concluded, 'My name is Robin Phillips, and I don't know what the play is about' (Good, p. 4). His effort is to create not 'an externally imposed directorial concept' but 'an exploration of the text within a certain context' (Knowles 1987, p. 50). The 'context' is a fully imagined life for the characters, within a fully realized society. While Granville Barker insisted that Shakespeare's characters have no offstage life, one often feels, in a Phillips production, that when the actors leave the stage they go not into the wings but into another room, where their lives continue; or, as actor Rod Beattie put it, 'With Robin's shows you have a past and a future and familiar earth beneath your feet' (Knowles 1987, p. 55). To create this sense of living experience, he draws on the personal lives of the actors, and on his own. He once asked an actor playing Romeo 'What kind of music turns you on?' and that music was used in preparing the love scenes; he told an actor playing Timon of Athens to draw on his own sense of being unappreciated by his country; he drew on his own experience of returning to his native England after a long absence to help an actor playing Posthumus in *Cymbeline*. Exploring the frustration of Lear and his knights at Goneril's house, he reminded the actors of receptions they had been given on tour where they were expected to be content with 'good bread sandwiches' (Good, p. 157). He illuminated the play's family tensions by recalling 'his deaf father for years drumming his fingers until his mild-mannered sister exploded' (*Globe and Mail*, 15 September 1979). In their different ways the Gielgud and Brook productions created a formal stage world, consciously theatrical, aware of its own artifice. Phillips aimed more directly at recognizable reality.

This included his choice of period. The nineteenth-century setting had been used before, by the Royal Shakespeare Company in 1976 (David, pp. 96–7), but for most of Phillips' audience the first view of the set, a panelled interior full of Victorian furniture, was as startling as the first sight of Brook's plain white walls had been. The New York critic Clive Barnes was overheard to remark, as he took his seat, 'Ah, yes, this must be "King Lear"! I'd know that set anywhere' (*Flint Journal*, 8 October 1979). In outline the set was simple and formal: three wooden walls enclosed the interiors; the middle wall was flown up out of sight for exteriors; otherwise the set remained unchanged through the evening. The upstage area was a platform two steps higher than the downstage area, the difference in levels being useful but not obtrusive. But within this simple framework a whole nineteenth-century society was evoked, down to the use of authentic Crimean war buttons (not reproductions) on the uniforms (Knowles 1985, p. 31). For some reviewers it was the wrong period. Lawrence de Vine missed the 'tooth-and-claw days of 800 B.C.' (*Detroit Free Press*, 6 October 1979); according to Richard Whelan, Phillips had picked 'a period traditionally associated with subtle machinations in politics and general social circumspection' (*Stratford Beacon-Herald*, 6 October 1979) and therefore incongruous with bold gestures like Lear's division of his kingdom. While Brook had created a primitive, violent world that was lacking in domesticity, Phillips, according to some, had smothered the play's violence in a setting that was too domestic, too civilized. But while there were small problems of detail, as there always are in updated settings – for example, the Fool's coxcomb rather oddly became the inside of his trouser pocket – there were many opportunities to send clear signals to the audience that a more remote and generalized period would not have allowed. Cordelia's doctor appeared drying his hands, and it registered at once that he *was* a doctor, and that Lear's case had (as it does in the text) a medical dimension. Gloucester (Douglas Rain, a trim actor) was padded with a small pot belly that evoked the life of the Victorian clubman.

But the usefulness of the period went beyond matters of detail. If Beckett was the *éminence grise* behind at least certain scenes in the Brook production, the spirit of Thomas Hardy touched this one; and Hardy would have been the first to insist on the link between his pessimism and that of the play. Phillips regularly brings in books, pictures, anything that will evoke the world he wants to create. At the first rehearsal there were several Hardy novels on the table beside him, and he quoted briefly from them (Good, p. 4). At the end of one rehearsal of the storm scenes, he 'quietly [read] an ominous, dank and chilly landscape sequence from *The Mayor of Casterbridge*' (Good, p. 19). (Characteristically, even in the storm Phillips did not go full-out for noise, either from the elements or from the actors.) The Hardy analogy meant that when we moved out of the comfortable drawing rooms we sensed not a bare, blasted wasteland but a familiar life close to the earth and to the animal world, a life of farming and hunting. At the first entrance of the disguised Kent, we glimpsed a few other poor people, who looked like discharged farm workers, and we briefly heard the clucking of hens.

If there was something novelistic (and particularly nineteenth-century) in the production's use of detail, there was also something of one particular nineteenth-century dramatist in the scenes of sexual tension. Watching a rehearsal of Edmund's scene with Goneril (IV.2), Peter Ustinov remarked, 'Strindberg, of course. "Miss Julie," this one!' (Good, p. 84). The incongruity some reviewers felt between the Victorian setting and the violence of the play may have been more apparent than real. Trish Wilson noted 'the first scenes bear a striking resemblance to stiff family portraits of the age' (*Kitchener-Waterloo Herald*, 6 October 1979). But these respectable-looking people were up to no good. Reviewing the 1980 revival, Gina Mallet recorded a dual impression: 'All those polite ladies and gentlemen standing around look like illustrations from a Victorian morality tale' but they could equally well have been 'illustrations for a book of pornography. That's apt. The evil in this production is pornographic' (*Toronto Star*, 15 September 1980). If we think of the enormous scale of prostitution in Victorian cities, if we think of the flood of pornography from Victorian presses, we realize that this production was particularly well equipped to deal with the dark sexuality of the play. The lighting was 'stark, eerie, always subdued' (Lyle Slack, *Hamilton Spectator*, 6 October 1979), as though a sickness were hanging in

[65]

the air. Gloucester was blinded in the comfort of his study, his eyes put out with a letter-opener, and the intrusion of such deep evil into such an ordinary setting was profoundly disturbing. When in the later scenes Edmund appeared in shirt-sleeves there was something distinctly feral about him. It was like the drawing in *The Tale of Jemima Puddle-Duck* in which the fox – who has previously been seen walking on his hind legs, dressed as a respectable gentleman, reading a newspaper – suddenly appears naked, on all fours, pawing over the eggs. When Albany also appeared in shirt-sleeves to denounce his wife we felt that we were seeing alarmingly deep into their private lives.

One production photograph shows Regan (Marti Maraden) holding a handkerchief to her lip. The thought in the actor's mind, I am told, was 'I think I've got a cold sore.' Discussing the period with his company, Phillips stressed its unhealthiness – the sweat, the dirt, the stuffy rooms. The constriction of the costumes – 'all that passion beating against whalebone' – produced a more darkly sensual effect than 'all that nakedness'. As Phillips imagined it, if Regan's costume were unbuttoned, steam would rise (Good, pp. 5, 144). As with the costumes, so with the furniture. The effect of constriction and clutter, so unlike the bareness and simplicity of Brook, was to show us a world bound down by things. In the first scene the division seemed to concern not just an abstract map but a good deal of property: 'Goneril and Regan were observed to eye possessively the sofa, the chandelier, and mother's favourite pictures' (Knowles 1985, p. 31). In the first scene Gloucester prepared for the division of the kingdom by laying out papers on a desk at one side of the stage. Instead of denouncing Cordelia from a throne, Lear dragged himself out of his chair and crossed to the desk, where he signed and stamped an order. The result was a diminution in the traditional scale of the scene, but an increase in the sense of real business being transacted. The most telling use of furniture came at the end. The entire fifth act was set in a room full of chairs, ranged diagonally across the stage, and stepped down in size to give an illusion of perspective so that, as Maurice Good observed, the fourteen chairs looked like forty (Good, p. 118). Edmund's new authority was indicated by his occupation of a desk at the front of this room – or, as the audience saw it, downstage left. The political fall of Lear and Cordelia was signalled when they were made to sit at the back of the room, rows of empty chairs separating them from Edmund as he worked at the desk. The image of two people under arrest, so often signalled conventionally by a soldier at each side, was unexpectedly telling. (The effect was sacrificed in the 1980 revival to give the actors a stronger downstage position.) When Regan, dying of poison, made her final exit, she had to knock over a chair to get out of the room. The feeling was of claustrophobia and explosive panic (and at a more practical level it cleared a path for Lear's entrance with Cordelia).

Class and social position, as so often in updated settings, were clarified. The poor (who, as we shall see, figure so largely in Kozintsev's film and are usually absent from the stage) were briefly glimpsed here in a small group of beggars, 'the context out of which Poor Tom emerged' (Knowles 1985, p. 34). We knew at once who the knights were: useless second sons of the gentry, turned to a military life, drilling on the parade square for a war they would never fight and spending their off-hours hunting. They were boisterous and hearty – one of them mocked Goneril by barking like a dog – but not so dangerous as Brook's knights. As he was later to do with *Cymbeline*, Phillips gave the play a stronger military colouring than it usually gets in production. The battle was the production's only fully stylized moment. Gloucester – indeed, the whole of V.ii – disappeared and the battle was indicated by a procession of soldiers marching across the stage carrying tall banners, while a brisk march played. Unlike Kozintsev or Kurosawa, Phillips was not interested in the violence of war as such; he was more interested in the structure and rhythm of military routine. As the women were tightly laced, so (to the amusement of the actresses) were the men. In the later scenes the blue uniforms of the French soldiers were the production's main visual statement. Lear woke in Cordelia's tent to find himself not in a long robe but in French uniform. On 'Am I in France?' he tapped the cuff suspiciously, drawing a laugh from the audience. The duel between the brothers became two officers in shirt-sleeves settling a point of honour in the guard-room; it was fought with sabres, and Edmund was dispatched with a cut across the stomach. It was preceded by a new speech for the herald who supervised the duel: 'The Code Duello has been read … There is no reconciliation … The affair will proceed' and on to elaborate instructions in English and French (Good, p. 113). Here for once the period detail was jarringly intrusive; and matters were not helped by Edgar's entrance in a black mask that made him look like the Lone

Ranger. (Interestingly, when Phillips did a new production of the play in 1988 he did not cut the mask but gave it to several other actors besides Edgar, creating a more conventionalized idiom in which the device worked much better.)

More effective was the use of steady, soft drumbeats at certain points in the later scenes – Cordelia's return, Edmund's soliloquy before the battle – tying the scenes together with a sense of mounting urgency. Phillips told the company: 'In the long second act, no one should forget that drumbeat that must run as a mental rhythm under it – most of it is to have that drumbeat pulse. And everyone should hear it, in themselves. Everyone, that is, except Peter. And Douglas' (Good, p. 200). Lear and Gloucester (Peter Ustinov and Douglas Rain) were off on their own; everyone else was caught together in a military and political action. Like Irving and Granville Barker, Phillips gave the play a formal ending, drawing on the military atmosphere. On the back platform, three soldiers carrying flags lowered them slowly as a funeral march played. The march continued into the curtain call (as the storm, which broke out at the end of the first act, had continued into the interval). The closure was formal, yet the play was not quite cut off; something of its atmosphere was allowed to seep forward into that moment when the actors become actors again and the audience knows the show is over.

The way the military dimension was used – stressing not violence but formality – is an important clue to the tone of the production. The first sound heard was a piece of quiet trumpet music, whose opening notes sounded like the Last Post. The mood was elegiac. This was not an active, vital world but an old, decaying one. The music in the early scenes was soft, even melancholy, quieting the effect of moments that are usually played with sharp attack – Edmund's first soliloquy, Lear's return from hunting, the opening of the storm. Bridging music in the storm itself was light and rapid but still relatively gentle. The first note of urgency from the orchestra came in the pulsing chords heard after the blinding of Gloucester, which suggested throbbing pain. The general softness of the music was also suited to the domestic scale of the action. If the family drama had been missing in Brook's production, it was abundantly present here – just as the universality given by his vast bare set was deliberately eschewed. In Brook, the daughters had each taken the ceremonial orb on making their speeches, suggesting an ancient ritual; in this production, as

Goneril and Regan were given their shares of the kingdom they kissed their father on the forehead. In his final confrontation with his daughters, Lear made them sit down on a bench with him, trying to be fatherly and domestic as he taught them about 'true need'. Though Gloucester did not recognize his son, Douglas Rain played the fatigue of their journey with 'a delicious undertow of familial argumentativeness' (Good, p. 29). In the blinding scene Rain took an ironic pause on 'I shall see the winged vengeance overtake such ... children?' which told us everything about how family relations had been poisoned.

A production's main chance to be Blake-like and archetypal comes in the storm. But here the special effects were simple – the simplest in any of the stage productions we are discussing – and the focus was on the characters and their relations with each other, not on archetypal man against the cosmos. The stage was filled with dry-ice fog, stirred by a wind-machine. Lear held a quivering twig in his hand. This was Ustinov's idea; he thought of himself as 'conducting' the storm (Good, p. 143) but the actual effect as I remember it was that the twig, like the movements of the actors in Brook's production, helped to create the wind. Thunder was heard, and occasionally the lights flashed full on to indicate lightning. But there was never any danger of drowning out the actors, and it was the actors themselves who at one point produced the most telling visual moment, as the Fool and Kent stood watching Lear, their heads bowed, with the steady patience of men who had been standing in the rain for hours. The storm was background for the actors, not (as in Brook) a character in its own right. As such it was not stylized or symbolic but realistic, part of the natural world. That world was also vividly evoked when the Fool studied the night sky before asking his riddle about the seven stars; it was not a disembodied idea but something he drew from the scene around him. More problematic was the sound of gulls in IV.vi, which fooled audiences into thinking Gloucester really was at Dover Cliff; Phillips' explanation that gulls appear quite far inland after a storm, though answering the objection in the realistic spirit in which it was raised, did not solve the problem (Good, pp. 213–14). Here for once the realistic idiom pinned the play down too closely.

The production had a symbolic dimension as well, but it appeared simply and unobtrusively in the colours of Daphne Dare's costumes, which followed certain principles. The King's party –

Edgar, Kent, Gloucester, the knights – wore shades of brown, the fabrics soft and comfortable. Edmund, Goneril and Regan wore black, grey and dark blue; Albany's colours were also dark, emphasizing that at first he was in their camp. The most dramatic use of colour was in the blue uniforms of Cordelia's army, of which her own dress was a lighter variation. As in the blue tent of the Granville Barker production and the symbolic colours of the Noguchi designs, blue stood for France. It had the effect of bringing freshness and light for the false dawn of Cordelia's return. In this respect Phillips' production buttressed its realism with an underlying formality, and implied an acceptance of the division of characters that Brook had challenged.

The nineteenth-century setting and the domestic realism that accompanied it were unconventional decisions signalling a fresh look at the play. So was the casting of Peter Ustinov as Lear. A multi-talented artist and a star of international standing, chiefly known to audiences for comic acting in popular films, Ustinov had never played Shakespeare before. But for many years he had wanted to play Lear, and he had distinct views about the part. His contribution to the opening rehearsal exercise (what is your name, and what do you think the play is about?) was, 'My name is ... (baffled pause) and the play is about senility' (Good, p. 3). We are back to Lear the old man, Garrick's Lear, but with an important difference. This mad Lear, wandering around with his shirt-tail hanging out, was not simply pathetic. Ustinov played not so much the pathos of old age as its difficult, embarrasssing, even dangerous qualities. He saw the inconsistency of senility as dangerous to Lear himself: 'the same man has to live with the decisions he made during lapses of concentration, and he is usually too stubborn by nature and by accident of birth to reverse those decisions' (Good, p. x). Lear's use of his own senility could be manipulative; Good pointed out that the near-heart-attack he suffered while banishing Cordelia could easily have been feigned (Good, p. 195). On 'dear daughter, I confess that I am old', he did an ironic parody of an old man. Ustinov told a interviewer, 'I've always thought that he was crazy from the very beginning and that the atmosphere in his court was awful – the way it must have been with Franco's followers in Spain or in Pétain's Vichy France' (*Toronto Star*, 18 August 1979). (Ustinov once wrote a play about Pétain, *Moment of Truth*, which he wanted to call *King Lear's Photographer*.) Lear was forgetful; in the first scene he had trouble

[70]

with 'Our dearest Regan, wife to … er … Cornwall.' One audience member suggested to me that he did it on purpose. His occasional deafness may also have been selective and deliberate. Lear's difficulty was also the actor's: Ustinov had persistent line trouble, and in the archive tapes from both seasons one can hear him fumbling, transposing, paraphrasing. It is sometimes difficult to tell where the character's forgetfulness ends and the actor's begins. But what in another performance would have been a painful handicap, here could be fed into the central conception.

In the opening scene there was no suggestion of Granville-Barker's 'magnificent portent'. The voice was senile, the consonants mushy. His anger took more out of him than he could spare; when he rose to denounce Kent or Cordelia, he staggered. He searched for words: 'this shall not be … (long hesitation) … revoked'. On the 1980 archive tape one hears, after the shout of 'Call Burgundy!', a small cough. His entrance from hunting did not have the crisp vigour of Gielgud's or Scofield's, and by the time he got to Gloucester's house he was dog-tired, trudging as though weighed down by his greatcoat. He could be quavering and pathetic with his daughters. In the mad trial, after the cry of 'false justicer!' he gasped with fatigue. It seemed fitting that for the reunion with Cordelia he was brought in not on a chair but on a stretcher. In his first scene he had seemed very comfortable; there was no parti-cular sensation at his entrance, and he sat in a chair, his knees apart, with a cigar and a brandy snifter, very much at ease. But in Gina Mallet's words, he was 'a dinosaur destined for the junk heap because he has no survival skills' (*Toronto Star*, 6 October 1979). One detail signalled this Lear's vulnerability: in IV.vi, where Gielgud 'gently fed the mouse' and Lee J. Cobb killed it with a slap of his hand (Rosenberg, p. 269), Ustinov suddenly pulled his hand back with a cry of pain. He had been bitten, not by the mouse but by a descending hawk ('Well flown, bird') that had snatched it out of his hand (Good, p. 30). In III.vi his first greeting to the dogs was friendly and delighted, then he recoiled in fright on 'they bark at me!' Being an old man, he was in his second childhood. There was a child's smugness on 'I can go with Regan' (*I've* got a plan, I don't care about *you*), a child's light chuckle on the running exit. But the most startling moment came on 'You think I'll weep; no, I'll not weep', which Scofield had delivered with grinding menace. Ustinov wept helplessly. Even through the uncertain sound of the 1979 videotape one can hear an unusual stillness in the audience at this point. The interval came shortly afterwards, making the final revelation of the king's helplessness, not the blinding of Gloucester, the climax to which the first act had been building.

Marowitz complained that Lear the father was missing from Scofield's performance; he was abundantly present here, from the schoolmasterly, lecturing tone (complete with pointing finger) he adopted in the first scene to his pathetic embrace of Regan in their final quarrel. In that scene, as I have noted, he sat on a bench with his daughters, trying to teach them. In his last moments he rocked back and forth as he cradled Cordelia's body. In all of this he was human, not titanic. Where Scofield had isolated the reference to 'our darker purpose', investing his authority with an edge of menace, Ustinov followed it with a small chuckle, as though the darker purpose were a private joke. He had no idea how the coronet could be parted. Gielgud in 1950 took it from a cushion, had Albany and Cornwall place their hands on it, then replaced it on the cushion. Ustinov waved a hand over it with an indecisive gesture, then simply gave up. Reviewers, predictably, complained that this approach was 'too naturalistic, not nearly massive, resonant or archetypal enough' (Jay Carr, *Detroit News*, 9 October 1979), lacking 'the special desperation of man against destiny' (Clive Barnes, *New York Post*, 17 October 1979). It was natural for reviewers to concentrate on this aspect of the performance, since it was here that Ustinov was at his most innovative and unexpected – for some, at his most perverse. Yet, following his own conception of the inconsistency of senility, he could also be strong, clear and direct. 'Darkness and devils!' was loud and quick, accompanied by a surprisingly fast cross. His anger with Cornwall was similarly clean and swift. There were no mushy consonants here; he could be quavering with his daughters, but not man to man. Good commented of a rehearsal of the storm scene, 'The sound is huge. At last, it's gallery time at La Scala' (Good, p. 51). Had it been a portrait of senility alone, Ustinov's Lear might have been pathetic or irritating. But it was something larger than that: a portrait of senility in a constant struggle with strength, clarity and passion.

Maurice Good saw in Ustinov's playing of IV.vi, the scene with Gloucester, an 'ever-recurrent release of inner gaiety' (Good, p. 29). This recalls Gielgud's 'happy king of nature'; but it also suggests the mischievous comedy that was a hallmark of Ustinov's performance. He told an interviewer, 'People say I'm playing it for laughs, but listen to the way it's written' (*Toronto Star*, 21 October 1979). Some of the laughs we can hear on the videotapes are predictable: on 'I'll not chide thee' (after he has been attacking Goneril for several lines) the audience reacts to Lear's illogicality; the reference to the 'scurvy politician' (IV.vi) draws a knowing chuckle. More surprising, but legitimate and revealing, are the laughs on 'her price is fallen', which shows Lear's callousness to Cordelia, and on his reply to Gloucester's 'O let me kiss that hand', 'Let me wipe it first', which, delivered quickly, becomes not so much self-disgust as comic self-deprecation. Like Gielgud, Ustinov had his 'points', emphasizing sometimes the absurdities of Lear, and sometimes Lear's discovery of the absurdities of the human condition. Some of the small touches of invention moved in the direction of comedy – the swift movement of the index fingers to indicate copulating flies, the pumping of the arms on 'to't, luxury, pell-mell'. He added in 1980 a little interested murmur when Regan said of Goneril's speech of flattery, 'Only she comes too short', and a trail of flowers dropped on the running exit in IV.vi. Lear's fussiness was indicated when on 'My train are men of choice and rarest parts' he paused to pick a bit of lint off an attendant's lapel, and when on 'Draw the curtains' (III.vi) Kent mimed the action and Lear pointed out he had only done one side.

The life of the performance lay to a great extent in details like these, rather than in an overall line of development. Like Scofield's very different interpretation, Ustinov's was open to the criticism that it did not change or grow. It was perhaps symptomatic that the 'Howls' were all identical, with no build. Ustinov's own view was that Lear by the end did gain sanity, even wisdom, but that finding the burden of sanity too great he retreated to the pretence of continuing senility (*Saturday Night*, October 1979; Good, p. xi). Like some of Scofield's darker purposes (such as his belief that Lear's anger with Oswald is really anger with himself for his treatment of Cordelia (Rosenberg, p. 100)) this did not register on the audience, and it is hard to see how it could have done. The affirmation that comes from a developing Lear was not particularly emphasized here.

But there was affirmation of a different kind. It is characteristic of Phillips' productions to show a strong communal life, and in this case it appeared in the love by which Lear was surrounded (Good, p. 91). Attendants were always ready to help him, showing concern and affection: two knights assisted him up the platform

[73]

steps as he prepared to leave Goneril; when he woke in Cordelia's tent two soldiers moved to stop him from hurting himself with the pin. In the final scene, on 'undo this button' several hands reached out to help. (All this reinforced the sense of futility when, as Edmund tried to reprieve Cordelia, a stage full of soldiers suddenly panicked, not knowing what to do.) This was a dimension that Brook had severely reduced, particularly in his cutting of Gloucester's servants; in the blinding in this production the servants flattened themselves in horror against the walls of the room, groaning as they shared the victim's pain. Phillips' characteristic blocking had the upstage area filled with attendants, facing us as they watched the action, 'a second audience' providing 'colossal on-stage concentration' (Good, p. 178). These attendants were used to indicate, simply and movingly, the restoration of Lear's dignity at the end of his reunion with Cordelia: as Lear turned upstage the soldiers all bowed to him, and he returned the bow. In his last moment Lear gave a sudden cry and fell back into the arms of his attendants; he died not in joy but in pain, but he died surrounded by love. Granville Barker had female servants place a soft support for Cordelia's head (Fordham, V.iii); the effect sounds conventionally touching. Phillips gave us something more moving: tender, helpless love and concern for an old man from a room full of young soldiers. Watching rehearsals of some of the play's bleaker scenes, Maurice Good was frequently reminded of Beckett (Good, pp. 78, 184); he felt that Douglas Rain's Gloucester in particular drew on his previous season's performance in *From an Abandoned Work* (Good, p. 160). But few viewers thought of Beckett as they watched the production, and its strong images of affection put it at the opposite pole from Brook.

Without attempting to re-adjust conventional sympathies as Brook had done, this production examined the other characters closely; Phillips was no more content with stereotype than Brook had been. In the Granville Barker production, Edgar had come on with a book; of the two brothers, he was the thoughtful one. Here, it was Richard Monette's Edmund who appeared with a book. Monette was cool, intelligent, deliberate; in one rehearsal he walked out whistling Mozart (Good, p. 68). He was the thinker; if anything, he thought too much. He lingered over words like 'base' and 'legitimate'. Rodger Barton's Edgar, in contrast, was hearty, relaxed and unreflective, at ease in his world. Even in his various disguises the same qualities showed through. He had the 'honest,

[74]

forthright look of a hero of Victorian melodrama' (Knowles 1985, p. 34). In the blinding of Gloucester, Regan and Cornwall were human. Phillips insisted that they were driven by fear (Good, pp. 31–3) and all through the scene they sought and received emotional support from each other. The reality of the blinding itself was conveyed by Douglas Rain's voice, which lost its characteristic snap and tension, becoming drained and flat; we realized how much the ordeal had taken out of his whole system. His red makeup in the Dover scene showed him on the verge of sunstroke: 'It's been a long walk outdoors, hatless, for an elderly gentleman from the foreign office' (Good, pp. 183–4). Characteristically, these details do not add up to an agenda for an interpretation; they suggest instead an open-minded probing of the text, as Phillips and his actors searched for whatever human reality they could find.

In 1979 at least, the most striking secondary character was the Fool, played by William Hutt. If Oswald was Uriah Heep (Good, p. 175) the Fool was Mr Dick. There was no attempt at a Victorian version of a Fool's costume. He had all he needed in the shock of white hair, the staring eyes, and above all the voice – a light, childish, patient sing-song, well above the actor's usual register. While McCowen had been bitter and unhappy beneath the wise-cracks, Hutt's jokes were real jokes, which he himself found funny. But sometimes the Fool's voice could drop; he could be quiet and serious. He greeted Tom's entrance with a high-pitched scream that conveyed a terrible fear of the unknown. The King and the Fool had a strong rapport, greeting each other as old friends (adding in 1980 a flapping hand gesture that was clearly a private signal between them), and later sharing a brief dance. In rehearsal, they reminded Good of 'two old dogs worrying at the same bone' (Good, p. 11). The riddle of the seven stars was a shared comic routine: the Fool expressed delight when Lear got the right answer, then stuck in the punch line, 'thou wouldst make a good fool' – to which Ustinov responded (in 1980) with a comic stumble off the platform. On 'my poor fool is hanged' Ustinov suddenly imitated Hutt's voice. Of all the Lear-Fool pairings in the productions we are discussing, this was probably the least hostile, the most affectionate.

In most of this account I have not noted differences between the two years of the production's life, since on most of the matters I have discussed it was consistent in its general aims, however the details may have altered. But there were changes, some involving re-casting, that made for significant shifts of emphasis. Phillips' insistence on quiet had led in 1979 to a languid pace that did not always serve the play well. In 1980 it was tighter and swifter and had more tension. The actor who played Cordelia in 1979 had a persistent quaver in her voice that was hard to listen to and showed the dangers of being too overtly emotional. In 1980 Lynne Griffin was strong and crisp, not unlike the businesslike Cordelia of Diana Rigg. The growth in the evil characters was particularly remarkable: Martha Henry now played Goneril, and in her confrontation with her father she first tried to control the stage with quiet dignity, then suddenly threw a screaming tantrum, with electrifying effect. Taunting Albany, she flicked his legs with a riding whip. Patricia Connolly took a small, hesitant pause when she asked if Edmund had found his way 'to the ... forfended place' that made the line profoundly obscene. The Fool, on the other hand, seemed quieter, saner and less funny. But though the production continued to develop, its essential characteristics remained unchanged. At whatever cost to traditional notions of scale and grandeur, it presented an open-minded, sometimes moving, sometimes disturbing exploration of the human dimension of the play.

CHAPTER V

Adrian Noble, Michael Gambon and Antony Sher

While Robin Phillips' production of *King Lear* centred on a recognizable society, fixed to a specific period, Adrian Noble, who directed the play for the Royal Shakespeare Company in 1982, created a stage world that was frankly a theatrical invention, drawing on recognizable images but combining them in a manner peculiar to itself. Brook, in a way, had done the same thing, invented a world; but while his had a single uniform character Noble's was deliberately eclectic. We began in a throne room. So does the play, of course; but after the informal, unregal openings the play had been given in previous productions it was a pleasant surprise to see what Granville Barker's audience would have seen in 1940: a throne at the centre, with other chairs placed symmetrically around it (Gielgud 1981, p. 110). The room was a large enclosed space, with five entrances on the back wall; the largest, the central one, was obviously the King's. This was a world of order, power and hierarchy. The King's entrance, through the central door, was marked by a long, bold fanfare of trumpets, drums and cymbals – even at one point a choir. When he appeared, everyone knelt. France and Burgundy, who normally appear without any particular fuss, had an entrance fanfare but it was shorter than Lear's; in this world there was a clear pecking order. Michael Gambon, who played Lear, was large and solidly built, an imposing presence. The map was also large (though not extravagantly so) and as he carved up his kingdom he gestured over it with a sword. His voice and bearing were strong, confident and demanding. Here at last was Granville-Barker's 'magnificent portent'.

The costumes, like Brook's, could not be pinned down to a century, but they belonged to an old world. There were long robes for the men, dresses along Elizabethan lines with puffed sleeves for the women, ruff collars framing the faces as in Renaissance portraits. But the imposing grey walls of the set suggested a nineteenth-century public building. Michael Billington called it 'a metaphysical Colditz' (*Guardian*, 30 June 1982), one of the military prisons of the Second World War. Later we would see these imposing walls ravaged by warfare, and we would feel we were in an East European city that had been bombed to pieces. Once we were out of the first scene there was a Russian feeling to many of the costumes, especially the greatcoats worn by the men; the soldiers, in caps and rough cloaks, looked like Russian peasants. As Lear's world broke apart, chronology broke apart with it, as though time itself were being scrambled – or, since there was a general move from mediaeval to modern, as though we were moving with unnatural speed from the ordered traditions of the past to the broken world we live in now. Instead of suggesting the modernity of an ancient period, as Brook had done, Noble separated the periods and took each in turn. The first sign that we were entering a new world came in I.iii when Oswald appeared in a simplified modern uniform, with high leather boots and an attaché case under his arm. Since its use by Polonius and Osric in Peter Hall's 1965 *Hamlet*, the attaché case had been RSC code for an establishment figure who was not to be trusted. Modernity was not just the prerogative of the evil characters; Cordelia had an electric torch which at one point she shone in the face of a messenger. But the two most striking transitions to the modern were Oswald's entrance and Lear's appearance in the storm. The King, who had been a mediaeval figure, then a nineteenth-century Russian one, appeared in the storm, and later in the scene with Gloucester, in waistcoat, trousers and shirtsleeves. Gloucester's blindness was indicated by black spectacles. If the political cynicism of Oswald located the play in our time, so did the madness and suffering of the two old men. In his later scene with Cordelia, Lear was dressed not in the traditional long robe but in pyjamas, with a blanket wrapped around him. Michael Gambon had enough personal dignity throughout that there was no need to add anything in the way of externals; what the costume stressed, accordingly, was not Lear the restored king but Lear the patient, who still needed to be looked after.

The deliberate anachronism followed Peter Brook's idea (more obviously than Brook himself had done) that 'a jarring of externals' (Brook 1968, p. 39) may be the best way to translate a complex work into stage terms. It also reflected, as Phillips' scrupulous creation of a single period did not, the combination of periods in the text, though it was more overt and extravagant on this point than the text is, and more deliberate in its use of periods to make a point than we may imagine the Jacobean theatre was. The production's modernity was also fed by its being in repertoire with Edward Bond's *Lear*. Apart from the three principal actresses, who doubled as Lear's daughters and the equivalent characters in Bond, there was little carryover in personnel. The productions had different directors and designers, and different Lears; they played in different theatres. But they were scheduled whenever possible to run on consecutive nights so that audiences could see them together, and there were some visual echoes, especially the 'rough, clumsy great-coats, the gear of an army on the march, exposed to danger, accustomed to discomfort' (Sinfield, p. 7). The planks and sandbags we saw Cordelia's soldiers loading could have been used to build Lear's wall in Bond's play. When in the blinding of Gloucester Regan took a long pin out of her hair and handed it to Cornwall, the appalling use of an ordinary domestic object recalled Bond's use of knitting needles in the torture of Warrington. In a more general way the production's loose sense of period recalled the equally deliberate anachronisms in Bond (though this was not reflected in the staging of Bond's play, which had a fairly consistent feeling of the 1940s.) Noble's focus on the political side of Shakespeare – Edmund delivered his first soliloquy leaning over the back of the throne, his second sitting on it; Goneril sat in the throne as she gave orders to Oswald – may have owed something to Bond's insistently political vision. Noble himself declared that he intended to 'bring out the contemporary political dimension' of Shakespeare's play, and that having Bond's in the repertoire 'was like a steady drop of cold water, preventing them from keeping *King Lear* in a separate historical pocket' (Sinfield, p. 7). While the production was in rehearsal Britain was at war with Argentina over the Falkland Islands, and the scene in which Cordelia's soldiers stacked planks and passed sandbags down a line was inspired directly by television shots of British troops loading up in Plymouth Harbour. The images of war, like the images of political oppression and madness, were modern – in this case, very specific and topical. There was nothing perfunctory or stylized about the battle itself. Noble decided he wanted to put the war on stage (Sinfield, p. 8) and he did so – with running crowds, drums, screams, flashes of light and explosions. As the last scene began, smoke from the battle still hung in the air. For Noble, as for Kozintsev in his film version, the war was too important to relegate to a few offstage noises.

The same explicitness could be seen in the production's occasional recollections of Beckett. Where Brook had taken from Beckett suggestions for a style of playing, Noble used visual images associated with the Absurdist playwright. The Fool (in a scene we shall return to later) died hanging out of a barrel, recalling the dustbins of *Endgame*. Lear's boots, removed during the scene with Gloucester, remained on stage to the end of the play, a silent tribute to Estragon (Sinfield, p. 12). In these and other cases, the production did its thinking in visual terms. In keeping with Noble's idea that the play 'was written in a period similar to our own, "when everything is about to be put in storage"' (*Observer*, 27 May 1982), the first scene ended with servants putting dustcovers on all the furniture, and the second scene was played amid the ghostly shapes this created. Lear's generation had been packed away, and a new generation, starting with Edmund, was rising. Brook's Edgar fled from distant barking dogs; Noble's, like a modern prisoner escaping at night, fled from searchlights. The terror of Tom's first entrance was signalled not, as in the Granville Barker and Phillips productions, by a scream from the Fool, but by the staging of the entrance itself. The hovel was indicated by a trap door, through which the Fool descended. Moments later the Fool was hurled out of the depths, followed by his hat and bag; then Tom exploded through the floor, scattering lumber and casting a giant shadow behind him. It was the modern equivalent of the entrance of a devil from the pit of Hell, and Tom's demonic side, which actors so often miss as they go for shivering pathos, was established at once. The large pit opening was also used in IV.vi, as Edgar led Gloucester over a plank that spanned it, externalizing the sense that they are taking a perilous spiritual journey from which they will emerge safe. There was the same externalized sense of danger when Cordelia's soldiers caught Lear in a large net, as though he were a wild animal. Lear's captors are normally more respectful; but in the text Lear is surprisingly elusive, and this may not just be arbitrary plotting. He has gone far beyond society, and Noble's device made him seem, for a moment, barely human.

This visual inventiveness constantly reminded us we were in a theatre; it was as though a sign 'Director at Work' had been hung over the stage. This feeling was particularly strong in the storm scenes: it was a theatrical storm, created not by the elements but by artists. Its dominant noises were not wind and thunder but music – crashing cymbals, electronic howls and whistles. At the beginning of III.ii Lear and the Fool were raised high on a small platform that made them look as though they were riding on the clouds. Unfortunately it also made them look as though they were standing on a bird feeder; reviewers and audiences divided as to whether the device was effective or incongruous (*Sandwell Evening Mail*, 29 May 1983; *New Statesman*, 2 June 1982). At the opening of the hovel scene Lear, the Fool and Kent ran on stage covered by a large blanket, looking like a demented pantomime horse and accompanied by an electronic whinny. Noble told an interviewer, 'When you get to the heath, you see a sort of Crazy Gang' (*Observer*, 7 May 1982); and this was one of his most powerful images – powerful because it was so bizarre and illogical. Later the characters seemed like mad children at play. Gloucester led them out of the hovel hand-in-hand, and as they circled the pit from which Tom had burst they looked as though they were playing a round game. On their way out they formed a straight line, with the Fool at the end, recalling the procession of death that ends Bergman's *The Seventh Seal*. In the farmhouse scene Tom shook feathers out of a leaking pillow; they hung in the air, lit by a single naked lightbulb that swung dementedly after Tom had struck it.

Noble saw the play's action moving from land to water (Fuzier and Maguin, p. 118); this makes sense if we think of Lear and Gloucester heading for Dover and Cordelia returning from the sea. But while Kozintsev could convey this powerfully in his film, the resources of the theatre limited Noble to a trough of water that ran along the front of the stage in the second act. Edgar drank from it, then washed in it as he prepared to change roles. Lear and Gloucester took off their boots and paddled in it. One reviewer hopefully suggested that the water was redemptive (Mark Amory, *Spectator*, 10 July 1982) but the real effect, I thought, was that it was fun to play in. It also recalled those Victorian theatre posters that advertised 'REAL WATER!', a display of stage technology for its own sake. It was useful for the final duel, a sabre fight varied by kicks and punches which ended with Edgar trying to drown his brother before attendants pulled him off. Both men, by the way, were stripped to the waist, suggesting, as so often in productions, an affinity between them – except that by a happy accident of casting Edmund was a redhead, with a lot of red body hair that Shakespeare's contemporaries would have recognized as giving him the colour of Judas. Sometimes the staging devices were designed to show us a scene from one character's point of view. This was Noble's intention in the storm: to show 'what it's like inside that head ... what it's like when the horizon tilts' (Sinfield, p. 10). The effect was clearer in Gloucester's entrance to the hovel, where clashing music accompanied Tom's reference to him as a devil, and let us for a moment think of him as Tom did; and in the blinding when, as Gloucester lost his second eye, the lights went dim.

The demands of all this on the backstage personnel can be seen in the promptbook, with notes like 'Plenty of time to reset' followed by a sketch of a happy face (implying this was unusual) and 'HERE WE GO AGAIN!' The simplicity of the Dover scene, in which Lear and Gloucester could simply sit down and talk, is indicated by the note '10 mins. to next Q's'. Productions of *King Lear* often elicit the complaint that the scale is too small. For Ned Chaillet the 'nearly operatic character of [Noble's] production ... pushes the performance past its normal human scale into something more portentous' (*The Times*, 30 June 1982). For Benedict Nightingale, 'The danger that Mr. Noble's imagination courts, and doesn't always avoid, is of substituting theatricality for truth of feeling' (*New Statesman*, 2 July 1982). Phillips had given all or most of the work to the actors; so, we may imagine, did Shakespeare's company. But in our theatre, where the resources exist to show the extra-human dimension the modern imagination needs help with, as Brook did with his wide set and rattling thunder-sheets, a production that passes up this chance may well be accused of reducing the scale of the play. Noble may have gone too far, but he went too far in a direction the play clearly offers; and the crazy eclecticism of his production brought out a dimension of the play itself, in which the risk of mingling clowns and kings, tragic grandeur and low buffoonery, goes as far as anywhere in Shakespeare.

What of the acting? In contrast to the quiet Phillips production the delivery was generally strong and punchy, if a bit loud. Even Cordelia (Alice Krige) was not soft, gentle and low but strong and vehement throughout, 'all too clearly her father's daughter' (Judith Cook, *The Scotsman*, 30 June 1982). Michael Gambon, who played Lear, had specialized in modern comedy and had not seen the play before; this meant he could approach the text with no pre-conceptions (*Wolverhampton Express*, 28 May 1982). Yet his performance, initially at least, answered to the most old-fashioned expectations. To use Granville Barker's image, he was an oak, down to the roots. His stage presence was massive, his voice powerful. When on 'darkness and devils' he grabbed Goneril she uttered a short cry of shock and fright. As he cursed her he knelt and pointed upwards, invoking the heavens in an old-fashioned way. 'I will do such things' was not so ineffectual as it often appears; Lear drew his sword. Anger came easily, even when he was appealing to the gods, whom he lectured on their duty to him. On 'I'll not weep' he almost did, but turned it into a shout. He used his whip a lot, threatening Goneril with it; and when he beat the Fool he beat him hard. But if he was 'ready to strike anyone' he was also 'ready to hug anyone' (Sinfield, p. 10) – the Fool, Gloucester, even Goneril (*Daily Telegraph*, 30 June 1982). Francis King noted a general tendency in the production for the good characters to 'make physical contact with each other, while their opponents remain isolated, each in a separate, solipsistic hell of evil' (*Sunday Telegraph*, 5 June 1983). But the question raised by Gambon's performance, as by those of Scofield and Ustinov, was whether this robust, oak-like Lear could change. His 'Howls', like Ustinov's, were all on the same note (and, strong though his voice was, he could not prolong the vowels as Scofield had done). In the first scene his manner did not change significantly when Cordelia defied him; he simply became louder and angrier. Waking in her tent, he conveyed little of the pain or bewilderment the text suggests; he seemed most himself when on 'I am mightily abused' he showed a flash of his old authority. Ned Chaillet observed, 'when he threatens to gather his tattered forces to reclaim his country, his threat bears force' (*The Times*, June 30, 1982). But it was the spiritual recovery that seemed to be missing; as Stanley Wells put it, the actor for all his power lacked 'inwardness' (*Times Literary Supplement*, 16 July 1982). Not all the reviewers agreed. Michael Coveney reported, 'He releases great emotional depth charges in the reunions with Gloucester and Cordelia' (*Financial Times*, 1 July 1982). James Fenton saw the inwardness that Stanley Wells missed: 'The unforgettable element remains Mr. Gambon's suffering face, with its ability to induce dysfunction: at a flicker of the eyes a kind of blindness is suggested, or a passing mad fit, or a great depth of misery' (*Sunday Times*, 4 July 1982). This suggests emotions presented with economy, but an economy that may have been too great to let the emotions register on some viewers. Robert Cushman found a similar economy in 'Come, let's away to prison', which was 'so quietly sensible as to be heart-rending' (*Observer*, 4 July 1982). Lear's links with Gloucester (David Waller) seemed particularly strong. Some were visual: Gloucester's denunciation of the gods was accompanied by a jabbing upward gesture that recalled Lear when he invoked the heavens. In a more obvious touch, Lear entered the Dover scene tapping with a stick, as though he too were blind. The effect of that scene was of two gruff old men sitting together, both chuckling as they shared a grim appreciation of the absurdity of a world they both knew. When Gloucester took off Lear's boots, Lear reciprocated by taking off Gloucester's shoes so they could paddle together in the water. Gambon in this scene was not overtly mad; rather, he was lecturing confidently, showing his old authority in a new way; like Gielgud he was 'happy in his madness' (*Daily Telegraph*, 30 June 1982). In the last scene he appeared most confident drawing on resources he had had from the beginning, such as the anger on 'Prithee away' and, more unexpectedly, on the final 'never'. He tried to get Cordelia to speak by shaking her. But the sudden colloquial naturalness of 'He's a good fellow' had the same moving simplicity Cushman found in 'let's away to prison'. In general, this was a performance that left some people untouched, others profoundly moved. The limitations that the first group saw suggested that, for all Gielgud's misgivings about his personal resources, it's not enough to be an oak; the ash at least can bend. So far as Gambon succeeded, he succeeded as other actors have done, by finding the humanity of the part.

The performance that roused the most discussion, however, was that of Antony Sher as the Fool. After the first read-through Sher decided that 'my own voice and personality didn't do the role any favours at all'; he was also plagued by the conviction that Shakespeare's clowns are totally unfunny. Noble had begun his own thinking about the part with 'the image of the strange banjo player in the film *Deliverance*'. He and Sher decided to experiment with different devices to find out what sort of entertainer the Fool was. Sher reports: 'We began with the red nose, and in the event never went any further, it was so immediately successful. There is something very liberating about wearing a red nose, both externally and internally: you look, feel and sound odd, exaggerated, caricatured' (Sher, pp. 153, 154, 156–7). As a red-nosed clown in a bowler hat and an ill-fitting suit, the Fool was one of the most clearly modern images in the production, and the most overtly theatrical. He was also more a role than a person, and this restored an effect Shakespeare's audience would have recognized: we recall those Elizabethan and Jacobean play texts in which a character (whether or not he has a proper name, like Pompey in *Measure for Measure*) is simply called 'Clown'. This Fool was a real comedian, a professional, who got an entrance round from the knights when he appeared. At various points the Fool and Lear worked as a vaudeville team, notably in I.v, when they appeared in front of a backcloth, with footlights casting giant shadows behind them (though the light was also cold, sinister and exaggerated, giving the comedy a frightening edge). Together they marked punch lines with a stamp of the foot and an outflung arm, 'as if they are playing the Palace as well as living in it' (Michael Billington, *Guardian*, 3 June 1983). When the Fool calls his master 'Lear's shadow' or when Lear refers to 'this great stage of fools' the play becomes metatheatrical, aware of itself as performance; the comic routines of Lear and the Fool brought out this quality strongly.

Sher's Fool, like the production as a whole, was shamelessly eclectic. Reviewers looking for clowns he reminded them of produced not single names but lists: Grock, Little Titch, Max Wall, George Formby, Michael Crawford, Chaplin, Rigoletto and Beckett's tramps. He played inventively with different styles and conventions. 'Have more than thou showest' was a rhythmic chant, with the knights joining in, foot-stamping and hand-clapping. 'That sir which serves and seeks for gain' was a brilliant imitation of George Formby, with the tiny Suzuki violin that was the Fool's main prop functioning as the ukelele that was Formby's. 'Fathers that wear rags' was a lullaby sung to a crying baby impersonated by the violin. Sher conjured 'the sweet and bitter fool' out of his hat. He placed the two halves of the egg on his eyes as comic spectacles, and juggled with them. Sometimes he sat on Lear's knee and imitated a ventriloquist's dummy, with Lear as the ventriloquist. He restored the Fool's vulgarity, which so many actors have suppressed: 'Lady Brach may stand by the fire and stink' was accompanied by a loud farting noise, the 'cut shorter' joke by a phallic gesture with the violin. The Fool was crippled, walking on stiff legs with toes turned in. He was allowed, as the Fool seldom is in the modern theatre, to speak his prophecy. And suddenly, towards the end of it, he could dance. Then a whistle blew, and the Fool was crippled again. He staggered out, shaking his fist at the heavens.

His close professional relationship with Lear led at least one reviewer to think of him not as a separate character but as Lear's conscience (Michael Billington, *Guardian*, 30 June 1982). The relationship was not always close or sympathetic; Lear could be gruffly unresponsive, and when he beat the Fool he beat him long, hard and painfully. 'Whoop, Jug, I love thee' was the Fool's plea for him to stop. Perhaps this was Lear rejecting his conscience. But Sher's performance took off so much on its own that he seemed to be a separate entity. The real danger was that all the attention lavished on the Fool threatened to make the play about him, not about Lear. One review was titled 'Lear in the Fool's shadow' (*Times Literary Supplement*, 16 July 1982); another, 'Upstaged by the Fool' (*The Times*, 2 June 1983). The production opened with a tableau in which the Fool and Cordelia were seen stretched out on the throne, their necks connected by a rope; it turned out to be a game they were playing – though of course the joke would become earnest in Lear's 'And my poor fool is hang'd.' The Fool was in the first scene, as he is not in the text, and had a brief, tearful farewell with Cordelia. At this point the production drew on the sentimental side of the popular tradition from which the Fool came, as elsewhere it drew on its vulgarity. As the Fool appeared earlier than he does in the play, so he did not fade unobtrusively as Shakespeare has him do. Trying to anatomize Regan, the mad Lear stabbed the Fool, who was sitting in a barrel. Dying, he hung out of the barrel, a grotesque jack-in-the-box. Edgar embraced him during his last soliloquy, then pushed him down into the barrel, covered it with a blanket and gave it a final pat as he left. All through the blinding of Gloucester we remembered that one of the props on stage was a barrel with a dead fool in it.

These inventions were striking in themselves, but they disrupted the balance of the play by putting a stronger focus on the Fool than Shakespeare seems to have intended. (Whatever Shakespeare might have thought of this, we know Hamlet would not have approved.) And there is a question as to whether Sher's own inventiveness finally worked against the character. Michael Billington put his finger on the problem: 'I sometimes find that Sher, brilliant though he is ... is so relentlessly virtuosic that you can't altogether understand what he is saying' (*Guardian*, 3 June 1983). This is a reaction to the London transfer, during which Sher himself felt that the production had lost some of its 'original boldness' and that he had lost his ability to make the audience laugh (Sher, p. 165). Certainly on the archive videotape, which was recorded some months after the Stratford opening, many of the Fool's routines (not all of them) pass over in relative silence. On the other hand, Kent's attack on Oswald – the two actors just stand together, while Kent (Malcolm Storry) spells out the insults slowly, each one seeming to be the end, each one succeeded by a fresh attack – brings the house down. The two problems, lack of meaning and lack of comedy, are related. Past a certain point, we won't find the Fool funny if we don't know what he's on about. The Formby impersonation (for example) was so good that our concentration went on admiring the voice, not on listening to what the voice was saying. And the sheer variety in the end produced a blurred effect. One of the secrets of clowning is economy: the clown must be immediately familiar and distinctive, and to that end he deliberately works over a narrow range and keeps his bag of tricks small.

I should add in fairness that I am now drawing on my own response to the production, which I saw relatively late in the Stratford run, when it may already have lost some of its edge; and that for most reviewers, and for most audience members I have talked with, Sher's Fool was brilliantly successful. Mine is very much a minority view, and I am quarrelling more with the detailed execution than with the underlying conception. In any case, though the performance stood out in bold relief from the rest of the production it was also in tune with its essential spirit. Noble's *King Lear* drew on Bond, on Beckett, on contemporary politics, and on the circus. In the process it showed how many areas of life and art the play could touch. But mostly it drew on theatre itself, with exhilarating and sometimes disturbing effect. The image of Alan Webb's Gloucester mutely staring at the opening white walls is one indelible image from my experience of the play in the theatre; Sher's circus-clown Fool, tossed about in the cosmic fury of an electronic, theatrical storm, is another.

CHAPTER VI

Grigori Kozintsev

The productions we have been discussing so far are gone, and the best we can do is retrieve information about them from tapes, reviews, photographs and memories. On the whole I have written about them in the past tense. The remaining productions are still available for viewing; I can write about them in the present. That is one obvious characteristic separating film and television from live performance. Another is that in the screen versions the play is being adapted for a medium it was not written for, a medium of which Shakespeare had no inkling. The makers of screen versions have not only the opportunity but the responsibility to re-create the text in new terms; simply to set up a camera in front of a stage performance can be deadening. As we shall see, the film adaptations by Kozintsev and Brook are much freer than the television versions; but all five offer a fundamentally different experience from that of *King Lear* in the theatre. The mysterious chemistry of the relationship between live performer and live audience is gone; in its place is the selective eye of the camera, deciding what we will see and what we won't. Though in the end he remained closer to the fundamentals of the play than Peter Brook did, the Russian film director Grigori Kozintsev in his 1970 film was in one sense not using Shakespeare's text at all; he was using Boris Pasternak's translation into modern Russian, so that he was taking the play not just out of its language but linguistically out of its period. (The effect is unfortunately distorted in the only print I have been able to see, where the English subtitles are direct quotations from Shakespeare; they imply a closeness to the original that is quite misleading, and even viewers with no Russian can spot moments when they obviously don't reflect what the actors are saying.) Freed from the literal surface of Shakespeare's text, Kozintsev was able to find, on his own terms, a way of re-creating what he saw as its essential spirit. In his book *King Lear: The Space of Tragedy* (English translation 1977) and in other writings he describes the process in detail, allowing us to study not only the film but the thinking that lay behind it.

In Kozintsev's own words, 'The poetic texture has ... to be transformed into a visual poetry, into the dynamic organisation of film imagery' (Kozintsev 1972, p. 191). The word 'dynamic' is particularly important for this film. On stage an actor can walk only a few steps before he is in the wings. On screen an actor can go on walking, and the camera will follow. In our collection of truisms about the difference between stage and screen, this makes the best starting point for a look at Kozintsev's film, a film 'shot through with the rhythms of walking, marching, running. Everything is shaken from its place. Everything is in movement' (Kozintsev 1972, p. 196). This picks up and expands the sense of movement we have in the play: Lear's journeys from house to house and finally into the wilderness, Gloucester's journey (as he thinks) to Dover, Cordelia's exile and return. Kozintsev opens with a shot of ragbound feet trudging along a dirt road. Lear's people, the poor of the kingdom, are on the move, through a stony wasteland. Gradually we see more and more of them, walking steadily forward through standing stones which include a rough carving with Celtic interlace design. Shot by shot, the screen image grows in scope and detail, opening out before us in a movement as steady as the movement of the people. When I screened the film for some students, and asked for their reactions, one of them wrote, 'The shots of the peasants travelling somehow moved me – I have no idea why!' She was aware that there was more at work than an obvious sympathy for poverty. It is the rhythm, the movement of the film itself that is being established, translating into screen terms, and over a broader range, Shakespeare's sense of Lear's relentless journey. Having seen the peasants we then see knights on horseback, with spears; we are moving in a different way, up the social scale. Gloucester and Kent walk down a staircase into a courtyard. Inside, Goneril and Regan are walking at a steady, dignified pace into the main hall of the castle. Cordelia runs down a flight of stairs and joins them, falling in with their pace but only after she has shown that her natural movement is swifter and freer than theirs. As in Shakespeare language is a clue to character (in Ben Jonson's words, 'Speak, that I may see thee'), here we know the characters when we see how they walk. Later we see Gloucester slowly walking a large dog as he broods in voice-over on the strange events of the day ('Kent banished ...'), and we sense a reflective melancholy beneath the sensual exterior suggested by his heavy face. When Lear wakes in Cordelia's tent, stage productions generally aim at stillness. We see him with Gloucester, then we see him run away; when we next find him he is restored and at rest, his journey apparently over. What Kozintsev emphasizes is the journey: Lear is carried on a litter of reeds past a foaming river, then through fire and the sound of clashing swords. Fixing steadily on his sleeping face, the camera journeys with him, and so do we. Even his reconciliation with Cordelia takes place in the open air, by a roadside; they are still in transit. This sense of constant movement was of fundamental importance to Kozintsev. He was a great believer in walking as a way of stimulating thought: 'I conceive Shakespeare's tragedies while I am walking; I hold imaginary conversations with friends who are no longer living and with favourite authors. I argue with them and learn from them'. He recalls stories of Dostoevsky walking the streets alone, waving his arms and talking to himself (Kozintsev 1977, pp. 44, 87–8).

As the camera can follow actors when they walk, it can also take us quickly into different spaces, freeing and extending the location of a scene. We can see, for example, how characters in different rooms shut each other out. Cornwall and Regan are sitting at a table; Edmund is pouring a drink for Cornwall. Through a closed door we hear Lear arguing with Gloucester over why his relations will not see him. For a moment the king is shut out from us too. The effect is reversed when at the climax of the bargaining session – 'What need one?' – Goneril and Regan walk into the house, Oswald closes the door behind them, and Lear is left to conduct 'reason not the need' as an argument with the elements, and with himself. This time we are shut out with him. But the most powerful use of multiple space is the blinding of Gloucester. We can imagine – or perhaps we would prefer not to imagine – what the director of a popular horror movie would do with this scene. Kozintsev does not try for graphic violence. We see that Cornwall puts out the first eye with his foot as Gloucester lies bound in a chair, but on the removal of the second eye we see only Cornwall's back. The real horror comes when, as Gloucester's cries ring through the house – his house – we cut to Goneril's room, where she is lacing up her boots. She pauses for a moment, then goes on lacing. Then we see Edmund, just as calmly, buckling on his sword. The moral horror of their indifference adds a new dimension to the scene. Then we are back on the move again.

Mortally wounded, Cornwall staggers over to Regan. His eyes go dead and he falls at her feet. She walks past him, out of the room, then takes a zig-zag track, avoiding people, through the house till she comes to Edmund's chamber. She rips his shirt open, and the next thing we see is Cornwall's dead body, stripped to the waist, laid out on a table, with Regan bending over and planting a devouring kiss on his lips. (Penelope Gilliat observes that in this film Goneril and Regan 'snatch kisses from men as if they were eating mouths' (*New Yorker*, 11 August 1975).) As in the Phillips production, there is a dark sexuality at work in the evil characters, an appetite that will not rest till it has devoured the living and the dead.

Kozintsev opens out not only the space of the play but its range of important characters. The poor we see on the roads in the opening shots are the 'poor naked wretches' of Lear's prayer. In Shakespeare's play we never see them. They are something for Lear, Gloucester and Edgar to talk about as part of their growing knowledge of the world, but they are not an active part of the drama. Was this because Shakespeare's audience had walked past them on its way into the Globe Theatre and would walk past them again on its way out? Or because, with the economy and represen-tative power of Shakespeare's theatre, Poor Tom can stand for them all? Phillips allowed us to glimpse a few of the poor, but the glimpse was brief and discreet. Trevor Nunn's 1976 Royal Shake-speare Company production introduced a whole troop of them parading across the stage, chanting one of the Fool's songs. But their effect was intrusive, and when the production was trans-ferred from Stratford to London they were cut (Bratton, p. 79; David, p. 104). Shakespeare's text really allows no space for the poor of Lear's kingdom on stage; but in Kozintsev's film they are a major presence. He was convinced that 'one cannot portray the life of a king without portraying the life of his subjects' (Kozintsev 1977, p. 34), and years before he made the film he imagined that Shakespeare must often have seen uprooted farm workers reduced to beggary and wandering the roads of England (Kozintsev 1966, pp. 12, 67). When in the play Lear addresses the 'poor naked wretches' they are an idea in his mind. In Kozintsev's film they are right there with him, packed into a dark hovel where they have taken refuge from the storm, a scene drawn from Dostoevsky's description of people packed into a prison wash-house in *Notes from the House of the Dead*. For Kozintsev this, not the thunder and lightning, was the climax of the storm sequence (Kozintsev 1977, p. 192). This also means that as Poor Tom, Edgar is not an isolated figure. Edgar sees a procession of beggars moving down the road. They are chanting some of the lines that in Shakespeare are Tom's; Kozintsev saw Tom's proverbs not as springing from the demented mind of one character, but as 'the voice of the Kingdom' (Kozintsev 1973, p. 14), the embodiment of peasant wisdom. Edgar strips off some of his clothing, covers himself with dirt, and falls in at the end of the procession, adapting his natural walk to the slow, limping gait of his new companions. Later Gloucester will join him in the procession, and finally Lear. The journeys that in Shakespeare are solitary wanderings into spiritual isolation have become purposeful decisions to fall in with a group. In the most literal sense, to learn wisdom is to join with the common people. We may attribute this to the convictions of a Soviet artist; but we should also notice that what I have just said about the spiritual isolation in Shakespeare's text is not the whole story: Gloucester falls in with a beggar and Lear falls in with a blind man; much of their talk is about the society they have left behind.

Kozintsev, whose film is made for a screen of Cinemascope width, can also open the play to the landscape and the weather. Appropriately, this is one of Shakespeare's most outdoor plays, and it was designed for a roofless theatre. Kozintsev insisted that 'tragedy takes place not amongst landscapes but among people'; for him the world of *Lear* was as densely populated as that of Balzac (Kozintsev 1977, p. 82). Indeed, we might say that the most important feature of Kozintsev's landscape is the people. All the same, he had a film director's eye for the right symbolic location. He felt that in the studio shots he and his colleagues 'had just about achieved a mediocre quality' but as soon as they moved to the bleak, stony Kazantip promontory in the Azov sea they found 'a Shakespearean landscape, the power of reality devoid of everything specific' (Kozintsev 1977, pp. 127, 130). Here, the real work could begin. This is the landscape through which the beggars move. The flat, desolate plain, looking like a dried-up river bed, on which the storm breaks out and Gloucester takes his final journey, was a tract of land near Narva in which all the vegetation had been killed by pollution from the State Regional Electric Power Station (Kozintsev 1977, pp. 230–1). As befits the play's universality, the desolation of Kozintsev's landscapes is both ancient and modern, natural and man-made. The weather makes its contribution too,

[92]

and not just in the storm scene. As Lear and his train set out for Goneril's house, distant rain hangs in the sky; they set out for Gloucester's through mist and winter trees: menace followed by desolation.

Many of the film's most important symbols are drawn from nature. Water suggests restoration and new life. While Adrian Noble was restricted to a trough of water at the front of the stage, Kozintsev shows Cordelia on her return to England against a background of foam-flecked sea and white gulls; Lear carried on a stretcher beside a running stream; Gloucester and Edgar meeting with a large body of still water behind them. Stage Lears enter crowned with flowers. In the film, Lear lies in a field of waving grass, his unruly white hair seeming part of it. Nature itself, like the poor people, is a real presence. But the lyrical shots of sea and grass are less characteristic of the film's view of nature than is the harsh stony landscape through which the beggars move, 'a mean, cruel and heartless nature ... the land of tragedy' (Kozintsev 1977, p. 131). Stone is a key image throughout. Early in his account of the film's gestation, Kozintsev describes how he was inspired by a visit to the stone garden at Ryōan-ji in Kyoto (Kozintsev 1977, pp. 3–4). At the point where Shakespeare's Lear, confronted with Cordelia's soldiers, makes a grotesque running exit, Kozintsev has him make an equally grotesque attempt to climb on to a large boulder, the only throne he has left in a land whose physical sterility suggests the emptiness of his rule (Schmaltz, p. 89).

In creating Lear's society Kozintsev took Peter Brook's route, a generalized older period, essentially mediaeval but with occasional Renaissance suggestions – though his costumes are more natural and comfortable, more like something from real history, than Brook's heavy leather outfits. The castles are stone, the houses brick and half-timber; Edgar flees over a wooden stockade. His earlier *Hamlet* film had been firmly Renaissance in design, but Kozintsev saw *Lear* as more 'timeless and universal' (Kozintsev 1973, p. 11). 'Rags and suffering – which century is it?' (Kozintsev 1972, p. 195). The play's universality means that one of its periods is ours; Kozintsev includes among the images that fed his imagination while he was working on the film troops putting down student protests, tanks rolling through a town, the killing of Martin Luther King, and photographs of a new policeman's helmet that covered the head with steel, leaving only a slit for the eyes – 'What century was this?' (Kozintsev 1977, p. 124). Kozintsev did not use such images explicitly, as Adrian Noble did; and though as I write this the film is over thirty years old, it does not yet betray the 'period' feel that it would have if it consciously reflected its own time. But he asked Dmitri Shostakovich, who wrote the music, to use 'the language of contemporary art ... to express the contemporary world' (Kozintsev 1977, p. 242). With no obtrusive links to the modern world, the film was to be, like Brook's production on its European tour, 'about us'.

Though the family tree on which we see Edmund brooding evokes a world of property and inheritance, there is no attempt to impress us with spectacles of wealth or power. Kozintsev wanted costumes that were 'not remarkable in any way' (Kozintsev 1977, p. 37). We see the domestic side of life in the great houses: kings and nobles sit by the fire and eat dinner. Dramatic confrontations take place 'Between mouthfuls – this is the heart of the matter' (Kozintsev 1977, p. 162). The table at Goneril's house is spread with a white cloth and formal-looking utensils, decent and civilized but not ostentatious. The daughter helps her father by putting meat on his plate, and then starts to lecture him about the manners of his knights. Simply and recognizably, a family row breaks out at the dinner table. Lear will be happier a few scenes later, when we see him down on the ground, eating roots and drinking from a spring. After the battle we see the four victors squabbling in a tent, around a small table, with pewter mugs of drink. Regan's mug is poisoned. Elsewhere there are armies, crowds, vast empty landscapes, but Kozintsev insists – as Robin Phillips was to do – on the importance of the domestic. The designs reflect something like Brecht's fascination with the textures of everyday life: 'wood, wool, iron, leather, fur' (Kozintsev 1977, p. 37). Kozintsev was interested in texture, not colour, and (like Brook) shot his film in black and white. The background for the opening titles is the rough cloth of the beggars.

As in the Phillips production, the setting for the love-test and the division of the kingdom is more domestic than regal. Instead of proclaiming his intentions from the throne Lear sits and warms his hands by the fire as an attendant reads his proclamation for him. We recognize two familiar points: the old man's need for ease, and the tendency of public figures to let aides and mouthpieces do their talking for them. There is a similar insight into the practical side of a public occasion when an interpreter, in a series of discreet asides, translates the proceedings for the benefit of the

French king. (Yet this device has a double effect, since it also reminds us that the scale of the issues is not just national but international.) The interview with the two suitors is a business meeting conducted around a bare table. Kozintsev thought of the first scene as taking place in a gambling house, with everyone's eyes fixed on the map as they would be on the cards. But as Lear's anger mounts, so does the scale of the scene. The map, though not enormous, is large; and a bell rings to mark each stage of the division, suggesting a ritual formality like that of Peter Brook's orb. The first outbreak of violence in the film comes when Lear in a fury shakes the map; the movement is unexpectedly noisy, and it fills the screen. Lear spits at Kent but then sits on the throne to banish him, the only time we ever see him there. Finally, he appears on the castle wall – which is huge, and lined with fires and smoke-pots – to proclaim that he has cast off Cordelia. As he appears the people fall on their knees, then on their faces. The more madly and desperately Lear proclaims his power, the more it is shown through the language of conventional spectacle. This power, the images suggest, is fundamentally unreal, even crazy.

Kozintsev seeks the universality of the play through the domestic and the familiar – 'A mother feeds her child – which epoch is that?' (Kozintsev 1972, p. 195) – rather than through spectacle or stylization. His vision is not in any traditional sense religious. By his own account, the universality which other imaginations can see in the Bible, in Blake and Michelangelo, left him cold (Kozintsev 1977, p. 63). At the end of his first soliloquy Edmund hurls a stone at the sky. On 'O reason not the need' Lear seems to be arguing his case to the same sky. But there are no answers for man out there; the heavens reply to Lear's question only with the darkness of the storm, which for Kozintsev was 'the voice of evil celebrating a victory' (Kozintsev 1977, p. 50). And the storm is curiously underplayed. For Gielgud and others it has been the supreme test, the one the actor is most likely to fail. For many students of the play it is the central, defining episode: we think of Lear in the storm as we think of Hamlet in the graveyard or Othello in Desdemona's bedchamber. But when Kozintsev was offered a shot of thunderclouds as background for the titles he rejected it in favour of the piece of rough cloth: 'the storm is certainly not the main point of the film' (Kozintsev 1977, p. 254). In a letter to Yuri Yarvet, the actor playing Lear, Kozintsev told him to get acquainted with the storm, 'enter into an argument with it' (Kozintsev 1977, p. 231). Scofield, we have seen, did just that. But in the finished film there is little sense of this. The shooting script has Lear thrown off his feet, then rising and carrying on; this shot is not used in the film (Yutkevitch, p. 196). Instead we barely glimpse Lear and the Fool, small figures seen through driving smoke. On the sound-track (as in Adrian Noble's production) it is the pounding music that speaks for the storm, not the thunder we expected. And the sequence, unlike the elaborately inventive storm in Brook's film, is relatively brief and simple. It is as though Kozintesev is impatient to get on to the hovel, and the poor people who shelter there; they are what really interests him. My students who saw the film – and who expected that if anyone would pull out all the stops in the storm scene it would be a Russian film director – were palpably disappointed.

But Kozintsev's reason for underplaying the storm becomes clear as we move into the later scenes of the film. It is not cosmic violence but man-made violence that concerns him. One of the seminal experiences behind the film was his visit to the museum at Hiroshima, where he saw depictions of primitive man learning to use fire, the first stage in the technological progress that would lead to nuclear conflagration. And so the dominant image of the first scene is Lear's hearth-fire, the ancestral fire, the origin of family and society (Kozintsev 1972, p. 195). The setting also evokes the folktale simplicity of the story itself: once there was a king and he had three daughters (Kozintsev 1977, p. 120). Charles Kean's production also began with the Lear family sitting around a log fire (Bratton, p. 57). But in the film the fire escapes and becomes a symbol of destruction, opposing the redeeming power of water. We see Edmund torch a straw-roofed house, and we cut quickly from the shot of Cordelia backed by the sea to a view of burning buildings. In a manner that probably speaks with special urgency to a Russian audience, war is waged not just by swordplay but by wholesale burning. The war sequence – offstage and perfunctory in the text – is the climax to which the film has been building. This, not the storm, is the chaos that really matters. As the procession of beggars, with Lear, Gloucester and Edgar in their company, trudges along the road they encounter a stream of refugees fleeing in the opposite direction. The steady progress of the principal characters is halted and turned; the movement of the action is reversed. Retracing our steps, we are also made to see that this last catastrophe had its origins in Lear's initial action: for the end of the war sequence, and the film, we return to the high-walled castle we saw at the opening, which is now under siege, its walls broken down, its ceremonial fires replaced by the flames of destruction. We have tracked the madness to its origins; and we recall that in the storm we saw not just clouds but smoke: the war is also 'the real culmination of the storm' (Kozintsev 1977, p. 208).

Kozintsev's way to suggest the universality of the story is to convey – unobtrusively, through symbolism that is suggestive rather than overt – a capsule history of the human race, from the fire of the ancestral hearth to the fire of Hiroshima. While so much criticism centres on Lear's personal journey, Kozintsev has declared, 'The process of tracing the spiritual life of Shakespeare's plays cannot be separated from the tracing of the historical process' (Kozintsev 1972, p. 192). Even the brief interpolated scene of the marriage of Cordelia, conducted at the roadside by a hermit, makes its contribution. The figures stand by a rough wooden cross; there is no church building: 'It is the first year of Christianity' (Kozintsev 1973, p. 12). Students of Shakespeare's text have seen another source of universality in the obvious parallels between the stories of Lear and Gloucester which, taken together, suggest general principles at work. Kozintsev uses the freedom given by his medium to pick up and develop this traditional view. In the first scene Lear settles himself by a large, blazing hearth. Gloucester, in the equivalent of I.ii, sits by a more modest hearth in his own house, clearly the most comfortable room he has, and the room where he will be blinded. Gloucester slowly walks a large dog, man and beast at leisure together; Lear's madness is startlingly evoked by a quick cut from his frightened eyes to the staring, crazy eyes of his dogs. Later, a shot of Lear and Cordelia walking along surrounded by soldiers is immediately echoed by a shot of Edgar and Gloucester walking in the same direction (left to right) across a barren plain.

Equally traditional is Kozintsev's moral analysis of the action. Though he and Brook – whose films were made almost simul-taneously – were in sympathetic correspondence with each other and admired each other's work, in this and in other respects they were poles apart. Kozintsev gives due weight to the cruelty and violence of the tragedy, but this does not lead in the direction of absurdity. For him, as for A. C. Bradley and the generation of critics who followed him, this is a story that ultimately makes moral sense, a story of learning and redemption, of the triumph of good over evil. Yuri Yarvet's Lear, no less than Gielgud's, develops, though the development is traced in screen images rather than actor's 'points', and the range of reference is as much social as personal. This is 'the tragedy of a personality who flattered himself into thinking he was heroic. He becomes great only when he understands that he is like any other man' (Kozintsev 1977, p. 62). The sight of the crowd of beggars falling on their faces before this small, beardless, ordinary-looking man, who stands high above them on a wall of monstrous proportions, dramatizes the sheer absurdity of Lear's regal power. So does the train of possessions he takes with him on his initial journeys. We see him striding through the stables picking out the horses he wants, the dogs, the hawks. The result is a long, foolish and (as his power wanes) steadily diminishing baggage train that follows him through the countryside like 'the train of a dying comet' (Yutkevich, p. 196). Lear's knights, so far as we can tell, are well-behaved; that is not the problem. The problem is that he drags so much useless property around with him.

His redemption begins in earnest as he encounters the poor, the people who have nothing, and falls in with them. In Shakespeare Lear tries to dramatize his common humanity by taking his clothes off; his attendants won't let him. For them, as later for the blinded Gloucester, he is still the king. But Yarvet's Lear achieves common humanity, simply and without fuss, by walking along with its other representatives, among whom he fits in easily. As he walks he chats with Gloucester, sharing not Beckettian despair but folk wisdom. It is significant that Yarvet had originally been cast in the small role of a mad beggar and didn't believe Kozintsev was serious when he was told the director wanted him for Lear (Kozintsev 1977, p. 75). Kozintsev wanted not an extraordinary Lear, a 'magnificent portent', but a Lear who could be anybody, 'like all of us, really', and whose reduction to common humanity would be not the end of his greatness but the beginning of it (Kozintsev 1973, p. 11). By a similar paradox, Lear and Cordelia achieve victory in defeat. In the equivalent of 'Come, let's away to prison' they are swept along in a great crowd, unrecognized, Lear chatting happily to Cordelia and Cordelia smiling back at him. At the sight of their happiness Edmund is visibly disturbed and confused. According to Kozintsev, it is this sight that explains Edmund's defeat. He is caught in the other side of the paradox, defeat in victory. In a shot that looks like a parody of a Hollywood swashbuckler from the 1940s, we see Edmund as a triumphant warrior with a sword in his hand, Goneril clinging excitedly to him. As he stands in victory, raised above the crowd on a cart as Lear had been raised above his people on a high wall, the soldiers shout his name. Not long after, at the end of the duel, we see him twisting in the dirt, contorted with pain, shouting, his face upside-down in a grotesque close-up.

There is no question here of a blurring of the lines between good and evil. Kozintsev uses echoing images to keep the distinction firm. When Lear tears his shirt open to reveal a glimpse of skinny chest, he is seeking to assert his common humanity. When Regan tears Edmund's shirt open it is in a very different spirit (Schmaltz, pp. 87–8). Good and evil are as different, as opposed, as water and fire. Even in the duel between the brothers, in which fight directors so often are content with the convention that Edgar, the good guy, nearly loses but comes back in the end, Kozintsev emphasizes the contrasting styles of the fighters: Edmund is aggressive and uses up his energy too early, while Edgar bides his time. The sisters are strikingly opposed. Goneril is the sophisticated one, hard-faced and well-groomed. Regan's face is wonderfully stupid, heavy-lipped and puffy with fat; her hair is dull and unkempt. As my colleague Martha Kurtz put it, she looks as though she spends her time eating chocolates and watching the soaps. Cordelia in the first scene is attended by a stern-faced, aged woman who silently urges her forward. But the oppressive upbringing this suggests has obviously had no effect on her; her movements are light, quick and natural. She never thinks of rebellion because 'she is herself a rebellion, isolated from the rest by her very naturalness' (Kozintsev 1977, p. 70). One critic was moved to speculate that there must be peasant blood in her veins (Yutkevich, p. 196). Kozintsev imagined Albany as a humanist, a book-lover who must come out of his library to engage in practical terms with the evil of the world. What we actually see is a rather modest collection of books on a shelf, but by the standards of this rough, simple world it is a library, and Albany seems to draw strength from it as he denounces his wife. A more dramatic image of the engagement of good with the world comes just after the death of Gloucester. Edgar kneels and prays for a moment by his father's grave. Then we see smoke rising in the background, we hear the chorus of lament that is Shostakovich's battle-music, and the young man rises from his knees and goes off to fight, his deliberate sense of purpose contrasting with the confusion of the battle itself (Welch, p. 156).

The great challenge to any interpretation that sees moral coherence in the play is the death of Cordelia. Kozintsev confronts this challenge squarely. He does not shrink from the anguish of her death. In fact, he emphasizes it by contrast with the death of Gloucester. We do not see Gloucester's attempted leap off Dover Cliff, perhaps because the director sensed it depended on theatrical conventions he could not use (Salgādo 1984, p. 80), perhaps because in Kozintsev's finally optimistic view, the idea of suicide is a non-starter (Kozintsev 1966, p. 98). (My students, frustrated at not having all of the play they knew, particularly resented this cut.) What Kozintsev shows instead is something the play keeps offstage: Gloucester, feeling Edgar's face, recognizes him and dies of joy. Edgar buries him in a simple grave, and puts a rough wooden cross over it. The old man dies happy, and his pious son honours him. The contrast with Cordelia's death is brutal. As the survivors sort out the aftermath of the war, we hear terrible, animal howls. 'The camera searches frantically for the voice' (Schmaltz, p. 89), the soldiers rush up the walls – a whole crowd of them, as useless as the stage full of soldiers in the Phillips production. Lear stands on the wall, the position from which he had denounced Cordelia as the action began. We see her hanging dead in an archway. He does not carry her, as in the play; death has separated them (this effect, as we shall see, goes much farther in the Brook film). After she is cut down, Lear's cry of 'never' echoes through the now empty archway. Through it we glimpse the sea-foam and gulls that formed the backdrop for her return to England. The first impression is of loss: we are seeing Cordelia's world without Cordelia. But the world itself goes on; the sea is still there. At the end of the film there is affirmation in the face of death. After the duel, we have seen Albany go up to Edgar as he washes himself; now the three survivors, Albany, Edgar and Kent, stand together. The bodies of Lear and Cordelia are honoured, carried together on an improvised stretcher, their eyes peacefully closed. Goneril and Regan are also carried on stretchers, but each lies alone. Their eyes are open – whatever they have found in death, it is not peace – and Goneril holds a dagger that tells us how she died. Kozintsev revives the Elizabethan stage custom of carrying off the bodies, hardly ever used in the modern theatre, and through it he makes a final statement of the opposition of good and evil. He also draws on his own distinctive images. In the opening procession of beggars we saw a mother tend a sleeping child, the film's first image of human kindness (Jorgens, p. 237). At the end it is the common people who are seen dousing the remaining fires with water and raising a pole in a gesture that looks literally futile but symbolizes the beginning of reconstruction.

Shostakovich's music gives the film some of its darkest colouring, especially in the war sequence where his wordless choir becomes 'the grief of the whole people'. But, Kozintsev added, the music also 'gives rise to faith: the evil times will pass, they cannot do otherwise if such a voice is heard' (Kozintsev 1977, pp. 242, 254). This quality of survival is also embodied in the Fool (Oleg Dal). Up to a point he draws on the tradition of frailty that used to pervade English stage productions. He is a thin boy with a shaved head and haunted eyes. While Antony Sher seemed to draw on every clown one had ever heard of, Kozintsev, who was fascinated by clowns, went through a long list of books on the subject and found nothing he could use (Kozintsev 1977, p. 71). What fired his imagination was 'the orchestra in Auschwitz that was made up of men condemned to death. They were beaten to make them play better' (Kozintsev 1973, pp. 13–14). When in the first scene an extra pair of hands appears from under Lear's cloak and stretches toward the fire, we sense that the Fool is in some way an aspect of Lear (Salgādo 1984, p. 63). When the Fool rides on the outside of Lear's carriage, shouting things his master does not want to hear until the king finally hammers on the wall to silence him, it becomes clear that the Fool is Lear's conscience. This happens on the way to Gloucester's house; on the way to Goneril's, the Fool had been dragged along with the rest of Lear's possessions, a rope around his neck. As Lear's panic mounts his conscience is getting closer. The Fool's approach is signalled by the jingle of the bells on his costume; Kozintsev called this 'the call sign of conscience' (Kozintsev 1977, p. 72). He is also, like Stephen Haggard in 1940, Lear's dog. The shooting script describes his costume as 'dogskins worn inside out' (Yutkevitch, p. 196). He steals some meat from Goneril's table and snarls at an attendant. (There is also something dog-like about Tom in the hovel; he crouches by Lear on all fours, and Lear touches his back as he would a dog's.) As dog and conscience the Fool is degraded and despised, yet he has the privilege of familiarity. When on the stage the Fool appears in extra scenes, he seems intrusive; the text has no place for him, any more than it has for processions of beggars. But in the cinematic freedom of Kozintsev's version it seems right that the Fool should be there, as he is, for the reunion of Lear and Cordelia, playing the healing music on his pipe. He is bent and ill, the pain in his eyes has deepened, but he is still functioning. At the end he huddles, sobbing, on the road. As the funeral procession goes by a soldier kicks him out of the way. But he picks up his pipe again, and its music, 'the sad, human voice of art' (Kozintsev 1977, p. 238) ends the film. Beaten and neglected, his voice gone, 'he who gets slapped' – as St John Chrysostom called the fool – survives.

Kozintsev's vision of the play is humane, and this is reflected in the making of the film. Whereas the actors in a film version of this play could easily be swamped by special effects, as they sometimes are on the stage, Kozintsev keeps his actors centre front. He was fascinated by the human face: 'The advantage of the cinema over the theatre is not that you can even have horses, but that you can stare closer into a man's eyes' (Kozintsev 1977, p. 55). His search for a Lear, which did not end until perilously close to the shooting date, was a search for the right face. When he found Yuri Yarvet he wrote, 'I have at last seen the eyes on the screen: the very eyes'. The voice was a problem: Yarvet was an Estonian who spoke Russian badly. In the end he was dubbed by 'the unique Moscow actor Zinovi Gerdt, who is completely in tune with the Estonian's performance' (Sokolyansky, p. 206). But the shock of white hair, and above all, the deep, pained eyes, framed by a network of wrinkles – these spoke the language Kozintsev wanted to hear. He was also attracted by Yarvet's resemblance to Voltaire, 'the bitter irony, the wit of Europe' (Kozintsev 1977, pp. 74, 76). Lear's first entrance is quirky and unexpected. Behind a closed door we hear laughter and the jingling of bells. Lear is playing a game with the Fool. When he enters there is a mask on his face. Its purpose, in theory, was to symbolize Lear's initial inhumanity (Kozintsev 1977, p. 47). Its actual effect is that its removal throws into high relief the face of the man – a Lear we have never seen before yet somehow recognize at once, a Lear of profound and vulnerable humanity.

Through much of the film, the soliloquies are done in voice-over as the camera dwells on the unspeaking face, though this convention is occasionally broken. At the end, Edgar approaches the camera to deliver his final speech, but says nothing. Kozintsev wrote to a friend, 'At today's shooting, Leonard Merzin tried acting the whole speech without uttering a word. And I recognized Shakespeare's thought in his eyes. Perhaps the audience would also read these lines in the look he directed at them?' (Kozintsev 1977, p. 238). It is the last of the film's many risks, not only confessing – as, implicitly at least, the original speech does – the inadequacy of language, but turning over to the audience the final task of interpretation. To me, Edgar looks thoughtful and determined. To Barbara Hodgdon he is 'a lonely presence' who 'tries to speak' but cannot (Hodgdon 1977, p. 297). Jack J. Jorgens sees in his eyes 'helplessness and sorrow' and an angry accusation of the audience for 'not feeling enough' (Jorgens, p. 244). Though the film is carefully thought out, its images marshalled in the service of a moral argument, it finally releases its audience to react in a variety of ways, as though the play itself has escaped through Edgar's silence, its protean nature restored. When it was first seen in North America, at the 1971 International Shakespeare Congress in Vancouver, Kozintsev's film had a tumultuous reception. One of my colleagues found herself in tears at the end, and hoped the man beside her wasn't embarrassed (she needn't have worried; it was Kozintsev). I have always been sorry I missed that screening. Many years later – at a screening I am not sorry I missed – it was shown to a university audience in Toronto. This audience, which included a large group of graduate students in English, laughed all the way through. At the screening I arranged for them, most of my own students were interested but unmoved. Some of them found it cold, pessimistic and ironic (they hadn't seen the Brook film). To be fair, they saw it under dreadful conditions: pauses to change reels, and an ordinary lens that distorted the wide-screen image by elongating it. It is a tribute to the film that at least it held their interest under these conditions, and though I asked them only for quick, off-the-top reactions, many of them wrote detailed critiques. A few were swept away by it, as I am every time I see it. For audiences who know the play well, and who are not prepared to take the film on its own terms, its many departures from the surface of Shakespeare – like the cutting of Gloucester's leap – are a constant irritant. Yet its account of the play's fundamental issues puts it for the most part with mainstream, traditional criticism. Only in its emphasis on the people, on the communal rather than the private dimension of Lear's salvation, does it give a distinct twist to the left. If this is a distortion of Shakespeare – and I am not convinced it is – at least

[103]

the case is made with compelling visual and moral eloquence. Or, as a colleague said to me at the end of a badly attended Sunday afternoon screening just before I began work on this book, 'That's worth all the Marxist criticism ever written.'

CHAPTER VII

Peter Brook

Peter Brook's 1971 film version of *King Lear*, though it used some of the same actors (notably Paul Scofield as Lear), and some of the same thinking lay behind it, is not a transcription onto film of his 1962 stage production but a new creation. It is also a bolder departure from traditional readings of the play, and at times from the text itself, than Kozintsev's film. Brook had originally thought of using a new script altogether, written for him by Ted Hughes, but in the end he kept more or less to Shakespeare's words. Something of the original intention survives in the compression of lines into paraphrases – 'Thy dowerless daughter, King, thrown to my chance, / Is queen of us, of ours, and our fair France' becomes 'Thy dowerless daughter, King, is Queen of France' – and more fundamentally in the rearrangement of scenes (the Edmund–Edgar plot does not get under way until Lear has left Goneril's house) and the transfer of speeches from one character to another. Brook's stage production took local liberties with the text but preserved, as does Kozintsev's film, the general curve and shape of the play. The film breaks single scenes into short episodes, redistributes them, and generally creates a structure of its own. Inevitably, the text is heavily cut. But it is also, at certain points, filled out, giving explanations that Shakespeare declines to give. Why is Lear alone with the Fool in the storm? What happened to the rest of his entourage? The play does not tell us, but the film does: the carriage Lear is driving – recklessly, with the Fool as a terrified passenger – loses a wheel, and the two of them set off alone, up a hill, away from the road. His solitary appearance in the scene with Gloucester is also explained. At the end of the storm sequence Lear and the Fool are again in a carriage together. Lear, on his own initiative, slips away; his words, 'make no noise', which in the play signal the approach of sleep, are an instruction to the Fool not to betray him. In a film that is not much interested in conventional realism, based on a play that is not much interested in it either, these moments when puzzles are explained may seem surprisingly literal-minded. But they highlight an aspect of Lear: the voluntary refugee, the man who *wants* to separate himself from society, whose irrational urge to cling to his office is matched by an equally irrational urge to throw it away. Like the pointing of certain moments in Brook's stage production, these inventions clarify, and what they clarify is more than plot.

Though Brook wrote to Kozintsev, 'I want to avoid background' (Kozintsev 1977, p. 25), he also needed to create a society that would have its own distinctive flavour and atmosphere, avoiding the extremes of period authenticity on the one hand and inexpressive neutrality on the other (Manvell, pp. 139–40). His thinking began with 'the contrast between the safe, enclosed places and the wild, unprotected places' (Brook 1987, p. 204). The result is a combination of Innuit and Lapp cultures, a world that is distinctive and yet free of period, 'in the sense that Eskimos have used the same functional shapes for the last 1,000 years' (Kozintsev 1977, p. 240). The use of anachronisms like carriages – albeit rough and primitive ones, covered with skins and running on solid wooden wheels – keeps the culture from being too specific. This is a world, finally, that exists only in the film. Though its simple technology suggests life at a subsistence level, it has evolved certain rituals, notably the ceremonial use of the orb in the first scene, one of the few details carried over directly from the stage production. If the dominant fabric in Kozintsev's film is rough cloth, here it is fur. In the division of the kingdom, the map lies on the ground covered with furs, and as Lear issues his orders Gloucester, smiling, uncovers the portion he identifies. The film was shot between January and April in a bleak area of north Jutland, not far from an abandoned fur farm (Jones, pp. 149–50). The cold was intense, and through the film we are constantly aware of it: those furs are not just ornament. There was a nineteenth century tradition that when Kent was left in the stocks Oswald stayed behind for a few moments, taunting him in mime to get laughs from the gallery (Bratton, p. 115). Brook produces a similar effect on his own terms when, as Kent begins his night in the stocks, Oswald deliberately takes his boots off. Given the weather, it's an appallingly simple form of torture. The cold is so intense that when in the storm scene it rains, this intrusion from Shakespeare's text has an unfortunate side effect: we feel a sense of relief that at last there is a warm spell.

Fire, like fur, is an answer to the cold, but the interiors in this film never seem as comfortable as they do in Kozintsev. There are large hearth-fires, but they don't seem to make much headway against the prevailing cold, and the intended contrast between safe and wild places is not very strong. Everywhere seems wild, to one degree or another. The fire, as in Kozintsev, becomes destructive: it is the key image of the war. At the end of Lear's reunion with Cordelia, on the words 'I am old and foolish', father and daughter put their foreheads together in a rare moment of tenderness; this is immediately followed by black smoke and the thunderous roar of flames. Burning ships and burning buildings establish the battle and Lear's defeat; the faces of Albany, Edmund, Goneril and Regan are blackened by soot. Kozintsev counters the fire image with water that is meant to be redemptive, and his shots of the sea and of running streams are attractive, a welcome relief from the stone wasteland; but the sea in Brook is flat and cold. The setting for the equivalent of IV.vi is a bleak, windswept beach. If it really is Dover Beach, then Matthew Arnold's poem about a world without faith seems apposite (Reddington, p. 370). The measure of the difference is that Kozintsev uses the sea for Cordelia's return, Brook for Lear's encounter with Gloucester and the grim aftermath of the battle. The land is also bleak; but while Kozintsev's stone desert is at least populated, here the only signs of human life are the square, solid castles. The film uses 'high-contrast black-and-white images in which the background, particularly in exterior shots, tends to resolve into pure white or pure black. In this way some of the non-specificity of locale of the Elizabethan stage is approximated' (Acker, p. 220). Or, to use a phrase associated with Brook, behind the characters is an empty space. Silence begins and ends the film, accompanying the opening credits and the last fade-out to a white screen (Jones, p. 151). In the stage production Brook cut music to a minimum. Here, apart from the Fool's songs and some strange electronic noises in the storm, there is no music at all – not even for the waking of Lear, where the only symbol of healing and new life is the light on the King's face. In a medium that almost invariably uses music, its absence is striking and self-conscious.

Equally self-conscious is the quiet delivery of the lines. In the opening scene, public though the occasion is, Lear and his daughters address each other in unnaturally quiet voices, the volume rising slightly only on his quarrel with Cordelia. The lead-in to the blinding of Gloucester, and the quarrel of the victors after the battle, are equally flat and quiet. While Yarvet's Lear, walking along with the beggars, chats amiably with Gloucester in a voice that can easily be overheard, Scofield, chuckling, whispers secrets in his ear. Range and expressiveness of a conventional kind are deliberately sacrificed; instead, individual words are isolated – 'dowers' in Lear's first speech, 'eyesight' in Goneril's. This is the most striking difference between Brook's stage and film versions. The suppleness and the clean lines of verse-speaking in the former are replaced by a broken, prosaic idiom, in which individual words stand out like pebbles in sand. One result of the low-key delivery is a self-conscious awareness of the film medium. In certain scenes, including the opening, it is as though the performances are unnaturally scaled down in a self-conscious attempt to adjust to the camera. There is no such sense of effort in Kozintsev. Unless we are deliberately studying his film for its technique we do not think much about the medium itself while we watch it; in Brook's film we do.

Both directors begin with Lear's people waiting to hear what will happen to the kingdom. In Kozintsev they are on the move, heading towards Lear's castle as the camera follows them. In Brook they are standing packed together, absolutely still, as the camera pans back and forth across them. While Kozintsev emphasizes the crowd as a whole, in Brook we focus more on the weatherbeaten faces. But the key difference is that in Kozintsev the people and the camera move together, and in Brook only the camera does. This makes us more aware of the camera. Throughout the film we go on noticing the camera's decisions, some of which are quite self-conscious. We are aware of it, for example, when it passes swiftly back and forth between Lear and the Fool as they sit on opposite sides of the room, making it virtually a third party to their meeting. As Lear contemplates Tom – 'Is man no more than this?' – the camera pans down his shivering body and on 'Thou art the thing itself' it reaches his loincloth. It has made its decision about where the essence of the naked animal lies. Brook wrote to Kozintsev that in editing he wanted to 'interrupt the consistency of style, so that [the] many-levelled contradictions of the play can appear' (Kozintsev 1977, p. 241). On matters of tone and atmosphere the film's style is in fact rigorously consistent throughout; possible contradictions seem to have been smoothed over. It is the surface of the illusion that is constantly disrupted. In a way that

[108]

can be paralleled in silent film and Brechtian staging, titles are occasionally used to identify a scene and summarize the action: 'Goneril's Castle. The banished Duke of Kent [sic] is now disguised as a servant. He seeks employment with the King, who is now living with his daughter Goneril.' The device is not used often enough to establish itself as a consistent convention, and so a deliberate roughness is created, as it is by the clunking prose of the title itself.

The most self-conscious passage is the storm. While Kozintsev plays it down, it is in one sense the climax of Brook's film, elaborately experimental and inventive, as flamboyant in its own way as the display of nineteenth century stage technology put on by Charles Kean – and with the same danger that as we concentrate on the machinery we will lose sight of the actors. The storm begins not with thunder but with a howling wind, recalling, perhaps, the powerful effect of the actor-created wind in the stage production. But as the storm reaches its height the invention becomes more elaborate. The screen goes dead black, or dead white. Lear is shot alternately in left and right profile. Close-ups and long shots of Tom are alternated, the shifts accompanied by a swooping noise like a speeded-up thunderclap. At times we see water on the camera lens, distorting the picture. We are not sure what is real and what is being created by Lear's mad perspective. At times we simply do not know what we are seeing: we glimpse a shape that could be 'a rock, a stone, a stump, a bush – but could equally well be some agonising human shape, a limb, a face, a burnt child, a screaming mouth' (Manvell, p. 148). The effect of what one reviewer called 'a riot of inexplicable artiness' (Jonathan Raban, *New Statesman*, 30 July 1971) is that the medium itself is breaking down, chaos in the universe conveyed by chaos in the editing room; and in breaking down it calls attention to itself. The black screen is as conscious a trick as the black page in *Tristram Shandy*, and so are the other devices. As Adrian Noble's storm was self-consciously theatrical, this one is self-consciously cinematic, solving the problem that no illusion can portray Shakespeare's storm by shattering illusion altogether. The difficulty is that so much attention goes to playing with the medium to create a generalized sense of breakdown that if there is a specific human drama in Lear's encounter with the elements, we miss it.

For Kozintsev the point of the storm comes when Lear finds himself sharing a hovel with the poor of his kingdom; for Brook, the point seems to be fragmentation and chaos. Kozintsev, constructing a vision of progress, keeps his characters in constant movement and the film as a whole has a sweeping line that follows the line of the play. In Brook there is what William Johnson calls a 'manic-depressive tempo' (Johnson, p. 43), frozen stillness alternated with sudden bursts of movement. In the first court scene in Kozintsev, we see the participants walking into the main hall, and once the action begins it goes on moving around the room – the hearth, the throne, the table. Brook's opening is deliberately static: Lear is a still figure at the centre of an inner chamber, and his subjects are standing outside waiting for something to happen. The action begins with the closing of a door, locking Lear and his court in. But at the end of the scene he bursts out of the room and we see a wall of faces, the equivalent of Kozintsev's common people. Everyone scatters away from the palace; things fall apart, the centre cannot hold. Goneril and Regan's conversation and Gloucester's lecture on the eclipses are private conversations, held in carriages as they leave. In the Dover scene Lear and Gloucester sit together, as still as they would be in a stage production. Then Lear, with a burst of crazy energy, runs into the sea. Jack Jorgens (who sees that last touch as Lear's attempt to reverse evolution) summarizes the general pattern: 'dead, static scenes are interspersed with Lear's driving movement from the tomblike throne to Goneril's castle, to Regan's castle [sic], to the stormy heath, to the edge of the sea' (Jorgens, pp. 248, 250). Kozintsev returns to the starting point, the castle of the opening scene, as though to signal that the business of the ending is to judge Lear's initial action and to understand its consequences. This is the equivalent of Shakespeare's reconstruction of the stage picture of I.i, as the bodies of Goneril and Regan are brought back on stage – though in terms of geography Brook's effect of ending far away from the starting point is closer to Shakespeare. In Kozintsev the movement is steady, embodying progress and learning. In Brook the movement goes by fits and starts, and the end of the journey brings us not (as in Kozintsev) to a public action in a crowded castle, but to a few isolated figures on a vast, empty beach. If we have returned to a point of origin, it is not the beginning of a story, or of anything social at all – it is the biological origin of life itself. Following some instinct, the characters come to the sea to die.

Brook's version takes a grimmer view of humanity than

Kozintsev's. The Russian Edgar can join a whole world of beggars and find himself in a curious way at home, as Lear and Gloucester will also do. As Brook's Edgar calls out to the horsemen who have ringed him in, 'Do poor Tom some charity', one of them laughs and strikes him down. Just before he is blinded, Gloucester (Alan Webb) attempts a social smile on 'you are my guests'; the irony is devastating. In Kozintsev the old social values of courtesy and simple decency are just starting to flake away in the tough new world of Goneril and Regan, Cornwall and Edmund. Brook's world is more pervasively, endemically brutal. It is perhaps for this reason that the violence is swift and simple, not protracted; it comes naturally. William P. Shaw notes, contrasting this film with Roman Polanski's more conventionally bloody *Macbeth*, 'every killing in the film (with the exception of the killing of Oswald) occurs with a single stroke' (Shaw, p. 212). Edgar and Edmund fight with axes, and Edgar despatches his brother with a single blow to the stomach. Goneril kills Regan by flinging her to the ground; the last look on the dead face as it stares up at us is surprise. Then Goneril, working herself up to it with a strange twisting motion, kneeling, swaying, kneading her dress with her hands, brains herself on a rock. The impact is followed by a quick shot of Cordelia dropping on the gallows, connecting the deaths 'as if Goneril and Cordelia were at opposite ends of a Rube Goldberg device for hanging' (Johnson, p. 44). The blinding of Gloucester, and the killings that follow, are so quick it is hard to tell what is happening. (In the tradition of using ordinary domestic objects in this scene, Cornwall blinds Gloucester with a spoon.) Here Brook relents a little, partially restoring one of the controversial cuts in his stage production: as Gloucester is put out of doors one of the servants breaks an egg and applies it to his face. But the old man gets no guidance as he stumbles out into the wilderness alone. In general, the violence is unnerving in its speed and clinical precision; it also lets us see a number of deaths, including those of the three daughters, that Shakespeare keeps offstage. But Brook does not dwell on it. He has deeper ways of disturbing us than this.

Where Kozintsev, building a morally coherent *Lear*, keeps us watching objective reality, Brook breaks reality down into subjective fragments. It is harder for us to get a full view of what is happening, since we are frequently restricted to the perspective of the characters themselves (Hodgdon 1983, pp. 144–5, 147). The cutting of Cordelia's asides in the first scene has this effect; we hear only what Lear does. Not only do the 'Close-ups and shallow depth of field give the film a solipsistic feel' (Jorgens, p. 244) but at times the camera gets right behind the eyes of the characters. Lear's speech on 'true need' is delivered not as a fatherly lecture (Ustinov) or a solitary meditation (Yarvet) but as a threatening confrontation with Goneril and Regan, virtually a curse. We see Lear in close-up, from their point of view. He sways from side to side of the frame, like a cobra about to strike. Then the reaction shots of Goneril and Regan show Lear's perspective on them, the camera swaying as he does; Lear for a moment *is* the camera. As we have noted, the stylistic craziness of the storm in part reflects Lear's own madness. During the mad trial in the hovel, we share his hallucinations. We see Goneril walking towards us, holding the orb; on 'Is there any cause in nature makes these hard hearts?' we see (in an interesting reassignment of the line's significance) a brief shot of Cordelia. We see the blinding as Gloucester does: Cornwall approaches him and the screen goes black. The camera also cuts out part of the whole picture the stage would allow us to see. This is inevitable, but there are times when we particularly notice the loss. In Brook's stage production, the Fool's reaction to Lear's 'O let me not be mad' – he gently took his hand – was a telling moment of human contact. In the film the moment is shot as a close-up of Lear; we do not see the Fool's response. At other times the selectiveness of the camera leaves us, for a while at least, disoriented. When we see the rows of faces under the opening credits we do not know who they are or where they are (Jorgens, p. 237). As Edgar tells Gloucester that they are climbing, we see they are walking on level ground. But at the opening of the cliff sequence we see them in close-up; we do not know where they are, and they could be at a cliff-top. Only when Gloucester falls does the camera pull back for a long shot of the old man sprawled on the flat beach. He has been fooled, and so have we. (Brook's stage production, we have seen, produced the same effect by utterly different means.)

If we learn anything from Gloucester's leap, it is not to trust what we are shown. And in general the jerky, fragmented quality of the film blocks any sense of progress towards understanding. It may be significant that Jack MacGowran's Fool, though a compelling presence – he speaks with a wry smile, and his eyes seem to have looked at the world for a long time, not much liking what they saw – does not have the intellectual sharpness of Alec

McCowen's. While McCowen pointed every line, at the risk of turning his songs to prose, MacGowran, as the carriage drives to Gloucester's castle, sings a loudly mournful song that sounds like an Irish lament, in which no words can be distinguished. Along with a blocking of understanding goes a flattening of the distinction between 'good' and 'bad' characters. The process began in the stage production but goes much farther here. What in 1962 was a suggestion of rapport between the brothers, a whistled signal, becomes, through drastic rewriting, a new relationship altogether. As Edgar and Edmund contemplate their sleeping father, Edgar says, in the words Edmund (in the play) puts into his deceptive letter, that children should be allowed to manage their parents. He says it lightly, and Edmund agrees with a chuckle. In this version both sons are impatient with their father, and Edmund doesn't have to invent his deception out of whole cloth. In the film in general Edgar (Robert Lloyd) is a much reduced figure. As Lear and Gloucester sit on the beach together, he watches from a great distance; on stage, he is inevitably closer, and has a stronger role in the scene. Lear identifies him as the 'rascal beadle' – a judgement on his moralizing streak? His optimism is devastatingly rebuked by Kent (Tom Fleming) who, on 'Vex not his ghost', grabs Edgar, towering over him, and flings him away. The young man looks small and feeble, very unlike the decisive hero of the Kozintsev film. He is a strong presence only in the duel when, his face concealed by a helmet, he becomes a menacing, nameless figure. Cordelia (Anne-lise Gabold) is quiet and dour, unlike the lively, free-running Russian Cordelia (Valentina Shendrikova) or Diana Rigg's feisty princess. Losing her asides in the first scene, she appears as Lear sees her, 'a sullen brat' (Wilds, p. 160). Of the good characters only Albany seems to emerge with new strength, and that is not because of any help the director has given him, but because he is embodied in the shrewd and knowing personality of Cyril Cusak.

The evil characters are softened and humanized. Irene Worth's Goneril is not quite so cold and schoolmarmy as she was on stage, though she is still stronger than Regan. She has moments of vulnerability: when Lear curses her she is clearly frightened. As Gloucester is blinded we see Goneril, riding away in her carriage, evidently sensing what has happened and feeling the pain herself. Susan Engel's Regan is softer, more gentle and reasonable than Patience Collier's was. When Lear comes to her at Gloucester's house she greets him with a warm, friendly embrace. She can descend quickly to depths of cruelty and resentment, but the surface is attractive. When she speaks to Gloucester after the blinding there are tears in her eyes. The most striking change is in Cornwall (Patrick Magee). In a reshuffling of the text as drastic as the new opening of the Goucester plot, he is allowed to linger for some time after his servant stabs him. What in the text is Edgar's judgement on Gloucester and Edmund –'The gods are just, and of our pleasant vices / Make instruments to plague us' – is spoken to Edmund by the dying Cornwall, as he lies in bed. He is detaching himself from Edmund and from his former life; it is the film's sharpest image of moral growth, bestowed on a character who in the play shows no growth at all.

Lear's knights, as before, are violent and unruly, but the effect is stronger. Since we see them riding into Goneril's courtyard and packed into her hall, we know how many of them there are and what a problem they present. Lear and his knights go on the rampage, as before; his line 'My train are men of choice and rarest parts' follows the riot, with an effect of heavy irony. Lear himself is a darker figure than he was on stage. Our first introduction to him is his canopied throne, seen from behind: a brooding shape, like a blunt pillar, in which he is enclosed. The face is first seen from below, in close-up. It is cold and proud, and the lower lip droops slightly as though he has had a mild stroke. We are aware that he is breathing quickly and shallowly, but the initial effect is of still, icy menace. When he rises to denounce Cordelia we see that he is wearing a hulking fur robe that gives him huge, unnatural shoulders. He could be the villain in a science-fiction movie. Over and over the same note of cold menace is struck. The curse on Goneril is not a burst of hurt passion, but quiet and controlled. 'Reason not the need' is so menacing (even the camera seems frightened of Lear and has trouble keeping him in the shot) that we lose the actual meaning of the lines, which are not just a threat. When on the beach he appears suddenly behind Edgar as a shadow cast on the ground, the effect is alarming. This is no happy king of nature but a strange creature with a low, grinding voice. This quality was present in Scofield's stage performance; it is more dominant here. His film Lear is also older than his stage one, more stiff and bent, and played over a narrower range. He is hard, dry and tough. His humour is cynical, as in the wry amusement of 'When I do stare, see how the subject quakes'. Yet there are still hints of something human. In the equivalent of I.v he wants to be amused by the Fool's jokes as they ride side-by-side in the carriage, and he smiles hopefully as each routine begins. (Kozintsev's Fool at a similar point had to ride *outside* the carriage.) On his threat to unleash 'the terrors of the earth' – a dangerous moment, where Gielgud in his 1950 opening had gone out of control – there is a sudden strain and loss of power in Scofield's voice. The old man is not so tough as he looks. After his final attack on Goneril and Regan he calls the Fool to him, and past the back of the Fool's head we see a single blinking eye, a touch of frailty as Lear is caught off guard.

Brook warns us from the beginning that his reading will not be affirmative. The initial dialogue is cut, so that the first word spoken is Lear's 'know' – which could easily be 'no' (Jorgens, p. 237; Wilds, p. 160). Later, when Kent in the stocks appeals to Fortune the screen goes blank for a moment. In other readings of the play there is some compensation for the darkness of the heavens in the contact people can make with each other. But in the last scene, where Shakespeare shows characters working together in an effort to understand and cope with what has happened, Brook gives us a radically fragmented vision. As Edgar picks up an axe and goes off to kill his brother he walks past the corpse of his father, which is simply lying there. There is no recognition, no relationship between them. Edmund not only dies without attempting to reprieve Lear and Cordelia, he has no conversation with Edgar; only his own words, 'the wheel is come full circle', as he sees who has killed him. The ending of Lear's life is at the opposite pole from Phillips' stagefull of concerned attendants. Cordelia drops on the gallows. Then Kent walks, alone, toward the camera. Then there is a very long shot of Lear walking alone on the beach with Cordelia's body. The howls are faint, a drifting sound, unshaped and unfocussed, without the rhythm Scofield gave this moment on stage. He lays Cordelia down on the beach, and they are alone in a bleak, empty space. Then the fragmentation begins in earnest. On 'This feather stirs' Lear looks at the feather, but doesn't hold it to Cordelia's lips; we no longer see her. On 'Is this the promised end?' Albany and Kent are standing over Cordelia, but Lear is gone. 'Never, never, never, never, never' is broken up, unrhythmic. Lear is kneeling alone, with no sight of Cordelia. If the setting evokes Arnold's 'Dover Beach', the action recalls Cowper's 'The Castaway': 'We perished, each alone'. On

'Look, her lips' Lear is pointing to the camera. Either there is no Cordelia, or we are watching from the perspective of a corpse. Where we do see her is when once again we enter Lear's hallucinations. On 'What is't thou say'st?' she is standing beside him, then Kent stands in her place. She appears again on 'my poor fool is hanged', then disappears. Here at least there is an affirmation of the value of Cordelia, in the imagination's refusal to accept her death. Versions of this hallucination are a common experience in bereavement; for once we touch on something like normal feeling. But there has been no strong Lear–Cordelia relationship in the rest of the film for these moments to draw on. We have seen them smiling at each other, and it's something; but not enough. The end is brutal. Lear's face, in close-up, alternated with shots of the survivors, who now have no contact with him, slips slowly down out of the frame, leaving us with a blank white screen. Without even the formality of 'The End' the film is over. We have confronted death in its bleakest form, without meaning, without consolation. There is no sense of a community that will mourn the dead and somehow carry on; the final emphasis on Lear means that the fading of life is the last thing we know.

Once again, but this time more relentlessly, and taking far greater freedom with the original, Peter Brook produced an absurdist Lear, a challenge to readings like Kozintsev's. With no topical details (the beehive hairstyles are gone) it nonetheless catches the uncertain, violent spirit of its time. Jonathan Raban's hostile review betrays as much in the images he uses. The film, he writes, 'looks like an over-exposed 8mm home movie which has been smuggled out of a disaster area. The film, we're told, was shot in Denmark; it could as well have been Vietnam, or Bangla Desh, or the pocky, inhospitable surface of the moon' (*New Statesman*, 30 July 1971). To say it reflected its time is not to say it was popular. It failed at the box-office, and while it gathered (and still gathers) admiring reviews it also elicited a depth of hostility best exemplified by Pauline Kael: 'Peter Brook's "King Lear" is gray and cold, and the actors have dead eyes. I didn't just dislike this production – I hated it'. For her the devices Brook uses to detach the viewer work only too well: 'The cutting seems designed as an alienation device, but who wants to be alienated from Shakespeare's play and given the drear far side of the moon instead?' Her review is titled 'Peter Brook's "Night of the Living Dead"' (*New Yorker*, 11 December 1971). Of all the productions we are considering, this is the one with the strongest, most single-minded view of the play. In pursuit of that view, it takes Tate-like liberties with the text. There is room for that, as for several generations there was room for Tate. For me the central difficulty is that the film's special world and its peculiar atmosphere – cold, bleak and inimical to humanity – are created with such authority and power that they crush the characters and the action. Certain passages are gripping (my reaction to the ending is, 'This is what it must be like to die') but we spend more time admiring the clinical authority of the director than reacting to the characters. It is a legitimate experiment, an expedition to the cold outer reaches of the play; but it leaves too much of the play behind.

CHAPTER VIII

Jonathan Miller and Michael Hordern

It is not for nothing that television is called 'the box'. Just as film is different from theatre, a production meant to be viewed on a small screen by one or two people in a private room inevitably has a different aesthetic from a production meant to be viewed on a large screen by (the producers hope) two or three hundred people in a theatre. The flexibility of the camera is a common factor, but the scale of the experience is smaller. Television programmes can be shot on location, as films are; but as it happens all three television *Lear*s we are discussing were made in a studio. Though they respond differently to that condition, in every case the studio-bound nature of the production is quite evident, creating an artifice as clear as the artifice of theatre, where even the most realistic set is still a set. At the same time, as in film, the camera gets close to the actors, and performances scaled to the back row of a theatre will look phoney. This combination of stylization with intimacy, both of which go further than they do in cinema, means that television will have its own way of answering the recurring questions about *King Lear*: is it titanic or human, generalized or particular?

The 1982 BBC production is part of a series of the complete plays of Shakespeare that was originally intended to be uniform in style and intention, offering 'straight' interpretations – nothing individual or eccentric – under a single director. The results in too many of the early programmes were stultifying, and the original aim was abandoned as different directors were brought in and more distinct individual interpretations were allowed. Jonathan Miller was in charge of the series for a while, and directed *King Lear* towards the end of his stint, using a set of conventions he had evolved over several productions. These include the use of a Renaissance setting even for plays like *Troilus and Cressida* and

Antony and Cleopatra and a low-key, realistic manner of acting. Miller's Lear is Michael Hordern, a skilled character actor with a gift for playing eccentric dons – he was the first George in Tom Stoppard's *Jumpers*, and probably the definitive one – an actor whom a director with more conventional ideas would probably cast as Gloucester. Miller and Hordern had done *King Lear* together on two previous occasions, at the Nottingham playhouse in 1969, and in a severely truncated BBC TV version in 1975; in each case with the same actor, Frank Middlemass, as the Fool. This means that the 1982 production, though startling in many ways to someone encountering the Miller-Hordern approach for the first time, has its own mini-tradition behind it, and is the result of a long period of experiment.

In a television interview given five years later, Miller defended his choice of a Renaissance setting for this play on the grounds that Christianity and sovereignty are both seventeenth-century themes. He also located his approach to the play in our own time, saying that while the nineteenth century was more interested in man against nature, we are more interested in man against society (*'King Lear'*, London Weekend Television, 1987). Accordingly, the BBC production is as bare of literal images of the natural world as Peter Brook's stage version had been, while giving us instead characters in solidly realistic seventeenth century costumes. They still speak of the gods, but this seems to come more from their reading than from their religion. There is no more primitivism or paganism of an obvious kind than there was in the Robin Phillips production. In 1940, when Gielgud, in Renaissance costume, crossed himself, the business was thought wrong for the play, and he reluctantly cut it. Here, Christian imagery is freely used. Cordelia, as she declares she is going about her father's business (a moment when Shakespeare's words draw closely on a text in *Luke*), crosses herself. The costume designer, Raymond Hughes, tried to make Cordelia a figure 'of almost nun-like simplicity: "she's not in the church but she's virtually married to Christ"'. Her first costume includes 'a wimple-like cap'. Later, she wears a coronet 'like a stylised crown of thorns' (Fenwick, p. 29). Poor Tom directly recalls the crucified Christ. He wears a crown of thorns, and in his soliloquy at the beginning of act IV, as he watches a woodlouse crawl over his hand, we notice a wound in his palm. When he blesses Lear, he makes a quick sign of the cross. According to the designer, Goneril and Regan have their bodices decorated with 'rather naughty images' of Adam and Eve (Fenwick, p. 29). (We have to take his word for it; the images are not visible.) Shakespeare's text provides some warrant for all of this in the religious language that surrounds Cordelia, the naked madman's practice of sticking pins in his arms, and the reference to Cordelia as one who 'redeems nature from the general curse / Which twain have brought her to'. But in the text these are light touches, Christian ideas half-glimpsed in a pagan world. In Miller's production we are in a Christian world; the updating is frank and decisive. In defiance of Peter Brook's objection to playing fast and loose with history, we are asked to imagine that around the time of James I there was a king of Britain called Lear.

We have seen that in other updated productions social identities can be clarified. Surprisingly (but in line with the general practice of the BBC Shakespeares during Miller's tenure) this does not happen here. The Jacobean costumes are rich and elaborate but generalized, almost standard-issue uniforms. The predominant colour is black. If we encountered Lear in a room full of his courtiers, we could not pick out which figure was the king. Nor is there anything to set the knights apart. Albany is if anything more plainly dressed than Lear's followers. He has a tiny collar, while Oswald has a large stiff ruff. As a realistic observation this is convincing – dukes when at home are generally less gorgeous than their footmen – but we lose the sense of a coded world. The generalized costumes, the ruffs in particular, achieve one result that is extremely useful for television: they put a strong focus on the faces of the actors, framing and isolating them. For a medium that deals so readily in close-ups of 'talking heads' the effect is ideal. By the same token the bareness of the setting makes the actors stand out in high relief. Miller wanted 'to find some counterpart of the unfurnished stage that Shakespeare wrote for' (Hallinan, p. 135), and the conventions of studio production allow this much more readily than do the conventions of a feature film. Lear's throne room is an empty space, with a table, two benches and a fairly simple throne, all at the same level. The floor is bare wood, and a grey cloth hangs in the background. Where Phillips gave us cluttered Victorian interiors, Miller gives us the feeling of an age when even in great houses furniture was sparse, and every piece counted. Using a Globe-like freedom, he does not distinguish one interior from another: the same wooden floor and hanging cloth do for them all. When we go outdoors we are still in the studio: the cloth is replaced by a plain cyclorama, and we can see where it meets the floor. A crumpled cloth on the ground suggests rugged country, and it appears to be the grey hangings of the interior scenes, put to different use. Cordelia on her return to England is seen against a filmy white drapery that suggests her tent, but (more important) establishes a delicate, airy atmosphere and a simple background for her face. A few barrels and a tripod suggest preparations for war.

This stripping-down recalls the economy of Peter Brook's stage production, and the special conditions of television allow further economies. Literally the production is in colour, but the costumes, though full of different textures, are uniformly black, varied by grey and brown tones in the interior and exterior scenes respectively. Only the red plume in the Fool's hat (for which he compensates by wearing a dead-white makeup) stands out. When Edgar appears for the duel his costume includes a red cross. These touches of relief – one gaudy, the other serious – stand out as they are meant to, and help to link two of the good characters. But the device is used so sparingly that the attention drawn to the Fool and Edgar seems disproportionate. The main colours, of course, are those of the human face; but even these are muted, since Miller and his lighting designer decided to desaturate the picture of colour by an unusual thirty per cent (Fenwick, pp. 26–7). Music is also used sparingly. Brief trumpet calls, when required by the text, announce entrances; a slow drum-beat sounds under the final credits. So far as the staging is concerned, Lear's division of his kingdom looks like an informal meeting on an ordinary day in a private house; nothing external signals that a momentous event is taking place. The rituals of chivalry, which even Phillips built up, are also underplayed. The mutual challenge of Albany and Edmund is done quietly, in close-up; they simply hand each other gloves in an informal and businesslike way, avoiding the traditional grand gesture of flinging them on the floor. Once again, the scaled-down playing increases the realism, but we lose the sense of a society that lives by formal codes and uses symbols like thrones, crowns and gages.

What we are left with is the drama of relations between people, of which the chief medium is the actor. Even the religious dimension has this quality. We are aware not of divine powers out there in the cosmos but, as characters use religious symbols on their own initiative, making the sign of the cross on their own bodies, of the personal beliefs of people. The focus is not on the heavens but on the actors. We are not even particularly aware of the camera that shows us these actors. It remains still for long periods, concentrating on their faces. In the last scene, for example, where the Olivier TV production breaks the concentration on Lear and Cordelia with shots of Kent, Albany or Edgar, Miller's camera puts all the characters together in one picture, with Lear and Cordelia in the foreground (Worthen, pp. 194–5, 201). The opening dialogue of Kent, Gloucester and Edmund is a single shot in the BBC version, while there are thirteen cuts in Olivier's (Cook, p. 183). Much of the Dover scene is a single shot of Lear, Edgar and Gloucester, with Lear switching from left to right of the group partway through. Occasionally the camera takes a noticeable decision, isolating Lear early in his address to his court or breaking the group of three at Dover – just once – to pick out Edgar's 'matter and impertinency mixed'. When the Fool speaks his prophecy straight to the camera the fourth-wall convention is broken (appropriately, since on stage the prophecy breaks theatrical illusion) and we become aware of the camera, the screen, and ourselves watching. But this device is seldom used; Edgar's asides are not to the camera, and he does not particularly lower his voice. He just speaks, and we just overhear him. Television allows further economies that the theatre does not. Even in the simplest stage production, there are brief interludes between scenes as actors (and sometimes furniture) get on and off. Here, we cut immediately from one scene to the next. Sometimes an actor will not even enter; the camera moves a little, and there he is. This device is used for Oswald's appearance in the Dover scene. We can imagine that Shakespeare would have approved of this technique: many of the cuts in the Folio are of bridging passages that ease the transitions between scenes.

One thing that is hard to get on the small screen, and that is of special importance to *King Lear*, is the awareness of other people on stage watching the principal actors. In the text, brief comments by those on the sidelines – Edgar, or Cordelia's attendants, for example – contribute to the orchestration of the scene, the sense that the personal drama of the leading characters impinges on other lives. We have noted how Phillips used a second, upstage audience of attendants, how the doctor in the Granville Barker production contributed to the reunion of Lear and Cordelia. The convention of reaction shots, used in the Olivier version and in

Richard Eyre's television adaptation of his stage production, gives us something of the necessary effect, but at the cost of breaking the flow. Instead of being aware, as on stage, of the simultaneous presence of several characters, we go back and forth from one talking head to another. Miller's solution is to bring the watchers into the shot wherever possible. This leads to a recurring type of picture in which, as two characters address each other in profile, from either side of the screen, a third character appears full-face in the background between them. In the first scene, as Cordelia addresses Lear, Kent is between them, smiling. He stops smiling and moves forward slightly with concern as Lear starts attacking Cordelia. As Lear and Goneril square off the Fool appears in the middle, looking as if he wants to get in on the conversation. Hardy M. Cook has defended this device as giving a strong sense of the group, the ensemble, appropriate for the social and political scale of the drama (Cook, p. 179). But I think there are problems with it. Used too often – and Miller uses it too often – it becomes an obvious trick, and the viewer's reaction becomes, 'There, he's doing it again'. The medium calls too much attention to itself, and the effect is the more grating in that Miller's use of the medium is normally so unobtrusive. Also, since there is generally room for only one watcher – at the most, two – there is a strong emphasis on that figure, far stronger than there would be on stage. The result is not so much an extension of the scale of the drama into the public sphere as the addition of several private dramas in the background as we become aware of one individual's concern with what the foreground characters are doing. The large screen of the feature film does not create this problem, but the small screen of television does. Also, if it is to work at all the device requires considerable tact, and there are unfortunate lapses in this production. The closeness necessary to bring the watchers into the shot is sometimes unnatural, and one is all too aware of a director's decision. In the waking of Lear, the Doctor and Kent are in the top of the frame, leaning over Cordelia and Lear, who are in the bottom. All four faces are given equal attention, making it look as though the supporting actors are trying to hog the camera. Matters are not helped by the fact that John Shrapnel's Kent affects a shaved head and a large earring as his disguise, making him the most striking and exotic figure on the screen. His intent stare registers more strongly than anything Lear and Cordelia do. In the text Kent fades into the background in the later scenes. But this Kent, just by his appearance, pulls the focus to himself whenever he appears, disturbing the delicate balance of attention the play requires.

The small screen, we might say, makes it hard to measure out the human element precisely enough; the container gets full too quickly. The non-human element is easier to control. In the storm scenes the focus is strongly on the actors. The thunder does not call attention to itself: it is not even allowed to begin (as in the Folio) part way through Lear's exit speech but has to wait till the end, just before 'O Fool, I shall go mad.' This also removes the suggestion that Lear's voice triggers the storm, making it more simply a natural event. In the storm proper the background is either invisible, or revealed as the plain studio set. The storm begins with a thunderclap and a close-up of Kent's face; and throughout the sequence it is the human face, wet with rain and grimacing with cold, that largely creates the storm for us. By moving in on the actors, the camera gets closer than the stage can do to Gielgud's ideal that Lear himself should be the storm; we are simply not aware of all that surrounding space in which we feel something cosmic ought to be happening. What is lost is Brook's sense of the storm as an outside entity with which Lear is in conflict. But Miller's storm has a dynamic of its own, created by strong contrasts between scenes. The first scene with Tom is wild and noisy, ending with a struggle as the madman starts yelling and has to be restrained. The second, the mad trial, is quiet and controlled. Whether standing at the back of the scene or sitting at the table for the trial, Tom is now upright, dignified and still, very unlike the trembling, shrieking madman of his first appearance; and of course the effect is even more unsettling. (Granville Barker evidently distinguished the scenes in the same way (Dymkowski, p. 164).) There is an equally striking contrast between the noise of the storm scenes and the quiet of the interior scenes interspersed with them. Suddenly the interiors, which had seemed perfectly normal, are unnaturally, frighteningly quiet: the air seems dead, the grey background ashen. Occasional distant thunder only emphasizes the stillness. The quick cutting that is part of Miller's method pays rich dividends here. It is the contrast Brook wanted in his film between inside and outside, achieved here more strongly and by simpler means. A point is made that I have not seen made so clearly in any other production: the characters who ought to frighten us are not those who are out in the storm, but those who are inside keeping dry.

Miller uses a similar economy in other scenes which some productions have built up elaborately. The battle, so important for Noble and Kozintsev, is simply not there. All we have is a close-up of Gloucester's face as a slow procession of figures crosses behind him in silhouette, already defeated. The fight between Oswald and Edgar is over in seconds. The duel between the brothers, in which we see little more than their heads and shoulders, with close-ups of Edmund's face, is not much longer. Of the blinding of Gloucester, we see only the back of the chair; the most violent thing in the scene is the loud anguish in his voice. Though Cornwall wipes his hands like a surgeon after an operation, we see no blood. The greatest horror, as in Kozintsev, is in the reactions of other people. On 'pluck out his eyes', a line that seemed painfully torn from Irene Worth's Goneril, this Goneril (Gillian Barge) gives a small giggle. Regan (Penelope Wilton) likewise thinks 'let him smell his way to Dover' is a great joke. She has watched the blinding itself with cool interest, and Cornwall does it as calmly as if he did this sort of thing every day.

Given the economy of the production, such things count. The camera watches these people very closely, and so do we. The production is full of small, revealing touches: the little ineffectual sigh Albany gives as he sits at the table having lost an argument with his wife; the way Kent forgets his rural accent and slips into standard English as he defends his dignity against Cornwall. In such small touches, power relationships are established. Gloucester is amused by Kent's 'I have seen better faces' joke until he sees that Cornwall isn't; he quickly goes poker-faced. Oswald, on his exit after the stocking of Kent, gives Gloucester (whose house this is) a superior smile. In the last scene Albany listens to Edmund's assertion of authority with visible dislike and impatience. Comfort can also be shown in small ways: as, in the background, Lear is greeted by Cordelia's soldiers, in the foreground Edgar strokes his father's head. The scale is different, though the plots are moving in parallel, and it is the private moment the camera closes in on. Again, where so much depends on detail, tact is important. (I remember, many years ago, a stage actor seeing himself on television for the first time and muttering, 'God, that camera is pitiless'.) There are some failures. As Kent starts his quarrel with Oswald he is whittling a stick, and we wonder why. In the ensuing fight, in which Oswald defends himself by holding a saddle in front of him, Kent hits the saddle repeatedly but makes no attempt to hit Oswald. The strangest detail is a tiny old man who watches Gloucester blinded, and expresses his horror by patting himself on the top of the head. We wonder who he is, and why he is doing that; the later discovery that he is Gloucester's tenant farmer is no compensation for the damage he has done to our concentration. Background figures like this can be interesting in paintings, where we have the leisure to study them; the imperatives of drama are different. Edgar appears for the duel in a strange white mask. It gives the young man come to do justice an air of infinite age and impassive melancholy, and as a costume for a fight it has impractically small eye-holes. J. S. Bratton has pointed out that the mask creates a link with the white makeup of the Fool (Bratton, p. 205). I muttered, 'Of course', as I read about it; as I watched, I'm afraid I simply wondered what Miller was up to. Now that I know, I continue to wonder if the Edgar–Fool relationship is important enough to justify the distracting strangeness of the effect.

The occasional eccentricities stand out more disturbingly in that the production as a whole is natural and, within its chosen limits, convincing. Miller sees televison as a chance to remove 'large-scale hectoring rhetoric' from the acting of Shakespeare: 'people haven't got to boom or sing … You can be much more naturalistic. People can speak quietly in their own voices without simply descending into an ordinary modern vernacular' (Hallinan, p. 134). As Shakespeare might have thought of it, we are moving from the Globe into the Blackfriars. The voices in this production are light, quick and natural, rising to shouts when required but avoiding the plumminess that sometimes afflicts Shakespearian acting. The low-key opening conversation of Gloucester, Kent and Edmund helps set the tone. There is nothing portentous here: Edmund seems amused by his father's jokes. When Albany denounces Goneril in IV.ii he does not make a tirade of it but sits down, thinking out what he is saying, trying to understand. As in Phillips' production, the quiet manner makes us listen and aids clarity. There are moments when a more full-out playing might be useful: Edgar's Tom impersonation reduces him too often to a weak, clenched whimper. But the domestic scale of the play is well served. Gloucester's family really seems a family. Norman Rodway's Gloucester makes a joke of 'I shall not need spectacles', and when he actually dons a pair he handles them as though he is not quite used to them. Evidently he does need them, and doesn't use them often enough; we sense an old man's vanity. For his speech on the eclipses, Gloucester and Edmund sit on a bench together, Edmund reacting with tut-tutting sympathy; the effect is not of a major statement about the cosmos, but of two people commiserating with each other in a familiar way about the wicked state of the world. (Later, when he parodies his father's astrological concerns, Edmund sits in Gloucester's old place on the bench.) In the Dover sequence Edgar does not lead his blind father but carries him piggy-back, the relations of parent and child ironically reversed. Edmund's military command is shown not by spectacle, as in Kozintsev, but by his appearance in shirtsleeves, at a desk, with a book and an inkwell. Like Phillips' Edmund, he is a working general who has paper to push.

It is appropriate that the Gloucester plot should move at this level; it is more surprising that the Lear plot does – though we have by now seen precedents for this. Michael Hordern described Lear as 'a dreadful old man ... Let's face it, he's a bloody awful father and he's just not used to being crossed either as a father or as a king' (Fenwick, p. 33). There is no thought here of a magnificent portent, and it is revealing that Hordern's account puts the first and heaviest emphasis on the father, not the king. His entrance, at the opposite extreme from Michael Gambon's, is without pageantry or music. We hear only footsteps on the wooden floor and the rustling of costumes. Lear comes on with his back to the camera, as do the other members of the court. As in Brook's stage production this is a quick, informal entry, a prelude to business. He wears no crown, and nothing in his costume distinguishes him from the other people in the room; he already has something of the ability to fit in with a crowd that Yarvet's Lear acquires only with the beggars. He has a beard of sorts, but it looks like three weeks' unimpressive growth, and it virtually disappears when he is filmed in profile. His later confrontation with Goneril – 'Does any here know me?' – is not an assertion of royalty but schoolmasterly exasperation interspersed with little sarcastic laughs, as though he were telling off a group of unruly boys. Hordern admitted, 'I find it difficult to wear a crown, metaphorically speaking ... so I was happy to go along with a rather more domestic opening to the play, which is wrong, I think.' Miller sees the effect rather as 'a person rattling around inside an office which was much too large for him' (Fenwick, p. 22). But the trappings of office are also small-scale. The map is about the size of an ordinary road map. Other Lears have divided the kingdom with a sword; Hordern pokes at the map with his finger. There is a throne, but it is not Lear's command post. He walks around the room having conversations as he goes; he singles out Cordelia by going to her, rather than by having her come to him. Even Ustinov used an armchair to make himself the centre of the room; this room has no centre.

Though there is nothing externally royal about this Lear he is not feeble. In the first scene, and in his confrontations with his daughters, he is strong, lucid and energetic. On 'I'll not weep' he is as good as his word; he remains angry and determined. Indeed, he hits this note so often that there is some danger of monotony. Lear is simply, stubbornly, fighting back. His knights do not misbehave; he himself is the problem. But there are moments of insight. On his reply to the Fool, 'nothing can be made out of nothing', he hesitates, suddenly remembering when he used those words before. In I.v, as the Fool jokes with him while they wait for the horses, he paces up and down, angry and preoccupied; then the joke about being old before he is wise arrests him for a moment. But though he will stop occasionally he does not change direction. In madness, he cracks with alarming completeness. Like Gielgud's Lear, he gets his madness from Tom; we see Tom close-up, in profile, and Lear full-face behind him, filling the rest of the screen, reacting excitedly to everything Tom says. He seems to be nibbling something, and when Tom jumps up and down Lear follows suit like a dog doing imitations. He seems quite sane when he speaks, quite mad when he listens to Tom, and the split is alarming in itself.

In the scene with Gloucester, where other actors have found a kind of philosophy, leavened with dry bitterness or wry amusement, Hordern is twitchy, jumpy and totally off his head. His entrance is prepared by soldiers running across the backcloth, evidently looking for him. Then suddenly, unexpectedly, he is there with Gloucester and Edgar. We didn't see him coming. His changes of tone and pace – sometimes fast and excited, sometimes slow and meditative – keep catching us by surprise. He feeds the imaginary mouse, nibbling along with it, then gives a cry of disgust, throws it down and stamps on it. On 'a dog's obeyed in office' he barks, 'woof, woof!' and Gloucester laughs. It is not so funny when on 'I remember thine eyes well enough' he tries to dig his fingers into the sockets. Lear is dangerous, out of control and liable to do anything. There is less rapport between the two men than we usually see; Lear is too far gone for that. Gloucester does not try to take off his boots. 'Thou must be patient' is a shout; Lear is scolding his companion, not comforting him. On 'I know thee well enough' he rebukes him for being so silly as to cry. In general, he handles Gloucester roughly. His preaching is a comic parody of the parsonical manner, with hands clutching an imaginary gown. At the end of the sequence there is a wonderful contrast between the shaggy, eccentric king nibbling a straw from his crown and the stiff, dignified young men who have come to take him away. The scene as a whole is brilliantly played as a clinical observation of madness; it is also busy and fussy, and what in other performances have been moments of discovery pass over quickly. 'It smells of mortality' is accompanied by a small gesture of disgust, as Lear wipes his hand, but the moment is not in any way isolated. We have a much stronger sense than usual that Lear really is mad; but we feel rather less than usual that his madness is a vehicle for insight.

His scene with Cordelia restores his dignity, and his sanity. He is sitting up in bed and seems quite calm. But there is little of the pain or bewilderment Lear also feels in this scene, and he is still not quite in touch: as Cordelia weeps, he says, 'Do not laugh at me.' As in the scene with Gloucester, we miss the sense that Lear is making new discoveries; he seems rather to be coming round after an illness. Here and in the last scene, Kent and others gather around closely, looking on with tender concern and bending over to keep in the frame. Again the watchers are intrusive; at the very end, the way Kent leans his cheek against the top of Lear's head makes his relationship with the king seem stronger than Cordelia's. And there is less than there might be for the watchers to react to. The 'Howls' are quick and angry; Hordern does not attempt a large or sustained cry. Emotion does not register strongly in his voice. But his melancholy eyes give us something of what the voice misses, and there are telling details: the struggle for breath on 'undo this button', though his shirt is hanging wide open; the simplicity of 'no life' as he lifts Cordelia's hand and lets it fall limply. These moments help; but it could be said of Hordern, as some viewers said about Scofield, that he falls short in the later scenes. Benedict Nightingale summarized his performance at Nottingham in words that could be applied here: 'As a picture of dotage it's distressing and persuasive, and I don't doubt that it has ample clinical justification ... one can almost see his tears and smell his urine.' But, he adds, 'Something hard to define is lacking in Hordern's performance: intensity of feeling, perhaps, a special vulnerability and capacity for suffering ... It substitutes mental affliction for spiritual anguish' (*New States-man*, 7 November 1969). Lear will not touch us if he does not seem real; but the observation of real behaviour, however finely done, will not give us everything we need.

Nightingale's reference to the clinical basis of Hordern's performance recalls the fact that Jonathan Miller is a doctor as well as a director. What it suggests, unfairly perhaps, is that Miller's special expertise has actually limited his insight. Frank Middlemass's Fool is certainly limited, in this case by a single, consistently sustained view of the character's function. A man of Lear's age, with plenty of experience behind him, he is the king's conscience, and never lets him alone. Middlemass describes his function as 'a sort of whipping of the king' and calls the Fool 'a very strict nanny telling the king he's made an absolute idiot of himself' (Fenwick, pp. 21, 22). For the most part he neither sings nor clowns; he lectures. His manner is hard, angry, hectoring. He stands there and shouts. But beneath the anger is concern: in the final confrontation with Goneril and Regan we glimpse the Fool over Lear's shoulder, looking pained. When Lear recoils from the barking dogs the Fool touches him, tender and worried. As his makeup washes off in the storm, so the inner man looks out towards the end. He has a sentimental relationship with Cordelia, appearing with her in the first scene, touching and comforting her; her asides are addressed to him. We can see the logic of this, but it weakens Cordelia dramatically. In the text she is on her own until Kent intervenes, and part of what we admire is her solitary courage. A better invention is the handling of the Fool's bawdy joke, 'She that's a maid now, and laughs at my departure, / Shall not be a maid long, unless things be cut shorter.' He aims this at the camera and, using the backcloth as a stage curtain, he prepar-es to nip behind it with a quick two-finger gesture. It is a frankly theatrical 'turn', the only attempt the Fool makes to be funny. It cracks the idiom of the production, and we glimpse for a moment something we've been missing: simple, corny, old-fashioned theatre. The BBC production uses its medium intelligently and is full of perceptive, sometimes brilliant insights. But as the Fool lectures more than he clowns (unbalancing the part as Antony

Sher did but in the opposite direction) so this production may be too correct, too intelligent, not quite vulgar enough. In this respect the Olivier production, which appeared the following year on a rival network, Granada television, can be seen as its mirror-opposite. It is to that production that we now turn.

CHAPTER IX

Laurence Olivier

Speaking of television productions of *King Lear*, people refer casually to 'the BBC version' and 'the Olivier version'. We think of the one as the product of an institution (though in fact it is highly individual) and the other as a showcase for a famous actor. In that, and in other respects, the Olivier production reverts to an earlier way of doing things. In many respects it is strikingly old-fashioned. Olivier himself freely admitted that its origins were theatrical (Olivier, p. 141), and as we will see it is less fully tuned to the television medium than the BBC version is. It draws to some extent on the 1946 Old Vic production, which Olivier directed and starred in: once again Lear enters chatting with Cordelia, and his manner in the first scene is comically whimsical. The production was directed not by Olivier, but by Michael Elliott, essentially a stage director, who had been associated with Olivier in his National Theatre days and who was a brilliant director of Ibsen in particular. But the production's theatrical origins go back farther than this. As Stanley Wells commented, 'Irving and Wolfit would have been at home in this setting; the most recent theatrical production that it recalls is Glen Byam Shaw's, for Charles Laughton at Stratford in 1959' (*Times Literary Supplement*, 8 April 1983). In terms of scenic conventions, we can certainly go back to Irving, and farther still. Olivier's design team fixed on 800 AD as the setting – exactly the year that Charles Kean had picked in 1858 (Cowie, p. 78; Carlisle, p. 284). This is a period for which we have comparatively little visual evidence, and our way of imagining it owes at least as much to the conventions of nineteenth-century illustration as it does to archaeology. Long robes tied at the waist, flowing moustaches, headbands – the look of the Olivier *Lear* is a Victorian look, illustrations from a popular and improving history book come to life. Its sets are closer to being totally realistic than those of any stage production we have discussed, and this too takes us back to the nineteenth century. The primitive, barbaric side of the play lights up, with a corresponding diminution in the sense of political and domestic business. The opening set suggests Stonehenge, with a circle of light behind it to represent the sun. In this setting the opening conversation of Gloucester and Kent loses its political and domestic ambience; we are in a temple just before the start of a ceremony. In the equivalent of I.ii, where in the BBC version Gloucester and Edmund have a family conversation sitting on a bench, the same characters in the Olivier version are surrounded by tall standing stones. Gloucester's 'I shall not need spectacles' sounds very odd. Here we need the Renaissance setting; the play's anachronisms move both forward and backward. As the camera moves in more closely on the faces, and we lose sight of the set, the lack of a domestic setting ceases to bother us; but we never feel that these people have a house. The domestic interiors we see later are primitive: log dwellings lit by torches, rough wooden stockades. They evoke the tribe and the war-band, not the family. In line with William Poel's objection, we cannot clearly identify these people socially. Only Oswald's occasional attempts at a posh accent help us place him; he is in standard Saxon gear like the others, and the metal collar round his neck does not really tell us who he is.

What we get is an appropriate setting for the play's pre-Christian, polytheistic religion. Stonehenge and the sun set the ambience. Edmund addresses 'Thou, nature, art my goddess' to the sun, which has risen a little higher than it was in the first scene as though to give precedent for his ambition. Lear regularly falls on his knees to pray. His invocations of the gods are not conversational formulae, but real prayers to powers he believes in. In general we sense that there are gods in this world, and people address them seriously. Nature is significant: as the camera moves in on Edmund for 'This is the excellent foppery of the world' we hear an owl. He may not believe in omens, but they work all the same. Later, carrion birds caw in the background of his meeting with Goneril. Outside there is generally a haze in the air; the sun is filtered through mist, and mist hangs on the hillsides. This is a technical device to conceal the fact that we are in a studio, in contrast to the BBC production where the line between the floor and the cyclorama is frankly visible. On the other hand, the device is obvious enough that there is no serious intention to fool us. Instead there is a balance of conventions: a studio setting pretends to be open country without really denying its character as a studio. The general mistiness also has its own effect, playing on our illogical but habitual assumption that the primitive world was wrapped in fog and twilight. A more surprising design decision is the delicate pastel colours of the costumes, which seem incongruous with the violence of the action. Many years previously the same costume designer, Tanya Moiseiwitsch, had worked with Tyrone Guthrie on a production of *Oedipus Rex* in which they considered for a while using 'tender juicy greens and yellows which would literally suggest the springtime of the world' as an ironic setting for the grim story of the play. The intention was abandoned for fear that 'the irony would misfire' (Davies, *et al.*, pp. 122–3); but something like the same intention seems to have been at work here. Illogically again, we think of the primitive world as a young world; and so the look of the production is pretty and fresh. But I think the fears about the *Oedipus* production were justified: the look is too lyrical, and if irony is intended it misfires.

The background may be hazy, but the details of this world are solid. The mad Lear and the blind Gloucester meet not in a bare existential space but on a green hillside with a large tree in the background (Barker's oak again?). When Lear wakes to music we see the musicians, looking like figures from an illuminated manuscript. As in Kozintsev's film, there are horses and dogs, but their presence seems more formidable in the tight studio space. Lear rides his horse right into Goneril's banqueting hall, and his train includes a large shaggy dog. He and his knights are noisy, but that is not the only domestic nuisance Goneril has to put up with. As Edgar flees, he is pursued by men with dogs; we see horses in Cordelia's encampment. Oswald arrives on horseback to confront Gloucester and Edgar. It is a useful social point, but it creates a technical problem: when he has to dismount to play the scene, the horse just wanders off. The fight between Kent and Oswald sets poultry clucking and dogs barking. In the mad trial, where Goneril is impersonated by a joint-stool, Regan is impersonated by a chicken, which Lear tries unsuccessfully to catch. The mouse for once is a real mouse, which Lear teases with his finger (though the cheese is still imaginary). We see in practical terms how Lear survives in the wild: he snares a rabbit, cuts it open, and eats what looks like its liver. In creating such a solidly physical world the production is actually responding to an aspect of the play's language, in which we are never far from the animal kingdom, a feather stirs on Cordelia's lips, clothing has pins and buttons. Cosmic though its implications may be, the experience of the play is grounded in practical everyday reality, and one of its concerns is the business of survival: what to eat, what to wear, where to find shelter. This is a dimension of the play which more abstract productions miss, and the camera has the advantage of showing us the smallest details. Realism touches the performance as well as the design. The soliloquy in which Edgar announces his intention to become Tom has nothing of the quality of a formal statement, as David Threlfall's delivery is shot through with short gasps: Edgar is out of breath with running. Kent's disguise, which is usually token and conventional, really is a disguise here: he shaves off his beard, and looks utterly different.

The use of realistic detail takes the production closer to the conventions of the feature film than to the spare, stylized television idiom evolved by Miller for the BBC series. The duel between the brothers is pure Hollywood. It goes on a long time, there is a certain amount of dodging around the Stonehenge pillars, Edmund gets Edgar down and nearly kills him; finally the good guy ambushes the bad guy in a surprise ending. While other productions have aimed at stylization and simplicity in the duel, this one goes for narrative excitement of the old-fashioned kind. Miller cuts immediately from one scene to the next. Such bridging passages as he adds are few and quick; Elliott's are more extended and realistic. Lear and the Fool, sharing a horse and accompanied by attendants on horseback, ride away from Goneril's. Lear is removed from the farmhouse on a cart, while the Fool stays behind, trembling with the fever that will soon carry him off. As in the Brook film, the characters' movements are shown and explained, but the production never departs as Brook's does into a narrative of its own, and the confines of the studio do not allow the journeys to develop, as in Kozintsev, into episodes with their own symbolic weight. What we have instead is padding between the scenes. It is a half-hearted use of the opportunities of the medium.

Film purists (who are as fussy as Shakespeare purists) find much to complain of in this production. William B. Worthen objects to the way the camera keeps moving away from Lear and Cordelia in the last scene, showing us the reactions of Kent, Edgar and Albany, breaking our concentration on the central figures. We have seen Miller's solution to the problem, which Worthen prefers (Worthen, pp. 194–5, 201). Hardy M. Cook likewise prefers Miller's 'relatively static camera' with its shots of two to four characters to Elliott's 'shorter takes and dominating one-shots' (Cook, p. 179). Worthen also objects to Elliott's persistent use of overhead shots in which our perspective is wrenched 'from the actors' plane by swinging the camera high above the stage, presumably so that we might share the vantage of the play's wanton gods' but distancing us too much from the action (Worthen, p. 198). The device recalls Olivier's trick in his Shakespeare films of pulling the camera away from the main scene on to the sidelines where (as in *Richard III*) we see two old monks chanting, or a woman scrubbing a door-step. There is another world going on outside the lives of the great. But in the Olivier *Lear* the overhead camera does not pick out another action; it sees the main action from an unexpected angle. Sometimes the effect is arbitrary, as when the camera pans down through a hole in the roof of the farmhouse, or marks a scene transition by lifting up and away from Edgar and Gloucester, then moving down to Goneril arriving at her house. Moments like these seem to be make-work projects for the camera, giving it something to do. More obviously significant is an overhead shot of Lear and Cordelia surrounded by sword-points; and as in Brook's film the camera is used effectively to preserve the ambiguity of the Dover scene. We see the two men walking over rough country, and for all we can tell they might have come to a cliff-top – until Gloucester falls and the camera pulls up overhead to show him sprawled on a flat patch of sand.

Both television versions follow the text closely, taking nothing like the liberties of the Brook and Kozintsev films. But of the two the Olivier version makes more attempts to open the play out in a cinematic way, to fill out background and action. The trouble is that these attempts are tentative: a television production is trying to be a feature film, without having quite the resources. Music is used much more heavily than in the BBC version, but it does not have the quality of the Shostakovich score. The music under the opening titles seems designed for an old-fashioned Hollywood spectacle, as do the barbaric, braying fanfares that accompany entrances in the first scene. In general the musical effects are conventional: a sinister theme tune for Goneril's entrances, pounding menace for the blinding of Gloucester, a mournful lament for the death of Cordelia. One feels that the scenes do not need to be decorated this way, and one misses the silence of the Miller and Brook screen versions. The battle is filled out, but not much: in a double-exposure with a close-up of Gloucester, we see a few soldiers fighting around a burning wooden structure; we hear shouting, drums and filmic music. Violence, as in other screen versions, is relatively restrained. We don't see Gloucester's eyes put out, just close-ups of Cornwall's face as he does the deed, and then the bleeding sockets. It should be noted that none of the screen versions we have discussed is particularly graphic at this point; they all use the camera's selectivity to shield us from what we would see on stage. There is a close-up of the blinding in the Brook film, but it is so quick the details don't register. I suspect this is not just an old-fashioned squeamishness of the sort that used to keep the blinding offstage altogether. It is more the equivalent of the distance from the event that the theatre naturally imposes. It is one thing to watch the blinding from several feet away; it is quite another to come within inches of it. That closeness, and the graphic detail that special-effects artists could create, would make sheer physical disgust our only reaction, overwhelming all the others. Shakespeare wants that disgust, but he wants it sharpened by moral horror. The question 'How is this possible?' should be looking for more than a technical answer. That having been said, the violence of *King Lear* needs to be more precise than it sometimes is in the Olivier production. Oswald kicks the stocks and Kent gives a small cry of pain; but it doesn't look as though it *ought* to hurt. This is nothing like the refined cruelty of the moment in the Brook film when Oswald takes Kent's boots off.

In the storm sequence, as in the BBC version, the main focus is on the actors, but not so exclusively. The camera pans over open country, then picks out Lear on a rise of ground. There are flashes of lightning, bursts of thunder, and rain falling in buckets. The landscape itself is generalized, consisting of a few low shrubs, just a background for the actors; but it is at least a landscape, not the frankly bare studio space of the BBC version. Generally speaking, Miller keeps his actors in a studio while Elliott puts his in a series of pictures. Each method has its strengths and its drawbacks: Miller's bare space tends to flexibility and economy, with a strong focus on the actors; but its bareness, paradoxically, is ostentatious, the result of a conscious, even slightly academic, decision. It has a different effect from the bareness of the Globe stage, which its audience would have taken for granted. As in Brook's refusal to use film music, we are aware of a deliberate denial of the normal resources of the medium. The blank space also makes its own statement: cold and empty, it leaves the world of the play a bit bloodless. Elliott's method is open to the objection that it is heavy and over-literal, cluttering the play. But it also gives the actors a more fully realized world to move in. Illusion that draws us in is not much in fashion in Shakespeare production these days; but in a play that tries to engage the audience's emotions as fully as this one does there is something to be said for it. Brechtian detachment isn't everything.

Though very different on the surface, Elliott's production is like that of Robin Phillips in creating a full context for the actors to work in, rather than developing a particular interpretation. As Stanley Wells puts it, it produces not 'an intellectual exploration of the text' but 'a framework in which the actors' energies may be fully released in the portrayal of individual characters' (*Times Literary Supplement*, 8 April 1983). The plurals are important, since this is not just a showcase for the star; a notable cast has been assembled. We find ourselves responding to powerful personalities rather than, as in the BBC production, admiring small details. The performances are for the most part solid accounts of the familiar view of the characters. The voices tend to be heavier than in the BBC production, and at times they quiver with emotion in a manner that suggests the stock Shakespearian acting of the 1940s and 1950s. In more recent productions – and Brook's 1962 *Lear* was, as we have seen, a turning point – we have been used to a lighter, drier, more conversational manner. The sound, like the look of the production, takes us back to an earlier time. At times we have to be content with stock villainy or stock pathos. Jeremy Kemp's Cornwall is obviously belligerent; you just have to look at him to know he's a villain. John Hurt's Fool is sane, bitter and sensitive, but not essentially comic. He cares about Lear and tries earnestly to get through to him. Like Middlemass, he functions as a conscience, not as an entertainer. When the conventional readings are filled out, it is more by the striking personalities of the actors than by any fresh thinking in the intepretation. This is true of Hurt's Fool, which draws on the actor's considerable gift for looking stricken and vulnerable; and of Leo McKern's Gloucester, who gives a salacious relish to his memories of Edmund's mother that few actors could match. Robert Lang's Albany goes effectively from sleepy bewilderment in the early scenes to a final decisiveness.

Where the production breaks with tradition, with brilliant

success, is in the treatment of Goneril and Regan. Normally Goneril is the brains, the executive, and Regan follows behind, lower, stupider and meaner. This was essentially the balance that Brook aimed for, and other productions for the most part have played variations on it. Here the balance is reversed. Dorothy Tutin's Goneril is dour and earnest, easily angered, easily upset. Diana Rigg's Regan, by contrast, is startlingly cool, witty and ironic. Regan's tendency to follow along becomes a gift for topping her sister. The lacquered quality that bothered some viewers in Rigg's 1962 Cordelia is a clear advantage here. In her love-test speech she is more light-hearted and ingratiating than her sister. Beneath the charm there is a deadly cool. As Lear goes into the storm, Regan's 'To wilful men / The injuries that they themselves procure / Must be their schoolmasters' is sweetly reasonable; but it is followed by a curt bite on 'shut up your doors'. Her erotic interest in Edmund is clear from early on. She kisses him at the start of the blinding scene, Cornwall's 'Farewell, Edmund' has an edge of warning, and Regan turns to face her husband defiantly. At the end of the scene she looks unconcerned as Cornwall falls dead at her feet. But as she starts to compete with Goneril for Edmund, tension mounts in her and the smooth surface cracks. At the end she fades visibly as the poison works on her; calm and smug, Tutin's Goneril has the edge at last. Of all the supporting performances, Rigg's is the only one that uses lightness, precision and irony. Against her, the other actors look a bit stodgy.

With one exception. Though Laurence Olivier's Lear has the scale and range that stamp it as the work of a great classical actor, his description of Lear as 'like all of us, really, ... just a stupid old fart' shows that he was not aiming for anything cosmic or portentous, and there was nothing solemn in his approach. He claimed that Lear was an easy part for him: 'He's just a selfish, irascible old bastard – so am I ... My family would agree with that: no wonder he's all right, they would say, he's just himself, he's got just that sort of ridiculous temper, those sulks. Absolutely mad as a hatter sometimes' (Cowie, p. 78). There is no need to wonder how much real autobiography there is in the performance, or how much pose (if any) there is in that statement. The point is that this Lear, like Scofield's, Ustinov's and Yarvet's, is recognizable and human. And there is no question that in other respects Olivier drew frankly on himself. In 1946 he had been, like Gielgud, too young for the part, and looking back on photographs he remarked that his makeup looked like Clapham Junction (Olivier, p. 137). By 1983 there was no need to fake the age. Olivier remarked, 'When you're younger, Lear doesn't feel real. When you get to my age, you *are* Lear in every nerve of your body' (Giroux, p. 99). Lear is a character who begins on the edge of death, and it is impossible to watch Olivier's performance without feeling that he too is on the edge. As one reviewer put it, 'each gesture can seem heroic, each line he utters a precious gift from the depleting stock of his time' (Richard Corliss, *Time*, 16 May 1983). In fact he had six years to live, but his strength had been wasted by a series of debilitating illnesses, he had given up stage acting ten years earlier, and Lear was to be his last major performance. Only the breaks required by filmmaking allowed him to sustain the energy to carry an entire role. The energy is considerable, the technique as brilliant as ever; only in the wayward memory (he paraphrases almost as often as Ustinov) is there a sign of failing resources. But as we will see, when Olivier *wants* to use his age, he does. In the performance, as in the part, we see one man's determination to defy mortality on his own terms.

The rituals of this Lear's court are as far as they could be from the informality of Miller's. The entrances are grand, and Lear's subjects prostrate themselves flat on the ground as he mounts his throne. The map is huge; it has to be spread on the floor like a carpet. Lear walks on it, dividing it with a sword. But he has come on chatting with Cordelia. Where Miller creates informality all the way through, here we have a formal court with an unpredictable and whimsical old man at the centre of it. On 'Tell me, my daughters' he leans back and makes himself comfortable. His eyes shift for a moment with a touch of comic mischief that recalls Olivier's Richard III. Regan's 'she comes too short' draws an amused 'oho!' He is ingratiating, playful and generally having a grand time. On Cordelia's 'nothing' he puts a hand to his ear as though he hadn't heard properly. 'Mend your speech a little' is a conspiratorial whisper, part of the game. When he realizes she is serious he is like a hurt, spoiled child. His hands flap ineffectually, and he is on the brink of tears, which turn quickly to anger. On 'this coronet part betwixt you' he takes the crown off his head and throws it to the floor. It lands on the map and rolls; no one picks it up. While Ustinov, with deliberate weakness, signalled his inability to solve the problem of parting the coronet, Olivier turns the problem (still insoluble) over to the others with a grand gesture that is also a symbol of breaking order, and a tantrum. In his later confrontations with his daughters his moods, like Gielgud's, shift rapidly, with every change sharply pointed. We can almost imagine Granville Barker giving notes. Lear goes from silent puzzlement to anger to child-like pleading. This is not just an actor showing off; these moods are all in the text, all tactics Lear uses on his daughters, and the reason there are so many of them is that none of them works. When he demands to see Cornwall 'now, presently' each word is pointed with a downward jab of the finger; then on 'hysterica passio' he is pathetically frightened. He notices Kent's release with a touch of human affection for him. 'Tamely' is jokingly light, recalling the mocking delivery of 'mildly' in his 1959 Coriolanus. There is a big climax, with a rolling 'r' on 'an embossed carbuncle in my corrrrupted blood' followed by a weak, childlike attempt at reasonableness on 'but I'll not chide thee'. We hear the rolling 'r' again on 'O rrreason not the *need!*', which is also a rising shout of anger. He uses the shameless tricks beloved by Olivier impersonators, pouncing on words and lifting them with a rising inflection – 'on thine all-*e*-GIANCE, hear me!' – or spreading the vowel on 'the te-e-e-rrors of the earth', after which his arms flail and he staggers weeping into the embrace of the Fool. Like Ustinov, on 'I'll not weep' he weeps. The passion and energy are in a constant struggle with physical frailty: on 'give me that patience, patience I need' he also needs breath. In the storm he continues to veer between anger and pleading, with an attempt at reasonableness when he tells Kent why he does not want to enter the hovel. But the rain flattening his hair makes him look smaller and more vulnerable; his dignity is gone. And there are touches not just of frailty but of informality: at the height of the storm, in the midst of a tirade, he scratches his nose. On 'We'll to supper in the morning' he manages a little smile.

In IV.vi, the scene with Gloucester, where in 1946 he had run in on bleeding feet (Rosenberg, p. 267), he is now more like Gielgud's 'happy king of nature'. We see him first alone, snaring his rabbit and then, happy and self-satisfied, leaning back on the grass and chatting to himself. He decorates himself with conventionally pretty flowers, white, yellow and blue. Songbirds twitter in the background. Then he wanders off, singing 'Come over the bourne, Bessy, to me'. There is 'a kind of self-contentment, a new-found serenity in his madness' (Stanley Wells, *Times Literary Supplement*, 8 April 1983). There is also a weary understanding on 'they flattered me like a dog' and he pats Gloucester's hand on 'thou shalt not die' as though saying to his companion, 'I know the world; let me tell you about it.' When Cordelia's soldiers come for him he is helpless and pathetic at first, then jollies them along with child-like cunning as he plans his escape. But beneath the self-satisfaction there is an undercurrent of pain. The sexual discoveries are jokes at first. The opening of his speech on the simpering dame is wry and knowing; on 'whose face between her forks presages snow' he makes a gesture as though parting a woman's legs. Then as the vision gets more terrible he succumbs to helpless, flailing pain. Just before he asks for an ounce of civet he gives a series of little cries as though he were going to vomit. The scene is punctuated with little sniffs and scratches, and Lear's costume – the only case in which the historical surface gives way to something contemporary – looks like pyjamas with a rough blanket thrown over them, giving him the appearance of a confused old man who has escaped from a hospital.

It is this underlying frailty that breaks through in the scene with Cordelia. Gielgud at this point was sitting in a chair, with clean linen and hair carefully brushed, his dignity restored (Fordham, IV.vi). Olivier is lying on his back, his beard shaved off, and what little flesh there is on his face sunken inwards so that the bones stand out painfully. Having looked seventy, he now looks ninety. Part of what he is to discover in this scene is the frailty of the foolish, fond old man, the frailty he has struggled against for so long. As he wakes his eyes are restless and searching; his hands touch his face, and he misses his beard. In the scene with Gloucester he was knowing and experienced; now he is finding new things. The word 'Cordelia' is one of them, and he dwells on it. 'Old' and 'foolish' are also new words, and he dwells on them too, but less happily. 'Old' is touched with self-disgust and 'foolish' leads into a sob. 'Let's away to prison' is intimate and affectionate, restoring something like the relationship with Cordelia we saw at the beginning, in their first entrance together. He is not just making new discoveries but getting old comforts back again – only to lose them, and to struggle against the loss as he struggled against the loss of his kingdom. On the last 'howl', an almost inhuman sound, his eyes seem to be searching for something, and so does his voice. He puts his head to Cordelia's chest, listening intently for life. On the first three 'nevers' the word seems to have no meaning; the fourth is a discovery, and the voice plays on it; the fifth is resignation. But the remarkable thing in Olivier's playing of the last scene is how often he smiles. He smiles as he bends close to Cordelia, urging her to speak; as someone reminds him of Caius (though he has no idea Caius is Kent); as he asks for the button to be undone. And he beams with pride on 'look, her lips!' as if to say, 'Isn't she beautiful? She's my daughter, you know!'

He dies, like Othello, on a kiss; and Stanley Wells, who notes the analogy, notes also 'something celebratory about his concern for Cordelia' (*Times Literary Supplement*, 8 April 1983). But what also registers in the last scene is the restlessness, the inability to accept what has happened, that we saw when his older daughters turned against him. Olivier, like Gielgud, stressed the importance of variety in Shakespearian acting: 'The actor must keep an audience engaged by constant changes of inflection, he must keep them forward in their seats; he must have an acute sense of when he is boring them' (Olivier, p. 134). But while Gielgud used this quality to show a growing, educated Lear, Olivier – who had, I think, more of the ironist in his makeup – uses it more to show Lear battling his experiences, trying different tactics to put off knowledge. At the end his delight in Cordelia struggles against the grief of her loss, and in his final moments it is the delight that wins. The camera moves back and up, and we see that Lear and Cordelia are on a stone slab, an altar in the centre of Stonehenge. The camera continues to pan back, and we see the full shape of the monument, as the attendants, carrying torches, kneel in a circle around the bodies. As in Kozintsev's film, we have returned to the beginning. As in Irving's production, there is a formal ending, concentric circles of men and standing stones around Lear and Cordelia. A pattern is complete; there is order of a kind. But the wind we hear under the last few speeches, like the muted thunder at the end of Brook's production, suggests that the world is still bleak and dangerous. And within the formal framework, we have seen a life end not with serene acceptance but with a continuing struggle. The production that surrounds Olivier's performance is largely conservative and conventional, solid rather than exciting; but the central performance, like the play itself, is dangerously, unpredictably alive.

CHAPTER X

Ian Holm and Richard Eyre

While the Miller and Olivier versions of *King Lear*, though they had as we have seen some stage background, were made specifically for television, the version discussed in this chapter, first broadcast in 1998 by the BBC, was closely based on a stage production. This puts it in a different category with regard to its use of the medium: it translates not only the play but a particular stage performance, with most of its key decisions intact, into television. That this hybridization is so successful can be attributed in part to the special conditions of that performance. Richard Eyre's production of *King Lear*, starring Ian Holm, opened at the Cottesloe Theatre, the smallest of the three spaces used by the Royal National Theatre, in 1997. The Cottesloe seats about 300 people, allowing an intimacy equivalent to the intimacy of television. (There was a similar factor behind the equally successful transfer to television of Trevor Nunn's production of *Macbeth*, with Ian McKellen and Judi Dench: that production began its life at The Other Place, the Royal Shakespeare Company's smallest auditorium.) The intimacy works two ways. At the Cottesloe the audience sat on either side of a long, narrow stage, a situation in which it is more natural for the actors to talk to each other than in a proscenium-stage production, where there is always some cheating out to the audience. This allowed the establishment of close personal relations, which survive the transfer to television even though the camerawork and editing break those relations down into close-ups and reaction shots. And in an auditorium like the Cottesloe the audience can get close to the action, allowing the actors to scale down the performance and play more subtly than they could in a large theatre. This subtlety also survives the transfer. As we shall see, one of this production's main strengths is the close observation of character relationships, particularly among members of Lear's family. This puts it at the opposite pole from Peter Brook's stage and screen versions, whose bleak vision put the characters in solipsistic isolation.

The stage production, hailed by Heather Neill as 'the *Lear* for our time, the one we have been waiting for' (*Times Educational Supplement*, 11 April 1997) – we have seen such claims before – quickly became the hottest ticket in town, with long lines of people waiting for returns. It was natural, then, that the television transfer should preserve as much of the original as possible. Richard Eyre remains as director, Bob Crowley as designer. There is only one major cast change: Victoria Hamilton replaces Anne-Marie Duff as Cordelia. One striking stage effect, on which several reviewers commented, had to be sacrificed. At the beginning of the storm scene the two end walls of the set crashed to the floor, changing the colour of the stage from red to dirt-streaked white, creating a burst of wind in the auditorium and drawing a gasp from the audience (Pearce, p. 121; Smallwood, pp. 249–51). This is replaced on television by a much smaller effect, appropriate to a smaller medium: the closing of a door and a close-up showing a bolt being drawn from inside. The crashing doors were pure theatre, and untranslatable.

In the Cottesloe two banks of audience members faced each other, and much of the visual background of the performance would have consisted of the audience. For television, the production had to move as it were indoors, to a set that closes the actors in. Richard Eyre takes Jonathan Miller's route rather than Michael Elliott's: the set declares itself frankly to be a studio set, with no pretence of creating a realistic world. It is a large room with plain, bare walls and imposing doors at one end. A long passageway allows for dramatic entrances. On a backcloth at the end of this passage we sometimes see the giant shadows of actors about to enter. The blinding of Gloucester begins with the rapidly moving shapes of his tormentors, a sinister effect. Edgar's entrance for the final duel is portentous: loud, slow footsteps, then the giant shadow of the nameless knight, who moves into the entrance passage as a dark, featureless silhouette with a light behind him. Red at the beginning (the key colour of the set in the stage production), the set changes to grey for the blinding of Gloucester, and retains that colour. For the waking of Lear, with its comfort and its hope of redemption, the set, within whose walls terrible things have happened, disappears behind pure white hangings. It disappears altogether for the outdoor scenes. We see Edgar running through a tangle of trees. As Kent and the Gentleman talk about Cordelia, they walk through similar trees, more widely spaced to allow freer movement, against a background of stars. We have seen two aspects of nature, its hostility and its beauty, and when Kent declares that the stars govern our conditions, he can gesture towards them. (They are not *just* beautiful.) The Dover Cliff sequence takes place on off-white sand, shrouded by thick fog through which characters make dramatic entrances. Edgar enters for his first meeting with Gloucester as a slow-moving, dim silhouette, gradually coming into view as he walks toward us. He hears voices, and as the camera takes his point of view we see nothing but fog. Gradually the shapes materialize: Gloucester and the Old Man. At first we are in something like Gloucester's sightless world: as it gradually clarifies, we follow his journey to understanding. Elliott used mist to blur the lines of the horizon for studio interiors that were pretending to be exteriors: here the fog is a strong presence in its own right, and makes its own statement.

So does the lighting. There is a pale greyness in the Dover Cliff sequence. Miller desaturated the colour for his entire production: here the main effect is reserved for the end. As Lear enters with the dead Cordelia the colour is so drained that we seem to be watching a black-and-white film, relieved only by Cordelia's red dress. The effect recalls the small girl in the red coat we follow through the black-and-white world of Stephen Spielberg's *Schindler's List*. The main set, like the three blank walls of Brook's stage production, is nowhere in particular: it can be a room, any room, and with its furniture removed it can be a courtyard. When it is a room its furniture consists of a long table lined with chairs. At the opening, the table and chairs are draped in red cloth: when we move to Goneril's house they are draped in white. This allows Lear's knights to get the tablecloth muddy, dropping their saddles on to it; when they have left, Goneril, with a quick, angry gesture, pulls it off. For the blinding of Gloucester the table and chairs are bare wood, and only two chairs are left, one at either end of the table. The heavy draping of the furniture has suggested, if anything, an upscale restaurant: it is a design concept rather than a living space. As the basic cruelty of Cornwall and Regan is revealed, the fashionable surface is stripped away.

The long table has dual suggestions in the first scene. We are in a board room for a business meeting; and we are at a dinner table for a family discussion. We are not in a throne room. There is no throne, and Lear's authority consists of sitting at the head of the table, making him the chairman of the board (with the puns inherent in those words) and the head of the family. Reviewing the North American broadcast for *The New York Times*, Ariel Swartley, while finding that the production lacked a convincing sense of the outdoors, was persuaded by the room: 'one can picture a room like this on the glassy upper floors of a corporate compound or, for that matter, on board next century's executive spacecraft'. While admitting that Eyre did not go for specific contemporary references, and that the room was 'an abstraction', Swartley could not resist the thought that there were such rooms in Buckingham Palace (occupied by a tabloid-embattled Royal Family) and the White House (then occupied by President Clinton), in which 'affairs of state and affairs of the heart might easily blur beyond all recognition' (4 October 1998). There is nothing in the production like Noble's use of the Falklands War. But while it is sealed off from time and history, its very abstraction, like Brook's, allows the audience to see reflections of its own world. That the reflections in this case seem comparatively trivial is related to the production's lack of a political dimension, a matter to which we shall return.

The costumes, like the set, are simple and timeless. The lines are as plain as in Brook's stage production, but while in that production only Lear among the men wore a long robe, here long robes are common. Edmund and Edgar are the ones who stand out, wearing shirts and trousers with a more modern line. This is what young men wear. In the first scene there are only three colours other than those of the actors' faces: the set and furniture are red, the men are in long black robes, the women in long grey dresses, identically cut. In her confrontation with Lear, Cordelia's dress shows a few dark stains from her tears. When France and Burgundy enter, they are both in red, matching the set. (Both actors are black: this may have been colour-blind casting, but the effect is to make them visitors to a world where everyone else is white.) Later there are variations. For her confrontation with Lear Goneril goes into red; Regan at that point goes into dark grey, nearly black; at the end Goneril is in black and Regan, dying of poison, is wrapped in a white blanket. Cordelia returns in red. Does this associate her with France, who wore red in the first scene? Or, more ironically, with Goneril when she turned against Lear? And if the latter, how does the irony function?

We touch here on a problem. The limited range of colour suggests that each colour ought to be significant, ought to be making
a statement. Edmund is in black, while Edgar prefers white; that
one is easy. But the suspicion grows that the only real statement
being made is the designer's preference for simplicity and elegance.
Set and costumes have a paradoxical effect. They take us, very
effectively, out of history into a timeless world. But in that world
we are so aware of the hand of the designer, with his firm control
over line and colour, that the sheer simplicity seems artificial and
self-conscious, something imposed for its own sake. It is not (like
the worlds created by Kozintsev and Phillips) a world we can
recognize or imagine anyone living in. It evokes neither society or
nature; even its trees look like studio trees, and its sand is
certainly studio sand. The abstraction of Brook's stage production
at least suggested a harsh, primitive world that the audience could
relate to the cruelties of its own time. The world of this production is hermetically sealed, not so much a world as a statement by
a designer. Its relation to its own time is to the slick elegance of
fashion shows and fashion magazines. In a few years, for all its
apparent timelessness, its abstraction may look as dated as that of
Komisarjevsky. Its austerity includes a lack of hand props, which
can be used to evoke familiar human reality. Gloucester has no
spectacles to put on; Cornwall gouges out his eyes with his bare
hands. Here at least there is a point in the simplicity: we are
getting down to basics (and Gloucester's spectacles tend to be a
distraction). But the overall effect is that simplicity has been
imposed for its own sake.

To some degree, the storm allows the production to break free
from its own elegance. Lashings of rain flatten the actors' hair and
costumes. Lear is at one point completely nude, with all the
vulnerability that implies. The storm creeps up stage by stage,
beginning much earlier than in the text. As Goneril and Regan
reduce Lear's knights from a hundred, to fifty, to twenty-five, to
none, the wind gets up. On Lear's 'O reason not the need' we hear
thunder. When he comes to 'but for true need' a flash of lightning
briefly illuminates the set and the actors, followed by more
thunder. In the storm itself we are in a dark, featureless world, on
flat ground relieved only by the large rectangular box that serves
as Tom's hovel. But we also hit a familiar problem. Lear and the
Fool have to shout against the storm, and meaning gets blurred.
The lesson of Peter Brook's stage production, that the storm

works best as a dialogue – with a corresponding need to introduce variety into the storm effects – seems once again to have been forgotten. That said, the sheer relentlessness of the storm has its own power. And, as in Miller, there is a telling juxtaposition between outside and inside. As in Adrian Noble's production, Gloucester leads his companions to the farmhouse, single file, in a *Seventh Seal* procession through the driving rain. Then there is a quick cut to Edmund and Gloucester, sitting at a table drinking wine. They are warm and dry, a candle between them.

In the storm, water – not healing but relentless and battering – becomes one of the production's key elements. The other key element, as in the Kozintsev film, is fire. Candles and torches are everywhere. The opening credits are projected over an image of a solar eclipse, whose circle then becomes the top of a candle, which Edgar is using to darken a glass plate so that he can watch the eclipse. Edmund will later make his own use of the candle, burning the letter he has just used to deceive Gloucester. In the farmhouse, Lear and Tom seek comfort together from a fire burning in a brazier. The processional entrance of the court in the opening scene includes attendants with torches. Edmund, after his fake fight with Edgar, is surrounded by torches. A recurring effect is a one-shot of an actor with a torch behind him. Sometimes the effect is simply decorative. But it can be telling, as when Lear denounces Cordelia, standing with a flame behind him that seems to exemplify his own dangerous passion. This is the first use of the device, and the most powerful. Later, as Edgar hides in a pit under a trap door, Edmund thrusts a torch down in order to talk to him. We see a close-up of Edmund's face, the torch held close to it, and the effect is suitably demonic. The elegantly designed world of the production, I have suggested, needs some breaking up: it helps that at times it is drenched by water and lit by fire. (Just as telling in its own way is the absence of flame in the last scene. There is no fire any more; just cold light and grey walls.)

The prominence of the scenic devices is an effect of the transfer to television; they loom larger to the selective eye of the camera than they would in the more open space of the Cottesloe. The screen also allows the device of the voice-over soliloquy, an option often taken in both film and television productions of Shakespeare. Edmund's first soliloquy, which opens the second scene of the play, is here broken into fragments, delivered as voice-over during the opening conversation of Gloucester and Kent. We start with the cosmos, the eclipse: then we are in the mind of Edmund. What we suspect as we watch the scene on stage is confirmed here: as the old men talk, Edmund is wrapped up in his own thoughts; he has his own agenda. When Gloucester, having introduced his bastard son to Kent, adds that he has another, legitimate one, we hear Edmund's voice, complaining of the plague of custom that puts Edgar before him. Later, as Gloucester reads the letter, we hear Edmund gloating: 'I grow, I prosper. Now gods, stand up for bastards.' Edgar uses this device as well, often enough that we notice the resemblance as one of the many links between the brothers.

Voice-over is also used to tighten scene transitions, as a voice from one scene overlaps into the first visual images from the next, or a voice-over begins the next scene before the previous one is quite finished. As Tom leads Gloucester off into the fog, we hear the voice of Goneril. Over a close-up of Albany, who has just defied Goneril, we hear Kent asking the Gentleman about the effect his letters have had on Cordelia. This vast, apparently sprawling play is full of tight interconnections, and the voice-over device draws them out. It also keeps the pace moving. So do the very quick cuts from scene to scene, the most stunning of which is from the quiet intimacy of Lear's reunion with Cordelia, 'I am old and foolish', to the noise of battle. Elliott, we saw, tried to provide moments of transition to ease us from one scene to another. Eyre goes in the opposite direction, aiming for quick, even jarring juxtapositions. Though he is not using the Folio text (many of whose cuts he restores) he reproduces one of its principal effects.

The pace and urgency are bound up with a pervasive anger. There is a surprising, even dangerous amount of shouting in this production, as though all the characters, not just Lear, are under a pressure that leads to regular explosions. When he finally decides to answer Lear's question, 'Who put my man in the stocks?' Cornwall shouts 'I set him there!' not as cold defiance but as the exasperation of a man who is sick to death of being asked the same question over and over. Irene Worth delivered Goneril's 'An interlude' with cold, amused disdain. Barbara Flynn, arms folded, raps it out in exasperation. Behind the shouts what we frequently hear a character saying is 'I haven't got time for this.' Edmund (Finbar Lynch) screams 'We sweat and bleed. The friend hath lost his friend' at Albany, exasperated at the latter's attempt to take over the scene. More surprisingly, Edgar blows up at Gloucester on what could be the gentle line, 'Sit you down, father. Rest you.' He is trying to read Goneril's letter, and at that moment he has no time for his father. Cordelia orders the search for Lear – 'Seek for him' – in an angry shout, like a drill sergeant with a bunch of useless recruits. (What are you waiting for? Get on with it!) It is one of many moments in which we see that she is her father's daughter. Everyone is on edge: there is so much to do, no time to do it, and the stakes are very high. If the voice-over device helps to create the pace of the action, the flashes of anger suggest the price that pace is exacting on the nerves of the characters.

Mass entrances – the opening court procession, Gloucester led to his blinding, Lear and Cordelia under arrest – are taken at quick-march tempo. In the final scene the action becomes physically explosive. The camera – which has behaved sedately enough till now, recording the action without calling attention to itself – seems to go out of control as it films the brothers' duel, swaying about and changing angle erratically. Goneril, trying to escape, falls and skids along the floor. Sheridan Morley called the stage production 'a brisk three and a half hours' (the *Spectator*, 5 April 1997), suggesting something very different from the reflective, deliberate pace of Brook's stage version, which was four hours with cuts. The television version uses the devices of its medium to keep the play moving; it also conveys an urgency that was built into the original production.

What was three and a half hours on stage, however, is two and a half hours on the screen. This version is heavily cut, more so than either of the other television versions we have looked at. One of the effects of the cuts – and this is in line with the production's refusal to create a recognizable society – is that the political dimension of the play is severely curtailed. Kozintsev, we have seen, added a whole community of wandering beggars to fill out the world Tom emerges from; even Phillips, without Kozintsev's political commitment, added some idle farm workers. Eyre goes to the opposite extreme. Edgar's soliloquy preparing his Tom disguise is cut to one line: 'Edgar I nothing am.' The countryside, the whole world of poverty the soliloquy evokes – all this disappears, and we are left with one man's problem. It is as though television's propensity for talking heads has led to the disappearance of social context. Much of Lear's coruscating political satire vanishes. He goes straight from telling the gods to 'Find out their enemies now' to 'I am a man / More sinned against than

[151]

sinning.' The intervening list of the gods' enemies, a catalogue of human wickedness, has vanished. He speaks his prayer to the poor naked wretches – it would take some nerve to cut that – but its viewpoint is turned to the immediate personal drama rather than to a vision of society. Lear tells the Fool to enter the hovel first, and the Fool, not used to such consideration, responds with a startled 'Huh?' By way of explanation, Lear's 'You houseless poverty' is directed not to the poor of his kingdom but to the man standing in front of him. In the prayer itself, Lear does not say 'Take physic, pomp; / Expose thyself to feel what wretches feel' – thus denying North American viewers, who saw this *Lear* under the sponsorship of a major oil company, a moment of piquant irony. This Lear is not concerned with social justice; he is concerned with his Fool. In the scene with Gloucester there is no rascal beadle, no dog obeyed in office. It is hard for the play, even in this cut version, *not* to make us think about poverty, suffering and injustice. But we have lost many of the specifics.

This is also a play about madness; but even that dimension is somewhat reduced. We focus on Lear's madness as personal suffering, rather than as a vehicle for satiric insight. For the Fool to be mad is an option; we have seen that it is not always taken, and it is not taken here. Michael Bryant's Fool is sane and lucid. More striking is the reduction of Poor Tom. He is not completely absent; when we first see Paul Rhys's Edgar in the role, he is stricken, whimpering and covered with mud. But in no other production discussed here do the mad scenes give so much of Edgar and so little of Tom. Most of Tom's mad ravings are cut; even those that remain do not seem all that mad: on 'Look how he stands and glares' Tom is not hallucinating about a figure we cannot see; he is commenting quite lucidly on Lear, who is indeed standing and glaring. As Edgar stands on the box which forms his hovel, so that Lear can survey him and ask 'Is man no more than this?' the rain washes off the mud. We are left not with a quivering, helpless human wreck but with a strongly built, good-looking young man. Even the scars on his shoulder look decorative: they are as carefully placed as tattoos. But if we get less of Tom, we get more of Edgar. He is a strong, comforting presence, putting a cloak around the Fool and a protective arm around Lear as they sit by the fire in the farmhouse. One of the many links between Edgar and Edmund is that both are watchers of the action, caught in frequent close-ups. Edmund's gaze is appraising, probing each situation for his own advantage. Edgar's face is harder to read – he seems a bit stunned by events – but in the eyes we can see concern and compassion. In the text, Edgar lies beneath the Tom of the storm scenes, surfacing occasionally in brief asides; in this production the effect is reversed, as a strongly present Edgar allows occasional glimpses of Poor Tom.

In politics and madness, *King Lear* is a play that goes to the edge, and over. This production can be accused of pulling back. It was a complaint about British theatre towards the end of the twentieth century that some of the political urgency of the 1960s (the period of Peter Brook's *Lear*) had gone. Kenneth Tynan wrote to his fellow drama critic Harold Hobson after they had both retired from the fray, 'The trouble with our successors is that nothing seems at stake for them' (Tynan, p. 648). Had he lived to see this production, he might (or might not) have joined in the general praise of the acting; but he might also complain that the play had been reduced to a domestic drama in a setting too controlled and elegant for its own good. It is, however, in the domestic drama that the real strength of this production lies. *King Lear* embraces the cosmos, society, and the troubles of a pair of families. It is in the latter that the intimacy of the production and the closely detailed work of the actors deliver, if not a *King Lear* for 'our' time (the time in question being the late 1990s) at least a *King Lear* for any time when personal relations, within families and between the sexes, are under close scrutiny. It is that scrutiny the camera provides; and it helps that of the three television productions under review, this has the strongest acting ensemble.

The opening scene has some court formality: after the quiet, surreptitious conversation of Kent and Gloucester, studying the map, Lear and his court enter, walking quickly but in a symmetrical pattern with the King at the centre, to a drum-and-trumpet flourish. At the end of the scene, after Lear's plans have blown apart and Cordelia has practically declared war on her sisters, there is a little, now ironic, touch of formality as Goneril and Regan, standing side by side, curtsy to the King of France and Albany and Cornwall, standing behind them, bow. However, the formality of this court is paper-thin. Ian Holm's Lear starts off the business of the scene with the first of many idiosyncratic gestures: he quickly drums on the table with his fingers, parodying the drum-beat of the opening flourish. This signals the start of business, and everyone sits down. But it also suggests an eccentric personal joke, recognized by everyone who has been dealing with him for years; and there is something in it of an animal staking out its territory. Lear's first commands are not just the expected formalities. 'Attend the lords of France and Burgundy, Gloucester', rapped out in exasperation, catches Gloucester by surprise. Clearly he was not expecting this, and is 'not at all used to being the errand boy' (Smallwood, p. 249). 'Give me the map there' is an angry shout. Goneril and Regan exchange glances, and Gloucester looks back. Reviewing the stage production, Mark Ford observed in the opening scene a set of 'subliminal glances ... dense and palpable as a spider's web' (*Times Literary Supplement*, 11 April 1997). We see those glances here.

Lear takes off his crown and puts it on the table. Later it will be the coronet he tells Cornwall and Albany to part; at that point he gives it a little push that sends it down the table an inch or two, and leaves it at that. There will be no grand symbolic gestures around the signs of monarchy. Lear's body language is that of a father, not a king. On 'Tell me, my daughters' he wanders around the table, not wearing his crown. On the words 'Which of you shall we say doth love us most' he pauses by Cordelia and gives her a quick kiss on the head. As Goneril speaks Lear stands beside Regan, his arms around her as though to assure her that no matter what Goneril says, he loves her too. As Lear traces Goneril's share on the map, Albany cannot resist discreetly leaning over to watch. When the division is done he gives Goneril a quick look that says, 'We did all right.' Goneril has spoken to Lear from across the table; Regan goes up to him and puts her arms around him, topping her sister not in speech but in physical intimacy. When Lear turns to Cordelia on 'What can you say' he takes the physical initiative himself, almost whispering in her ear, giving her a hug and a kiss. At this point it all breaks apart. Cordelia has had no asides to prepare us for her 'Nothing'. Brook's film also cut her asides, giving an impression of surliness. Victoria Hamilton's Cordelia, as she starts to defend herself, is anything but surly: she is strong, principled, passionate, keeping an argument going even as her face runs with tears. Lear tries not to listen, putting his fingers to his ears (a gesture he will repeat when Kent starts to lecture him) but, though she registers the gesture, she does not let it stop her. She goes on arguing, and Lear's hands come down. She has forced him to listen. Lear's confrontation with Kent goes from private to public, from a close-up argument, tense and urgent but quiet, to a startling display of regal power as Lear climbs on the table to declare Kent's banishment, with a downward gesture that forces the offender to his knees. Lear's confrontation with Cordelia is more intimate. We see them, in turn, in close-up, Cordelia angry and determined but with tears in her eyes. As they stare each other down, Lear has two close-ups. In the first, we see only anger in his eyes; in the second the anger shades into grief.

That last touch, which in a way encapsulates the whole quality of the opening scene, is one of many in which angry confrontations are shot through with hurt family feelings. In Goneril's complaints to her father about her housekeeping problems, she is close to tears. Cursing her, Lear circles around her and we see her struggling unsuccessfully to control her sobs. (The Fool, in the background, looks none too happy either.) When he attacks her in their second confrontation just before the storm, he allows a moment of tenderness on 'thou art my flesh and blood, my daughter', to which Goneril responds with a smile of relief. It is a last glimpse of a relationship they might have had. When Edgar kills Edmund with an unexpected sword thrust to the stomach, Edmund screams in shock and pain. The screams continue, getting more insistent and hysterical. In the confusion we think it is still Edmund screaming; then we realize it is Edgar, struggling against the soldiers who are restraining him as he tries to get at the brother he has just killed. When he kills Oswald, a killing about which he can feel no remorse, Edgar gets his white clothes covered in blood. This seems to externalize the much deeper shock and horror he feels at what he has to do to his brother. Edmund, meanwhile, has come to terms with his death and is leaning back against a wall, smiling.

If Eyre follows Miller in his use of abstract settings, he follows Elliott in his preference for reaction shots over long takes. Occasionally bystanders will appear in the background watching the scene and filling it out, though without the self-consciousness that makes Miller's use of this device artificial. We can often see the Fool in the distance, as in Lear's curse on Goneril, his presence a silent rebuke. Two attendants stand behind Lear and Cordelia as they come together in her tent. But it is more characteristic of Eyre to cut away to a close-up reaction shot, and these shots become an important part of the drama. When Gloucester says of Edmund 'He hath been out nine years, and away he shall again' he does not bother to look at him. But the camera does; and we catch a barely perceptible change of expression that shows Edmund is surprised and offended. Later, when Lear and Cordelia defy him, we see a close-up of Edmund smiling. We may think at first that he appreciates their courage, but as the scene goes on the smile acquires a different meaning: he knows how to deal with these two. Occasionally a reaction shot will be a slightly pedantic foot-note: when Lear, waking, says he should know Cordelia 'and know this man' the camera cuts for a moment to a close-up of Kent. Eyre breaks up the last scene, as Elliott does, with reaction shots of Albany and Edgar, just to remind us they are there. But the reaction-shot device, at its best (and it is usually at its best with Edmund) establishes relationships. Or, at times, non-relationships: when the blind Gloucester says 'If Edgar live, O bless him' the camera cuts to Edgar, whose expression is intent but curiously unreadable. They are in the middle of the Dover sequence, and he is not yet ready to reveal himself.

Relationships are also established, as we have noted in the opening scene, by body language. In general this production responds acutely to the play's concern with the body. On 'Thou art a lady' Lear runs his hand downwards through the air, suggesting he is tracing the outline of Regan's body. He makes a similar gesture as he contemplates Tom. There is a lot of hugging and kissing in this production, as well as a lot of shouting. We seem to be watching the love–hate relationships of an extended family. Lear does not just contemplate Tom: he embraces him. In the opening scene he embraced his daughters as they were sitting down and he was standing behind them: this gave the gesture of affection an air of dominance and control. But as Lear embraces Tom, Tom towers over him, and Lear seems to be submitting to a new authority, seeking protection from someone more powerful. At first Tom tries to run away and Lear follows him; their relation-ship established, Tom takes Lear by the hand to lead him off. Later, in the farmhouse, he puts his arm around him. In the Dover scene, as Gloucester breaks down sobbing, Lear gives him a quick kiss on the head. In the final scene, grateful to Edgar for undoing his button, Lear kisses him on the lips. Hands establish the Gloucester–Edgar relationship, building on the basic fact that Edgar is leading a blind man by the hand. (Brook tried to avoid this by putting them at either end of a long pole.) On 'Give me thy arm', Edgar takes Gloucester's hand and presses it to his forehead.

As Edgar leads Gloucester to what is supposed to be the edge of the cliff, the camera picks up their clasped hands in close-up; the device is repeated when Gloucester gives Edgar a purse. In Lear's reunion with Cordelia, and later when they are under arrest, there is a recurring device: after watching them together for a while, the camera breaks their dialogue down into close-ups and reaction shots, so that we see only one of them at a time. When they finally come together, for a handclasp in the first scene and an embrace in the second, the camera pulls back and lets us see them united.

Relationships, then, are closely observed; so are the principal characters. Goneril (Barbara Flynn) and Regan (Amanda Redman) are strongly distinguished. Goneril is the exasperated housewife, whose characteristic gesture is to fold her arms indignantly. As in Brook, she has cause for complaint, though Eyre's means are much more economical than Brook's. We see little of the knights, but what we do see establishes them as a rough lot. They come running in from the hunt, barking like dogs, shouting and banging on the table, dropping their saddles on it. Their way of supporting their master is to mob Oswald and force him out; they greet Lear's 'Does any here know me?' with laughter. For the most part we do not see their faces: when we do, they look like thugs. Goneril, then, has a case, and her complaints to Lear do not sound like excuses; they ring with angry conviction. She is, as I have noted, genuinely upset when Lear curses her. But Eyre never tempts us, as Brook wanted to, to change sides. As always, the camera is alert to facial expressions, and when Lear cries out that he will 'do such things' Goneril gives a faint smile, with a slight raising of the eyebrows, that says, 'What could *you* possibly do, you stupid old man?' She may be upset by Lear's attacks, but Albany's, which are less emotional and driven by true moral conviction, produce nothing but impatience.

If Goneril is the exasperated housewife, Regan is the sexy society hostess with an eye for the younger guests. She comes from the world of 'how are you darling, it's been ages' and a peck on the cheek. She is blonde and elegant. Her earrings are larger than Goneril's, and in the first scene, though their dresses are identical, Goneril's is buttoned to the top, while Regan's is open one or two buttons down. (For all its cosmic sweep, this is a play in which buttons matter.) In the opening scene she shows Lear the strongest physical affection. But when she is crossed the charm flakes away and the sensuality becomes that of an animal. If Goneril's characteristic gesture is to fold her arms, Regan's is to bare her teeth. Goneril's anger includes hurt feeling (though we suspect increasingly that hurt feeling too is a weapon), and she makes some (token) effort to rein it in; Regan's anger is unrestrained and openly vicious.

In this production relationships matter, and we see the sisters most vividly in their relationship with Edmund. This begins quite early: as Goneril and Regan have their private conversation at the end of the opening scene (in the play they are alone at this point) Edmund, a torch behind him, watches them. By the end of the scene they both become aware of him. As Regan's sexuality is more overt than Goneril's, she goes for Edmund first. While he denounces his brother, she studies him, and there is no mistaking the expression in her eyes. She is interested in the wound on his arm, and takes a close look. When the house is disrupted by the Kent–Oswald brawl, Regan enters in a long white nightgown and Edmund (his own shirt open to the navel) puts a cloak around her. When Edgar makes similar gestures to Lear and the Fool, the effect is comfort. Edmund's chivalry is not quite that. In the lead-in to the blinding of Gloucester, Edmund, circling the table, touches Regan's back, and she throws her head back with a quick gasp. When after the blinding the dying Cornwall holds out a bloodstained hand to her, and she ignores him and walks away, we have seen it coming.

Goneril makes her move later, and does a more thorough job of it. The sexual electricity between Edmund and Regan has been quick, intense and transient. Goneril, enlisting him, puts a medallion around his neck and takes a moment to put her hands on his head. Then they go into a long, slow kiss. As they part, her hand touches her face and runs down his arm – Lear's gesture of tracing a body, but this time not in the air. By the final scene they are exchanging knowing glances as a matter of course. We know that Regan has lost when Edmund delivers his soliloquy, 'To both these sisters have I sworn my love' in voice-over as she approaches him (and the camera). The effect of the words is an amused detachment from both sisters; the effect of the staging is to apply this detachment to Regan. As though she knows she is losing, Regan gets increasingly desperate. Grilling Oswald about Goneril's letter, she tries different tactics: seductive, surly, and finally pleading; in the end, 'give him this' is a kiss on the lips. (Oswald has become another of the production's watchers, adding a disturbing element of third-party voyeurism: during Goneril and Edmund's long kiss, he watches, his expression unreadable. When Regan kisses him, he seems disturbed, then smiles faintly. His enigmatic reactions are a shifty undercurrent in the production's already disturbing sexuality.) Finally Regan tries for a long embrace like Goneril's. But she is gasping, angry and desperate; kissing Edmund, she seems ready to bite him; she is on the brink of madness. She is also the target of mockery, as the kiss triggers Albany's sarcastic 'Our very *loving* sister'.

In the last scene Regan is obviously ill. On 'My sickness grows upon me' she embraces Edmund, who throws her off. She collapses in a heap, and we have to be quick to see her dragged off. Her sister disposed of, Goneril goes into a long kiss with Edmund, defying her husband, who is standing right there. Edmund gives Albany a triumphant look; everything is out in the open. The triangle has ended, it seems, in naked conflict with Goneril as the clear winner. Yet our final image of the sisters is ironically domestic and affectionate. Their bodies are brought out on a cart, partly covered by a blanket, lying close together, with their faces uncovered. They look like two children tucked up in bed. Edmund climbs on to the cart to join them, and the picture becomes less innocent – yet still, in a strange way, loving. The production's conflicts have been strongly based in family relationships, and in place of Brook's solipsistic fragmentation, Eyre takes us back before the beginning of the play, to something the play never shows, a glimpse of childhood bonding. The irony is obvious, but not simple: is the horror we have seen a betrayal of this childhood image? Or did the natural ties of family somehow lead to this?

While exploring the evil characters with a moral acuteness that matches Kozintsev's, Eyre, without making Brook's concessions to them, gives them nuance and complexity, and keeps us thinking. And he does not, like Brook, weaken the side of good. Paul Rhys's Edgar, we have seen, is a strong and comforting presence. David Lyon's Albany is not a milksop, not even a worm who turns; he is decisive and intelligent throughout, and from the first outbreak of domestic trouble his defiance of Goneril is serious. Most of all, Victoria Hamilton's Cordelia is no pale, wan figure of saintly virtue. As Lear and Cordelia are led off under arrest, surrounded by soldiers, there is an overhead shot of the tight, fast-marching group as it heads for the door. Suddenly the group breaks up. It takes a moment to realize what has happened:

Cordelia has landed a punch on one of the soldiers, and sent him reeling backwards. Her outbreak intimidates their captors long enough to buy a few minutes for her last dialogue with her father. For many another Cordelia, this moment would be forced and out of character. Here, it fits.

On stage and screen, Victoria Hamilton has a strong presence. I once saw her single-handedly rescue a touring production of *The Master Builder*, in which she played Hilda Wangel. The other performers (the distinguished leading man included) had been walking lifelessly through the first act. As soon as Hamilton entered, there was a sudden surge of energy, the performance woke up, and so did the audience. Kozintsev has Cordelia running in for the first scene, then falling in with the steadier pace of her sisters. Eyre reverses the effect: Cordelia marches in with the group, then suddenly breaks ranks and runs to her place at the far end of the table. The asides that Eyre has cut make Cordelia sound worried – 'Then poor Cordelia'. This is not the manner of Hamilton's Cordelia. Her defiance of her father is a strong, intelligent argument. It provokes startled glances around the table. As I have noted, she refuses to let Lear get away with the gesture of putting his hands over his ears; she goes on talking, and he has to listen. As so often in the production, the family conflict includes pain; Cordelia's tears flow freely. But she does not let them stop her. She takes the initiative in seeking an ally, holding Kent by the arm. He responds by taking her hand. As he goes into exile, they embrace. Her farewell to her sisters is angry and passionate, with a real bite on 'I know *you.*' Through all this she is her father's daughter, with all his strength of will and feeling, and twice his intelligence.

Kozintsev's Cordelia returns from exile, still in flowing robes, with the sea as background. Here, as Kent and the Gentleman describe her in voice-over, we see Cordelia kneeling in prayer in front of a bank of candles, with the stars behind her. But if she is a religious figure, she stands for the church militant: she is wearing armour, and the suggestion of Joan of Arc is irresistible. Her later appearances are in a red dress, making her, in the drained colour of the last scenes, the most striking figure on the screen. Lloyd Rose, besides drawing the Joan of Arc analogy, refers to her 'fierce goodness' and adds, 'Yet her gamin looks ... emphasize her vulnerable girlishness, and in her final scenes with her father she is all sorrow and tenderness' (*Washington Post*, 11 October 1998).

Yes; but there is still some of the old anger. In the final scene, 'Shall we not see these daughters and these sisters?' is a cry of rage. (Why are we being treated like this?) It takes Lear, with a descending cadence of 'No, no, no' to calm her down. It is possible to see Cordelia in this scene as the practical one, wanting to deal with the situation at hand, and Lear as retreating into a fantasy world. Here the balance is reversed: Lear's amused detachment from the pacts and sects of great ones seems quite sane, a way of coping with a mad world by seeing its triviality. It is Cordelia who is still caught up in conflict, and Lear needs to bring her out of it. On the page, Lear does all the talking; on the screen we see a dialogue between his words and the strong, shifting emotions on her face. In the end Lear succeeds: in one of the production's most poignant reaction shots, he gets Cordelia to smile. That done, they turn and defy Edmund together. The death of this Cordelia is not the breaking of a butterfly: it is the snuffing out of a vital, passionate spirit, and it has seldom seemed so outrageous.

Lear's other critic and ally is the Fool, and Michael Bryant makes him as strong a presence in his own way as Cordelia. Dressed in rough earth-coloured clothing, with a working-class accent, he seems more Lear's gardener than his fool, and he brings into the elegant sealed world of the initial setting an air of the potting shed and the manure heap. With his bottom-heavy shape and his conical cap, he reminded one reviewer of a Russian rocking doll and another of a garden gnome (Pearce, p. 122; Robert Tanitch, *Plays and Players*, May 1997, p. 9). As he walks, he flaps his arms in a way that suggests a bird too heavy to fly, but trying. In close-up his face looks older than Lear's. Though there is no suggestion of motley about him, he tries to remember that his job is to be entertaining. He has a small – a very small – repertoire of dance-steps, at one point dancing on the table as though to parody Lear's gesture of climbing on the table to banish Kent. For the egg-joke he produces an egg from behind Lear's ear and places it on top of the king's head, as though he were going to break it. But while we have seen other Lears (Ustinov especially) fall in with the Fool's routines, entertaining this Lear is hard work. Lear responds to one routine with an angry, heavily sarcastic 'Ha, ha, ha!' The Fool accompanies the seven stars riddle with a little dance step, which Lear – again, sarcastically – imitates as he gives the answer. Getting a bit desperate, the Fool tries to enliven his joke about the nose standing in the middle of the face with a cry of 'Yay hay, woo hoo!' Lear stares at him, expressionless. In some other productions Lear and the Fool achieve a rapport through the jokes. Here their rapport is of a different kind: a shared knowledge that the jokes aren't working.

As the Tom Edgar impersonates is saner than usual this fool, when he is not trying to liven things up (and he never tries very hard) has a quietly bitter wisdom. At his first entrance he looks on with disapproval as the knights force Oswald out; he knows this just means more trouble. He sits at the table beside Lear, giving him serious advice. Like Frank Middlemass, he is the king's conscience, but he does not fall into that actor's habit of monotonous shouting. Like Alec McCowen, he finds the logic of lines that look a bit crazy on the page. On 'out went the candle, and we were left darkling' his gestures show that Lear is the candle and his entourage, the Fool included, are the 'we' who are left in the dark when the king goes into eclipse. Bryant ends a realistic performance by suggesting realistic grounds for the Fool's disappearance: in the farmhouse scene he is ill and exhausted. His words come limping out, and his eyes glaze over as he tries to stay awake. We need not think of him as literally dying; it is enough to know, as we do, that he is finished. His memory lingers: Lear runs on for his scene with Gloucester wearing the Fool's conical cap as though he has replaced him, taken over his voice and his way of looking at the world. At 'this great stage of fools' Lear takes off the cap, and begins to cry as he turns it over and over in his hand. The Fool is no longer someone imitated, but someone remembered and mourned. Then the cap is just a cap: 'This is a good block.' In the final scene, on 'my poor fool is hanged', Lear holds the rope as he held the cap. The gestures are not strongly alike; the memory is fading. But it is still there, part of the production's concern with the interconnectedness of people: in this case, a dying king and a fool whose jokes he never found funny.

While in Peter Brook's production Alan Webb reduced Gloucester to a shifty time-server, and Leo McKern in the Olivier production let us hear the voice of an ageing lecher, Timothy West's Gloucester, as part of the general strengthening of the characters who serve the side of right, is serious, intelligent and businesslike. He is given, like Cordelia and the Fool, to conducting sensible arguments. He is a bit humorless: if there was good sport at Edmund's making, those days are long behind him. Other Gloucesters have shown Edmund a rough, if condescending affection in the first scene; this Gloucester is brusque with his bastard son, talking about him without looking at him. Trapped and pinioned by Cornwall and Regan, he is more angry than frightened, but he tries to answer their questions patiently. Even when he is blind and on his way to Dover, determined on suicide, his 'From that place / I shall no leading need' is brisk and businesslike.

In the Dover scene, Eyre does not play mind-games with us as other screen productions have done. When Gloucester falls (after a grimly convincing first effort that proves to be a false start – how many people could do this at the first try?) he falls into thick fog, which clears to show him lying on the ground. But there is no element of surprise: an overhead shot has already showed us, before Edgar describes the cliff, that the ground ahead is flat. It is as though something of Gloucester's own sensible realism has crept into the staging of the scene: of course this isn't a cliff. Gloucester's realism leads to the most striking moment he and Edgar have together – characteristically, a close-up and a reaction shot. Hearing Edgar in yet another new character, Gloucester asks 'Now, sir, what are you?' with a patience just edged with weariness. It is the voice of a man who has had enough confusion for one day, who wants to get things settled, and who hopes that this time there will be a sensible answer. Edgar responds with a short, quiet laugh. He too sees the absurdity of what he is doing. Through the whole sequence the play traps Edgar and Gloucester in a relationship that seems impervious to questions like, now what is Edgar doing, and why? For a moment the two actors take their characters out of that relationship, to register its absurdity before they carry on. Building on this rapport, Gloucester shortly afterwards puts his hands up to Edgar's face, as though he has recognized him and wants to confirm it; Edgar gently removes his hands, and it is hard to tell whether the recognition is complete or not.

Up to a point this Gloucester, though he suffers, suffers less than most. This, despite the fact that the blinding is almost impossible to watch. The scene begins with soldiers tossing dice on to a table, and for a moment (in a production generally short on Christian references) we think of the Crucifixion. Cornwall and Regan are sensually excited by what they are doing, and Cornwall in angry close-up suddenly looks like a rodent. Given the character West has established, a sensible man is being attacked by animals. Cornwall gouges out the eyes with his hands: while we are spared the actual sight, we see the results; and the fast action and quick cutting mean that we may not be able to look away fast enough; we may also think we have seen more than we actually have. The servants who comfort Gloucester are cut; a single attendant leads him out. All this is brutal; and yet there is less emphasis on Gloucester's pain than we might have expected; somehow he has found the strength to endure it.

The real pain comes later. The battle, the most elaborate in the three television versions, is a fast-moving confusion of gunfire, trumpets, smoke and explosions. Gloucester, who has endured so much, lies the sand with his hands over his ears – Lear's old gesture, which he needs as Lear never did – screaming in pain. The camera moves in for a close-up of his open mouth. Gloucester, like Albany and Cordelia, has been unexpectedly strong; but now, as though with blindness his hearing has become unnaturally acute, he has reached his breaking point. And it is characteristic of the personal focus of this production that its strongest image of the horror of war is the suffering of one man.

The overall strength of the cast means that the play's larger drama is explored in range and depth; but its centre is still Lear. Ian Holm came to the part at the age of 66, with a long career behind him. In the late 1950s and early 1960s he emerged as a leading Shakespearian actor at Stratford-upon-Avon. In 1959 he was the Fool to Charles Laughton's Lear. When Peter Hall created the Royal Shakespeare Company in the early 1960s Holm became one of its most prominent and versatile players. His range of parts included Puck, Gremio, Troilus, Richard III, Hal and Henry V. He originated the part of Lenny in Harold Pinter's *The Homecoming* (in the same production, Michael Bryant played Teddy). In 1976 an attack of stage fright drove Holm out of the theatre and into film, where his versatility and his gift for intense concentration led to a string of memorable performances. He returned to the stage in 1993, in Pinter's *Moonlight*, where he played the difficult father of a dysfunctional family. The play (which also concerns a lost daughter) might have been picked as preparation for *Lear*. Short of stature (like Garrick and Kean, not to mention Yuri Yarvet) Holm would have seemed odd casting to anyone looking for a titanic Lear. At least one reviewer was self-conscious about this (*New York*, 12 October 1998) but Sheridan Morley, reviewing the stage production, found that the unconventional casting simply helped to create a highly distinctive figure: 'a little, angry bearded gremlin, he seems to defy all preconceptions about the king as he pads about the stage, mannered and mad and majestic by turn' (the *Spectator*, 5 April 1997). He hunches forward, as Scofield did: the effect here is to create an air of defensive menace that warns us not to be fooled by his stature.

In the opening scene, as the centre of the drama of family tension with its glances around the table, he is volatile and unpredictable. The variety of attack adopted by Gielgud and Olivier is for Holm a way of conveying instability. On 'crawl toward death' he gives a little bark of a laugh; but when the others laugh in response, he silences them with a glare. You never know where you are with him. The Fool, we have seen, finds him hard work; but he is amused by Kent. He finds, like Ustinov, some of the wit of the part, including the moments of comedy Lear himself is unaware of. His throwaway delivery of 'But I'll not chide thee' would trigger a laugh from a live audience, if there were one. But his keynote, characteristic of the production as a whole, is anger, which like the other actors he finds in unexpected places. When he offers to hire Kent 'if I like thee no worse after dinner' 'dinner' is a sudden, angry shout, a reminder to the unseen household that he has been here for two minutes and hasn't been fed yet. He can turn the anger against himself. On 'beat at this gate' he bangs his forehead on the table, a gesture he repeats in the mad trial, banging his head with a stool. As he turns against his body, his body sometimes turns against him: when Regan starts to attack him, he suddenly has trouble breathing.

This is a highly emotional Lear, with a short fuse and an unpredictable temper. But, being volatile, he can achieve sudden insights into himself even as he attacks others. 'Woe that too late repents' quick, quiet, and directed inward almost in a whisper. He repeats 'Nothing can be made out of nothing' not, as Scofield did, as a stubborn repetition of an old idea, but as a new thought, caught in a moment of reflection. 'I did her wrong' is quiet, simple and serious. His regret over the banishment of Cordelia is very real, very early. But his progress is derailed by madness: on 'That way madness lies' he starts twitching, and his madness, as we have seen, is more a matter of suffering than of new insight. It sends him into hallucinations: in the mad trial, while Goneril is a joint-stool Regan is something he clutches, unseen, in his hand. In the scene with Gloucester he fires an imaginary arrow, imitates the noise of its flight, and follows it with his hand until he finds himself touching Edgar. Through most of this scene he is quiet and serene, very much in a world of his own (*Washington Post*, 11 October 1998). 'Every inch a king' and 'Let me wipe it first; it smells of mortality' are offhand. As Gloucester lies in the sand Lear sits beside him, relaxed. When Gloucester cries, Lear gives him a quick hug and a kiss on the head. But he is still dangerous. On 'I remember thine eyes well enough' he removes Gloucester's bandage, and Gloucester cries out in pain. 'Kill, kill, kill, kill, kill' has the old fury: he pounds the sand, as in his first confrontation with Goneril he struck the table with his riding whip.

The cutting in the television version removes some of the range of the Lear–Gloucester scene, so that it seems less central than it has in other productions. But this only throws into higher relief Lear's reunion with Cordelia. Lear begins this scene not as a king or father restored but as a mental patient under restraint: his wrists are strapped to the chair. Cordelia quickly undoes the straps; but restoration does not come easily. His first words, 'You do me wrong to take me out of the grave' are accompanied by a sideways look of angry suspicion. 'I am bound upon a wheel of fire' is a sudden cry of anguish. This is not a torment Lear is thinking about but one he is undergoing right now. He seems at this moment madder than ever. If there is any consolation it is in the certainty that he is dead. The emphasis he places on 'You are a spirit, I know; when [sic] did *you* die?' shows that he thinks of this as a dialogue of the dead. As Cordelia weeps, he asks her not to laugh at him; he is still not quite with her. Appropriately in a production where there is so much hugging and kissing, it is physical contact that starts to bring him around. He touches the front of Cordelia's dress on 'I feel this pin prick' and then brings his hand to his temple as though digging the pin into it, trying to feel the pain. (The gesture recalls his habit of putting his hands over his ears, and his self-punishment of banging his head on the table.) He touches Cordelia's face to feel her tears, and brings a finger to his mouth. But his clearest recovery is through comedy – this time a comedy of which he is in control. As he and Cordelia stand facing each other, holding each other's hands, he quickly pumps his hands up and down, recalling his first gesture of drumming on the table. He is trying to get her to laugh, and through the laugh is small and rather sad, he succeeds. His last words in the scene are spoken as they walk off together, in close-up: 'I am old and foolish.' This is a conspiratorial whisper, with an upward flicker of the eyes and a quick raising of the eyebrows – ironic, self-mocking, a secret shared. (Let's hope no one else finds out.) The quick cut from this to the noise of the battle is devastating.

When they are under arrest, as we have seen, it is Lear who tries to bring Cordelia around, and once again he makes her smile. 'As if we were God's spies' is another conspiratorial whisper, finger to the lips. Again there is physical contact: on 'Have I caught thee?' he throws his arms around her neck, and we see that his wrists are tied with a thick rope. (We will see the rope again.) Having achieved happiness, he guards it fiercely. As the soldiers approach him, he snarls like an angry dog. That note carries over into the final scene: 'Howl, howl, howl, howl!' is not so much a keen as a snarl of anger, as Lear denounces the 'men of stones' who are not mourning as they should. The anger is transposed into a different key, a quiet bitterness, as he drops Cordelia on the cart with her sisters, lifts her hand and then lets it fall limply. 'She's dead as earth' is a rebuke to those who have tried to tell him otherwise. And when he thinks for a moment that she lives, his rage returns as he accuses the others of interfering when he might have saved her, and pushes Kent away from him. He is still, as he always was, angry with the world. And he is more volatile than ever: the scene is shot through with moments of tenderness. He calls 'Cordelia' in a sing-song voice, as though they were children playing hide and seek. To the others, he lays down the law, declaring that Cordelia's soft voice was 'an excellent thing in woman' with an authority that links with his boast that he killed her executioner. He has lucid moments, registering Kent (now out of his disguise) with real clarity, but drifting off when Kent tries to identify himself with Caius. He registers with equal clarity the sight of Goneril and Regan, then covers them up with an air of disgust.

Above all, his relationship with Cordelia, established in close and moving detail in their last two scenes together, continues after her death. 'Never, never, never, never, never' has a mounting intensity, but the last 'never' is choked off as he starts to feel a rope around his own neck. He is dying as she did. On 'prithee, undo this button' Lear imagines that Edgar has relieved the pressure, and kisses him on the lips. This leads him to Cordelia's lips, and as he speaks the final 'Look on her, look, her lips, look there' in joy he is not looking at the body on the cart but staring into space at a Cordelia only he can see. They have died together, both hanged, and are now alive together somewhere else. With a little smile, like the smiles he could sometimes get from her, he collapses in Edgar's arms. The physical contact that denotes affection continues, as Edgar eases Lear into Kent's arms, and Kent lowers him on to the cart. ('Vex not his ghost' is not anger this time but gentle, concerned advice.)

At this point everyone who has died in the last scene is lying on the cart. Kent, who has entered the scene bent and ill, on the point of death himself, uses 'I have a journey, sir, shortly to go' to motivate his final act of service. He takes the handle of the cart and starts to drag it away. We see it disappear into the distance as Edgar speaks the last lines, close-ups alternating with voice-over. The last image is of the cart disappearing into the fog. In a way this gives formal closure. It echoes an equally striking image that ended the storm sequence: Edgar watching, and commenting in voice-over as the party bearing Lear disappears into the fog, moving away from the camera until all we can see is Gloucester's torch. There is a similar repetition, equally formal in effect, between the first image of the court marching towards the camera and the later image of Lear and Cordelia under arrest, marching toward the camera amid a party of soldiers. In the last image a close-up of marching feet echoes a similar close-up as Gloucester was led to his blinding.

But formal closure (like the circle of spears in the Irving and Olivier productions) is not the only effect. In the image of the bodies on the cart the production finally makes a decisive breakout from its sealed, ahistorical world into history, our history. As the cart disappears, we see legs and arms dangling over the side. It does not look like the preparation for a state funeral; the suggestion is that all these bodies will be dumped into a mass grave. They have lost the individuality they still have in Kozintsev's funeral procession. In an earlier time they might be plague victims; in a production done at the end of the twentieth century the image recalls the horrors of that century, and we remember that *King Lear* acquired a new dimension with the opening of the death camps. One detail near the end resists the impersonality: Edgar picks up Lear's dangling hand and lays it on his chest. We are reminded, briefly, of the importance of relationship, which has been so central to this production. But as the cart disappears, it seems that all these relationships, as painful and vital as they have been, and all the closely realized individuals who have been created for us with such care, come one common end.

CHAPTER XI

Cross-cultural dialogue: Akira Kurosawa's *Ran*

Shakespeare's ability to travel is well attested, and the material of *King Lear*, playing as it does on such basic themes as old age and family tension, makes it recognizable in cultures remote from his own. Other writers have used *King Lear* as a source or at least an inspiration. Turgenev's short novel, *A Lear of the Steppes* (1870), transposes the story to Russia, where it becomes the tale of land-owner, an impulsive giant of a man, who after a premonition of death divides his property between his two daughters (there is no third, Cordelia figure). They turn against him and drive him out of the house. He responds by literally tearing the house down, and dies in the wreckage. Jane Smiley's novel *A Thousand Acres* (1991), set in the American midwest, tells of an old but powerful farmer, Larry, who has three daughters, Ginny, Rose and Caroline. The first letters of the characters' names give the reader a nudge, equivalent to Turgenev's title. Larry divides the farm between Ginny and Rose, and cuts himself off from Caroline, who disapproves of the scheme. This time it is the father who turns against the older daughters. He then reconciles himself with the youngest, and tries to get the farm back. A storm breaks out, Larry's mind collapses, a secondary character is blinded in a farm accident, Ginny tries to poison Rose – the links with Shakespeare are persistent and detailed. But there is a major twist: Ginny, the equivalent of Shakespeare's Goneril, is the narrator. Lear curses Goneril with sterility; Ginny has had several miscarriages, likely caused by the well water on her father's farm. Smiley, writing a work of her own, can go farther than Peter Brook in turning the sympathies of the original around, something Turgenev does not do. Ginny and Rose are the ones with the grievance; Caroline, the Cordelia figure, is cold and difficult and her reconciliation with her mad father is distinctly creepy. In Lear's demand for total love there is a suggestion of incest, though this appears more often in criticism than in production. In Smiley the incest becomes literal: Larry molested his daughters when they were children. As productions of *King Lear* can reflect the preoccupations of their time, Smiley, writing from within late twentieth-century American feminism, not only changes the angle of the story but reverses its basic sympathies. Being universal, the story travels; being a story, it is told in ways that reflect the concerns of the teller and the audience whose community it enters.

This is particularly true of dramatic versions, whose contact with their audiences is live and immediate. In the late nineteenth century Jacob Gordin produced two cross-cultural adaptations for the American Yiddish Stage, *The Jewish King Lear* (1892) and *The Jewish Queen Lear* (1898), better known by its original subtitle, *Mirele Efros* (Berkowitz, pp. 31–72). In the first, the great Jacob Adler, playing the title character – who in addition to being cast out by his ungrateful older daughters, goes blind – moved the audience to tears as Garrick had done. After one of Adler's performances, 'years after the play's debut ... the bank was filled with young people sending money to their parents back in Europe' (Berkowitz, p. 50). Gordin, like Tate, produced a happy ending of family reconciliation (including the news that the hero's blindness is curable) that in this case answered the audience's need for reassurance: uprooted by emigration to the New World, they needed to see an image of tradition maintained. *Mirele Efros*, about a mother who has trouble with her entire family, ends with a reconciliation at a bar mitzvah, and a similar message about the importance of tradition (Berkowitz, pp. 56, 59). In both cases the original play's material, heavily adapted but still recognizable, locked directly into the audience's own concerns.

Cross-cultural adaptation, however, is not always easy. In 1989 an attempt to re-tell *King Lear* in the special idiom of Kathakali, a dance-theatre form developed in the southern Indian state of Kerala, produced controversy. The production, conceived by an Australian playwright-director and a French actor-dancer, involved several distinguished Kathakali performers (Zarrilli, p. 18). It toured Europe, where it was received with acclaim in France in particular (Zarrilli, p. 27); but when it appeared at the Edinburgh Festival the British press for the most part found it vigorous but remote, hard to relate to Shakespeare or to anything else they understood (Awasthi, p. 172; Zarrilli, p. 27). It was also controversial back home in Kerala. Tradition-minded audiences were disturbed by a moment, drawn from Shakespeare, where the King removed his makeup and part of his costume; and in general the King's failure to act like a king, and the tragic ending, seemed inimical to the spirit of Kathakali. (Zarrilli, pp. 29, 35–6). For one observer, Kathakali's special codes of gesture and makeup could not be used to express characters from another culture, and its stress on performance over text, where the performance depended so much on established convention, meant that it could not 'absorb new thematic content' (Awasthi, pp. 175–6). Yet one can see that the production made a serious effort to find Kathakali equivalents, for example in make-up: for the Lear figure, a mixture of green and red (a 'combination of kingly and turbulent aspects'), for France, basic green (heroic kingliness), for Cordelia, gold (radiance), for Poor Tom, black (closeness to animals) (Zarrilli, p. 21). Behind the individualized characters of *King Lear*, it can be argued, are the abstractions of the morality play, and finding equivalents in a different theatrical code that also deals in types does not seem a completely hopeless task. Nor was the performance totally impenetrable, even in Edinburgh. One reviewer, who had watched with 'remote fascination', found that the King's cry over his dead daughter crashed through all the barriers and created a moment of 'agonized theatrical communication' (Zarrilli, p. 34). Grief needs no passport.

Cross-cultural adaptation, then, involves a tricky negotiation between the familiar and the unfamiliar, and the enterprise can founder if an audience expects straight fidelity to Shakespeare, or if the codes (cultural and performative) of the receiving culture are too fixed to pick up signals from the play. Flexibility is needed on both sides. The difficulties are obvious; yet it can be said that historically the success rate has been remarkably high. In a sense all the performances discussed in this volume are cross-cultural adaptations, since no one now lives in Shakespeare's England, and the play has to make its way in worlds its creator never dreamed of. Some cultures have been especially receptive, Japan in particular. A glance at the annual international bibliographies in *Shakespeare Quarterly* will show the remarkable volume of work on Shakespeare by Japanese scholars; the Shakespeare Society of Japan is older than the Shakespeare Association of America; and during a visit I made to Japan a British resident told me that he had seen more Shakespeare productions in Tokyo than he would have done in an equivalent period in London. Why this should be so is a question requiring a more detailed answer than I can attempt here, though it is worth suggesting that a Japanese audience is better equipped than a modern Western one to understand a formalized society in which the sense of obligation is strong. What we can do is move in on particular cases, and in any discussion of the Japanese reception of Shakespeare, the filmmaker Akira Kurosawa comes immediately to mind.

Though he spoke only Japanese and made only one film outside his native country, Kurosawa claimed to feel at home anywhere in the world (Kurosawa, p. 61). In his autobiography he lists nearly 100 films from the period 1919–29 that particularly impressed him. A few Japanese titles appear towards the end, but for the most part the films are European and American classics: *The Cabinet of Dr Caligari*, *Die Niebelungen*, *The Gold Rush*, *Greed*, *Metropolis*, *Potemkin*, *The Passion of Joan of Arc* (Kurosawa. pp. 73–4). His samurai films draw on the conventions of the Western, and the Western returned the compliment when *The Seven Samurai* became *The Magnificent Seven*. He was a strong believer in the importance of the screenplay, and insisted that 'In order to write scripts, you must first study the great novels and dramas of the world' (Kurosawa, p. 193). On three occasions the dramas he studied were by Shakespeare. *Throne of Blood* (1957; original title, *Castle of the Spider Woman*) is an adaptation of *Macbeth*; in any list of Shakespeare films it stands high, and for some it is at the top. *The Bad Sleep Well* (1960), a tale of corruption in modern Japanese business, is an independent work that, without being an adaptation of *Hamlet*, draws occasionally on motifs from Shakespeare's tragedy, displacing them with ironic effect. *Ran* (1985) falls somewhere between the two.

Ran is usually discussed as an adaptation of *King Lear*, and given the closeness in story line and occasionally in dialogue, the temptation to do so is obvious. Yet it is worth stressing that Kurosawa's thinking began not with Shakespeare but with a Japanese source, the legend of Monotari Mori (1495–1571), 'whose three sons are remembered in Japan as the ideal of family loyalty'. One of the tales about him is his demonstration of the importance of family unity: he shows that while a single arrow can easily be broken, a bundle of three arrows cannot (Goodwin, p. 196). (There is an eerie cross-cultural moment right there: the same test, using a bundle of sticks, is used to convey a similar message in Sackville and Norton's *Gorboduc* (1561), the first regular English tragedy and an important forerunner of *King Lear*.) This triggered Kurosawa's thinking: what if the sons, contrary to the legend, were disloyal? One of Monotari Mori's maxims was that 'a leader should not trust anyone, particularly not family members' (Goodwin, p. 196). The resemblances to *King Lear* struck Kurosawa as he worked on the script (Goodwin, p. 197), and at that point Shakespeare as it were joined the team. But it was not Kurosawa's original intention to adapt *King Lear* as he had adapted *Macbeth*. The film is best seen not as a cross-cultural adaptation but as part of a cross-cultural dialogue, in which the first speaker is Japanese. And it should be said at the outset that the dialogue continues in the writing of this chapter, as it has in most Western-based criticism of *Ran*. This will be, inevitably, a Westerner's reading of a Japanese film made by an artist who was steeped in Western culture but still – just as inevitably – Japanese.

Like the Kathakali version, *Ran* has been greeted in some quarters with misgivings. Peter Holland points to the interesting irony that many Japanese academics dislike it for its lack of fidelity to Shakespeare (Holland, p. 58). For Darrell William Davis, who sees in this film the destruction of the heroic code on which earlier Japanese films were based, the infidelity is not to Shakespeare but to Japan: 'the grafting of King Lear [sic] onto a monumental evocation of Japanese history calls the Japaneseness of that history into question' (Davis, p. 244). Its relation to Japanese history has been controversial. It has been seen as a faithful reflection of a period of civil war (1392–1568), drawing on particular details like the breakdown of the code of loyalty, the advent of gunpower (*Throne of Blood* uses only arrows, though it uses them memorably; *Ran* is full of artillery fire), and the emergence of 'politically powerful women' (Hapgood 1994, pp. 235–6). But while R. B. Parker claims an 'obsessive authenticity of detail' in the film's handling of period (Parker 1991, p. 76), Darrell William Davis claims it is abstracted from historical particularities of time, place and person (Davis, p. 237). Samuel Crowl sees in *Ran* a mythic past like that of the American Western, 'a past largely created by film and thus accessible to a modern audience' (Crowl, p. 112). The very existence of such a debate returns us to *King Lear*, in whose production history we have seen a negotiation between the particular and the universal, and a concern over the choice of period. In chapter I I suggested that the universal is best reached through the particular; and this means that cross-cultural dialogues work best when they do not deal in abstraction. What is particularly Japanese in *Ran* can link up with what is particularly Shakespearian. Brian Parker calls its historical period 'not unlike that of Shakespeare's War of the Roses' (Parker 1986, pp. 415–16). And when James Goodwin identifies Kurosawa's fundamental concern as 'an inversion to Japanese ideals of family and political loyalty' (Goodwin, p. 197) we can substitute 'Elizabethan' for 'Japanese' and get a statement that is equally true of *King Lear*.

An outline of the story of *Ran* will show how it moves in and out of *King Lear*. The Great Lord Hidetora, head of the Ichimonji clan, has three sons: Taro, Jiro and Saburo. He decides to surrender his power: Taro will possess the First Castle, Jiro the Second Castle and Saburo the Third. Taro will be head of the family, and the others will support him. (There is no question of equality among the brothers.) Saburo rebels against the scheme; so does Hidetora's faithful follower Tango. The Great Lord banishes them both. Two neighbouring lords, Fujimaki and Ayabe, have competed for Saburo as a son-in-law. Ayabe withdraws his offer, but Fujimaki, admiring his spirit, invites Saburo to join him. Hidetora's plan is to stay with each son in turn, beginning with Taro. But conflicts arise, particularly with Taro's wife Lady Kaedi. (She harbours a grudge against Hidetora, who destroyed her family; the First Castle used to be hers.) Hidetora journeys to Jiro, who offers to house him but not his followers. Tango, who has rejoined Hidetora, urges him to go to Saburo; but Hidetora accepts the counsel of his treacherous adviser Ikoma and goes to the Third Castle, now occupied after Saburo's exile by forces loyal to Taro. Entering the Third Castle, Hidetora has entered a trap. Taro and Jiro join to lay siege to the castle, and in the resulting carnage Hidetora goes mad and retreats into the wilderness, accompanied by Tango and the fool Kyoami. During the siege one of Jiro's followers shoots Taro dead. Jiro is now the head of the clan, and occupies the First Castle. Taro's widow Lady Kaedi seduces him, and demands that he murder his wife Sué. Her plan is foiled when Jiro's follower Kurogane (who resents Kaedi's influence over his master) returns not with Sué's head, but with the head of a fox statue from a temple. Saburo returns from exile to look for his father. Jiro's forces advance on Saburo's. There is a tense standoff as Saburo claims he only wants his father and will withdraw peacefully once he has found him, and Jiro, pretending to agree, plots his brother's death. Meanwhile Fujimaki and Ayabi watch from the surrounding hills: Fujimaki to aid Saburo, Ayabi for whatever pickings he can grab. Saburo finds Hidetora, but in the midst of their reunion he is killed by a sniper; his father dies of grief. Jiro and Ayabi fight for possession of the First Castle. During the battle Kurogane beheads Kaedi, and he and Jiro prepare to die.

It will be apparent as we go on that this account omits much; but it should already be clear that while *King Lear* plays out its conflicts in the domestic sphere, with one battle (often perfunctory) near the end, *Ran* is a story of war. That there are three sons, not three daughters, is owing to the Japanese starting point. This is a male world: though the matching of Saburo with Fujimaki's daughter is an important plot development, the lady in question is never seen, never even named. The hierarchies of this world include birth order: the brothers' names mean First Son, Second Son and Third Son, and their castles are named accordingly (Goodwin, p. 198); but gender hierarchy is at least as important, given Kaedi's violation of it. When Taro lets her start trouble with his father, the Fool Kyoami sings a mocking song comparing Taro to a gourd swinging in the wind. Jiro is persistently criticized by his men, Kurogani in particular, for letting Kaedi rule him. Kurogani, presenting the fox-head, warns Jiro against shape-shifting foxes who take the forms of women and ruin men. Moving in to kill her, he calls her 'fox-devil' as Lear in the mad trial calls Goneril and Regan 'you she-foxes'.

The story confines itself to the ruling, warrior class. In strong contrast to Kozintsev's film, it shows nothing of the life of the lower orders. When Hideo Oguni, who collaborated with Kurosawa on the screenplay, pointed this out, the director replied, 'It is not a story that concerns peasants' (Parker 1991, p. 77). The peasants are in fact conspicuous by their absence. When he thinks that the food Tango has brought him is charity from his people Hidetora is insulted and orders their villages burned. But Tango tells him the villages are empty: intimidated by Taro's orders not to assist Hidetora, the peasants have fled. The charity Lear and Gloucester think of showing to the poor undergoes a double reversal: Hidetora thinks the poor are being charitable to him, and far from being a virtue this is an unforgivable offence to the class hierarchy. He has no moment that makes the social point of Lear's appeal to the 'poor naked wretches', with its regret that 'I have ta'en too little care of this.' Hidetora's moments of guilt stay in the military context: he is haunted by the victims he has slaughtered, and at a moment structurally close to Lear's 'poor naked wretches', when Hidetora is taking shelter from the storm, he declares, 'Because of me, my loyal men died a useless death.'

Hidetora's guilt takes us to one of the key differences between the two works. Hidetora has a past; Lear has virtually none. Shakespeare's characters begin their lives, in effect, when they enter the first scene. Apart from Goneril's observation, 'The best and soundest of his time hath been but rash' (and given the speaker, we can make much, little, or nothing of that) we have no sense of what Lear was like as king, or what things were like in the Lear family nursery. Kurosawa does not deal with the second question (though Jane Smiley does), but he is very interested in the first. He makes it clear that Hidetora became the Great Lord not by inheritance, much less by divine right, but by wholesale slaughter. Kurosawa found the lack of a past for Lear a major problem in Shakespeare's play: 'How did Lear acquire the power that, as an old man, he abuses with such disastrous effects? Without knowing his past, I have never really understood the ferocity of his daughters' response to Lear's feeble attempts to shed his royal power' (Goodwin, p. 197). (The search for explanations through past events may be not so much a Japanese preoccupation as a twentieth-century one; Jane Smiley shares it.) Hidetora has not only made himself what it is; he has made the world what it is. In his attack on his father in the opening sequence, Saburo declares this is a world without loyalty or feeling, and Hidetora has made it that way. Lear's remorse over his neglect of the poor is oddly detached from Shakespeare's play: it appears unprepared, a new idea. It is not an issue until it occurs to Lear half way through. Hidetora's guilt over the savagery of his conquests is one of the governing ideas of *Ran*.

As there are three sons and three castles, there are three principal characters who exemplify different responses to Hidetora's cruelty, and it is significant that (unlike Hidetora and his sons, or Tango, or Kyoami) none of these characters has a single exact equivalent in Shakespeare. Taro's wife Kaedi harbours revenge. The First Castle belonged to her family; Hidetora, having married her to Taro, then murdered the rest of her family. Her objections to Hidetora's presence in what she thinks of as her house start the chain reaction that wipes out the Ichimonji clan, and at the end, just before Kurogane beheads her, she declares that she has done all she set out to do. She offers no resistance; she dies completely satisfied. Samuel Crowl relates her to Edmund, and to Asaji, the Lady Macbeth figure in *Throne of Blood* (Crowl, p. 111). Christopher Hoile sees her as an amalgam of Goneril, Regan and Edmund (p. 32). Brian Parker adds to these suggestions Margaret in Shakespeare's first tetralogy, and this identification, from outside *King Lear*, may be nearest the mark (Parker 1986, p. 416). But she is ultimately a creature of *Ran*, born of its particular story as a response to Hidetora's guilt.

Her opposite number is Hidetora's other daughter-in-law, Lady Sué, wife of Jiro. Hidetora slaughtered her family too, but she is as dedicated to Buddhist peace as Kaedi is to revenge. After her initial appearance in the castle courtyard, Kaedi is always seen indoors. The First Castle matters deeply to her; it is not just her setting but her cause. When Hidetora comes to the Second Castle and looks for Sué, he opens a pavilion where he expects to find her; what he finds instead is a picture of the Buddha Amida, or Amitabha, 'the Buddha of Boundless Light whose great powers will bring believers rebirth in paradise' (Goodwin, p. 205). Sué herself is not there. We never see her indoors (Howlett, p. 365). She first appears on the walls, against a pink sunset, singing a hymn to the Amitabha. The background of sky recalls Kozintsev's Cordelia against a background of sea: there is the same sense of openness and freedom. Sué has freed herself from resentment at Hidetora's treatment of her: everything that happened, she declares, was decided in their past lives, and Buddha embraces all. (There is something here of Edgar's attempts at acceptance, though for Edgar it is more of a struggle; something too of Cordelia's 'No cause, no cause'.) When we first see her, Sué's back is to the camera, giving her an air of remoteness; and through the entire film we never see her face closely, as we see Kaedi's. She belongs to another kind of life, hard for us to grasp. It is surprising, and correspondingly important, that when Hidetora comes to the Second Castle he first seeks out not Jiro but Sué. When they appear together on the walls, they are both wearing peach-coloured robes, suggesting some kind of bond between them. To look at her, he declares, breaks his heart; it is worst when she smiles. Her hatred would be easier to take. He cannot share her faith, telling her that we cannot rely on Buddha's mercy. And yet, in the fact that he has sought her out, and in the similar colours of their garments, we may be seeing an aspect of Hidetora that emerges nowhere else: a longing for the spiritual enlightenment, the detachment from the world of who's in, who's out, that Sué represents.

The third character is Sué's brother Tsurumaru, whose eyes Hidetora gouged out. Kaedi inhabits a castle, Sué the open air. Tsurumaru lives alone in a small hut, the hut where Hidetora, Kyoami and Tango seek shelter from the storm. He is an eerie, otherworldly figure, with a great mop of dark hair that hides his face – the style, according to the screenplay, of a temple acolyte (Kurosawa et al., p. 59). We hear his voice before we see him, and it is the voice of a young man. His bent body and the pear-like shape given by his costume make him look like an old woman. Tango at first thinks he is a woman. A strange stillness surrounds him. When the travelers come to his hut, the wind that has blown through the last few scenes suddenly stops. Tsurumaru recognizes Hidetora's voice as Gloucester recognizes Lear's, but with a difference: it is the voice of the man who put out his eyes. His reaction to Hidetora is neither Kaedi's nor Sué's: he prays to the Buddha to be free of hatred; but he can never forget, and he can never sleep in peace. Three castles, three sons, and now three reactions to Hidetora's cruelty: revenge, detachment and inconsolable suffering. Tsurumaru declares his flute is 'the only pleasure left to me' and he offers to play it for the travelers as the 'hospitality of the heart'. That may suggest some kind of reconciliation: but the music is a piercing lament that terrifies Hidetora, driving him backward until he breaks the wall panels and falls outside the hut. Tsurumaru's appearance has been related to figures of Noh drama, ghosts and madwomen (Goodwin, p. 208; Richie, p. 217), his flute, again in Noh tradition, to madness and the supernatural, including the summoning of spirits (Hoile, p. 31; Phillips, p. 274). The blinded Gloucester has become the mad, demon-driven Poor Tom; but while Lear bonds with Tom, a poor naked wretch he can take some care of, all Hidetora can do, faced with this image of his past crimes, is flee in panic.

The warlord who spread terror is in the grip of terror himself, and this development has been anticipated from the beginning of the film. We begin not with a court scene, ceremonial or otherwise, dividing the land, but with a boar hunt, set in lush green hill country. The first shot, under the opening credits, is a freeze-frame of four horsemen symmetrically grouped on a hill. Then the image moves slightly as one of the horses twitches. As the credits continue, this shot is succeeded by other shots, equally still, some even more distant, of other horsemen poised and waiting. The music is quiet and tense. The first thing that moves is the boar, and as the camera picks him up, it too moves for the first time. Then the hunt begins. We may recall the tense stillness, followed by rapid movement, that opens Peter Brook's *Lear* film (Hapgood 1992, p. 37); here the switch comes much earlier. Other boars dart past, Hidetora and his party chasing them. Then the camera picks out Hidetora, in our first clear view of him, staring intently at the quarry, drawing his bow. Immediately, in blood red writing, the main title fills the screen: *Ran*. Chaos. Chaos is the title, and the theme; and Hidetora is chaos. He is also the boar, associated in the Japanese zodiac with 'a reckless person who makes a headlong rush' (Arai, p. 3). Joking with his followers after the hunt, Hidetora compares the boar to himself – old, tough and indigestible. The identification later takes a deadly turn when Jiro's counsellors urge him to turn against his father: 'Sound the horn or become the quarry'. In this world you are the hunter or the hunted. Later we will see Hidetora fleeing over a plain and hiding among rocks.

The hunt is succeeded by a still, formal scene as Hidetora sits with his sons and chief followers, and with his guests Fujimaki and Ayabe. They make a composed but not quite symmetrical picture: Hidetora in the centre, a line of five men one side of him and a line of two men on the other. Already something is slightly askew. While Macbeth, and his counterpart in *Throne of Blood*, disturb a formal occasion by screaming at an unseen ghost Hidetora disturbs this one by simply falling asleep. The powerful old man is suddenly, simply, old. The guests tactfully withdraw. Then Hidetora, in a panic, bursts through the cloth barricade that defines his encampment, breaking the enclosure of the space he controlled (Howlett, pp. 362–3); he has dreamed he was wandering alone in a frightening wilderness. (The dream will come true.) He dreamed that Taro's voice called him back, and this makes him realize how much he values his sons. We next see him at the centre of a larger group (still with the two asymmetrical lines closest to him) announcing his plan to surrender his power.

The speed of the boar hunt is an uneasy memory behind the decorous slowness of the conversations that follow it; Hidetora himself breaks the decorum first by sleeping, then by fleeing in panic from his dream; and the whole opening sequence is intercut with quick shots of storm clouds boiling up in the sky, getting bigger and darker each time we see them. It is as though the first and third acts of *King Lear* have been collapsed, to show that the storm is latent in the division of the kingdom. Chaos is not something that develops as the story goes on: it is the grounding reality of Hidetora's world, from the beginning. Saburo's protest, too, is anticipated. Even before Hidetora announces his plan, his third son appears as a troublemaker – unlike Cordelia, whose resistance begins as her father speaks and when it breaks out catches everyone by surprise. The fool Kyoami's first routine is an imitation of a hare; Saburo responds to it with the insulting suggestion that Fujimaki and Ayabe are two hares, who are going to be eaten by Hidetora. That his joke builds on Kyoami's routine suggests a link between them, equivalent to the persistent theory that in the first performances of *King Lear* Cordelia and the Fool were doubled. Jonathan Miller brought the Fool into the first scene as Cordelia's ally. What in that version is sympathy and support has a characteristically harder tone in *Ran*: Saburo and Kyoami are both impudent, both inclined to break decorum.

Among the brothers, Saburo is the odd man out. When Hidetora, consoling himself after his dream with the thought of his sons' loyalty, touches each brother on the shoulder, Saburo, still disturbed by the dream, pulls back. As Hidetora prepares to announce his surrender of power, the others sit but Saburo stands to one side. (At this point there is a shot of a storm cloud.) During the public announcement all three brothers sit; but Saburo's stance is a little more casual. In a formalized world, such things matter. As the others flatter their father, Saburo laughs and scratches his neck. When Hidetora, following the legend of Monotari Mori, demonstrates the importance of family unity by showing that one arrow can be broken but three together cannot, Saburo takes the bundle of three arrows and breaks it over his knee. It is his equivalent of Cordelia's 'Nothing', violent and externalized while hers is quiet, with its full meaning hidden. His attack on his father's plan has more of the toughness of Kent than the pleading of Cordelia: 'You are either senile or mad'. The very fact that he attacks the surrender of power marks a difference from Cordelia, who is concerned only to defend her silence. Saburo, a leader's son, has to comment on political matters; Shakespeare leaves that to Kent. Saburo's objection is grounded in a brutally frank declaration that this is a world without loyalty or feeling, and that

Hidetora made it so. In particular, he should not trust his sons, because they take after him. This gives a dark twist to Cordelia's 'You have begot me, bred me, loved me', as Hidetora's response that he has spoiled Saburo or he would not be so arrogant gives a dark twist to Lear's declaration that he loved Cordelia most.

Saburo's appeal is not to decency, love or family feeling but to a stark awareness that there are no such things in Hidetora's world. He sounds not a saint but a cynical realist. The screenplay, however, assures the reader, 'His words sound cruel and heartless, but behind the seeming heartlessness there is love' (Kurosawa *et al.*, p. 13). The screenplay frequently differs from the film in detail, but it contains some revealing editorial comments; this is one of them. The difficulty is that the method of the film, which avoids close-ups and keeps the camera at a distance from the players (we shall return to this) does not allow for the sort of close look at Saburo that would reveal the subtext, the love beneath the harshness. It makes the point in a different, characteristically external way. When Hidetora sleeps, Saburo cuts branches from a sapling and plants them in the ground to shade his father. As he cuts the tree, the shot includes Kyoami watching him: they are bonded in their impudence, and in their underlying loyalty. Saburo in exile gets screen time for which Cordelia has no equivalent. As he and Tango sit together Saburo, using his cynical voice, calls Tango a fool for defying Hidetora and getting himself banished. But his reason for saying so is not cynical: Tango, he argues, should stay with the Great Lord and give him good advice. Saburo has more edge than Cordelia (even than Victoria Hamilton's Cordelia) and a harder tone. But they are alike in their fundamental purpose, and it is no surprise when Saburo later in the film comes to his father's rescue.

As there are three chief responses to Hidetora's cruelty, there are three chief responses, among his followers, to his surrender of power; and in this case the characters, like the act itself, have clear Shakespearian equivalents. Tango is the Kent-figure, and just as blunt in his initial rebellion. When Fujamaki, offering Saburo his protection, asks Tango to join him, Tango refuses: he 'cannot abandon the Great Lord'. There are differences, however. Tango makes a token reference to disguising himself, but when he returns to Hidetora, though he is dressed as a hunter, he makes no attempt to conceal his identity. Kent's disguise, unusual for a Shakespearian tragedy, is a device imported from comedy and romance. The blunt military world of *Ran* has no time for such frivolities, and the code of loyalty Tango follows has no need to operate indirectly. The Kent of Peter Brook's film, more brutal than most, killed the followers who were accompanying him into exile, and physically attacked Edgar. Tango's violence is a clean, direct expression of his loyalty. Jiro has become head of the family in large measure through the treachery of Taro's follower Ogura (the Oswald figure) and Hidetora's follower Ikoma. Jiro thanks them both, then dismisses them, on the grounds that having betrayed one master they might well betray him. As they go into exile, Tango spots them from a distance, hunts them down, and kills them. Shakespeare's Kent never gets farther than beating Oswald; Tango, like Saburo, has more edge than his Shakespearian equivalent.

Saburo's reaction to his father combines harsh criticism with underlying love; Tango follows a straightforward code of loyalty; Kyoami is the most complex of the three. We have seen his link with Saburo; he is visually bonded with Tango as when they search for Hidetora they ride together on one horse, Kyoami behind, clinging on. When Tango and Kyoami both urge Hidetora to go to Saburo, not to the Third Castle, Hidetora strikes Kyoami with his whip ('Take heed, sirrah, the whip!'). We next see Kyoami and Tango, exiled again, sitting together as Tango and Saburo did earlier. Kyoami is sobbing; Tango says bitterly, 'All we did was tell the truth'. For all this three-way bonding among the figures of loyalty, however, Kyoami is the wild card in the deck – as we shall see Lady Kaedi is on the other side. He has some precedent in Japanese tradition: commenting on him, Kurosawa equated him to licensed entertainers kept by warlords and allowed freedom from the rules of etiquette (Goodwin, p. 207). His dialogue draws on the style of Kyogen, the farcical counterpart of Noh (Goodwin, p. 207). But he also comes from outside: he is introduced in the screenplay as 'a servant-entertainer, the equivalent of the fool in a medieval European court' (Kurosawa *et al.*, p. 9). This is the only Western analogy the screenplay draws. His first routine, the song about the hare, is introduced by music that has no visible source. The audience looks around, puzzled. Literally, the music might be coming from behind the cloth barrier that encloses the encampment. But there may also be a metafilmic joke: the music comes from the soundtrack, and the characters hearing it (as by convention movie characters never do) are suddenly puzzled at finding themselves in a movie. It is the only such moment in *Ran*, and allows Kyoami to disrupt not only the decorum of the occasion, but the decorum of the medium. (Frank Middlemass's Fool, we have seen, is the only character in the BBC *Lear* to play straight to the camera.) Leaping, dancing and gesturing, Kyoami has a freedom of movement totally unlike the formal body language of the other characters (Kehr, p. 25; Rothwell, p. 198). He is played by Peter, the first actor to be cast, a popular transvestite performer whose public personality included 'childlike temperament' and 'outrageous behavior' (Goodwin, p. 208). Peter was raised as a girl, in the family tradition of Jiutamae, a dance form for women, and for men dressed as women, of which his father was a distinguished practitioner (Kehr, pp. 25–6). What looks to a Westerner like a challenge to decorum has in fact a decorum of its own. Peter's gender-crossing is not a breaking of cultural norms but an art that is itself a recognized part of its culture. In the film, however, Kyoami is disruptive in other ways: in a world of warriors, he has no weapons or armour, his emotions are as free and open as his body language, and when he cries (as he does frequently) he cries like a child, his fingers in his eyes. This, combined with the fact that Peter is practising a recognized artistic skill, forms an equivalent of Saburo's double nature, an impudent breaking of decorum that has tradition behind it.

In keeping with the screenplay's identification of a Western equivalent for him, Kyoami's routines are sometimes very close to those of Lear's Fool. He tells Hidetora he was a fool to give away his house and land. He tells a fable of a bird that hatched a serpent's egg, closely equivalent to the Fool's routine about the hedge-sparrow feeding the cuckoo. The most interesting twist comes in Kyoami's equivalent of the Fool's ironic advice to Kent to let go his hold when a great wheel runs down a hill. The Fool makes it clear that this is wise advice, and bad advice, and that whatever a wise man might do, 'I will tarry; the Fool will stay.' Kyoami has a similar routine about a rocking stone; but he is alone at the time, it is advice to himself, and he tries to leave. Then Hidetora calls out in his sleep, and he returns. Throughout his later scenes with Hidetora Kyoami is torn between really wanting to leave and knowing he has to stay. When he returns, it is not with Tango's straightforward loyalty, but with an air of defeat that leaves him in tears. His better nature has triumphed, and he wishes it hadn't. Tucking Hidetora up in bed – 'Good boy, sweet dreams' – he complains, 'All my life I've been his nurse.' He then joins his master and lies beside him in bed, sobbing bitterly. A child in his naked emotions, he has been forced into the role of parent, and the child he has to look after is an impossible one who gives nothing back. But he stays.

The Fool's routines can be decoded as deep, bitter wisdom. Kyoami's are that too, but more openly. When Hidetora goes mad, Kyoami editorializes, as generations of critics have done: Hidetora is better off mad, since in a mad world only the mad are sane. He sees Hidetora's madness as a chance for his master to see more deeply: 'The failed mind sees the heart's failings'. In fact Hidetora is so far gone that he has nothing like Lear's articulate insights into the human condition. In the passages equivalent to Lear's scene with Gloucester, it is Kyoami who carries the burden. Gloucester cries, and Lear tells him to be patient: we are born crying. Here it is Kyoami who cries. Hidetora wonders who is crying, and Kyoami replies, in effect, everybody: man is born crying, and when he has cried enough he dies. Later Hidetora declares, 'I'm lost' and Kyoami responds, 'Such is the human condition.'

Like Saburo and Tango, Kyoami exemplifies loyalty; but it is harder on him than it is on them. They can function in the manly world of action, in which they are at home. He is reduced to the role of surrogate parent, for which is unprepared, and guardian, at which he is not very good. He is supposed to watch over his master, but just when it matters most he loses him. All he can do is confess failure, sobbing, and ask for help. What he can do, as the outsider in this world, is see what it all means. In that vein his insights are as basic and terrible as Lear's. Productions sometimes see the Fool as an aspect of Lear – the extra pair of hands appearing from Yuri Yarvet's cloak. In *Ran* this goes farther, as Kyoami takes on Lear's burden of wisdom, a burden Hidetora is too mad to carry.

Tango, Kaedi and Jiro have their own reactions to Hidetora's surrender of power, and they are the predictable reactions built into the Lear story. Hidetora's authority crumbles as Lear's does. He begins in the First Castle, occupying the outworks as Tango occupies the keep. Even this compromise does not work: a procession of his concubines gets in Kaedi's way, and she forces them to defer to her as Hidetora watches in shock from a window. There is simply not enough space for everybody. Kaedi provokes more trouble. Taro has let Hidetora's followers take the Ichimonji banner. (Its key symbol, ironically, means 'one' (Kurosawa *et al.*, p. 8).) Kaedi wants it back, to establish that Taro is now head of the family; later she will address Hidetora as 'The honorable father of my husband' as Lear for Oswald is 'My lady's father'. In the ensuing fight over the banner, Kyoami sings a mocking song about Taro's vacillation. One of Taro's followers attacks Kyoami, and gets an arrow in the back. Then we see Hidetora with his bow at the window, the Hidetora of the boar hunt, the old ferocity in his eyes. This is Goneril's 'Did my father strike my gentleman for chiding of his fool?' with the violence turned up. It is also the last flash of his old power. Taro and Kaedi invite him to a meal with them, not to honour but to humiliate him. He sits on the floor, at a lower level, while they dominate the room; they make him sign a pledge of obedience, and at the urging of the treacherous Ikoma (whom Kaedi then thanks) he does. His anger boils, but cannot issue in action. All he can do is kick over a candlestick on his way out.

While Taro remarks complacently that the view from the castle is better now that he owns it, the initiative for rebellion really comes from Kaedi, allowing Kurosawa to find an equivalent for Shakespeare's combination of child against father and woman against man. Hidetora makes a double protest: 'Is this a son's attitude?' and 'The hen pecks the cock and makes him crow.' Kaedi's manner in the early scenes is quiet and polite; when she speaks, she begins with a slight hesitation. But when Hidetora enters the room where he will be humiliated, the camera picks her out before it picks out Taro (Howlett, p. 364). She sits in the position 'nearest the wall traditionally reserved for the senior person in the room' (Rothwell, p. 199). In the First Castle the question is space; in the Second, the question is whether Hidetora is to have an entourage at all. Jiro's position is that he will admit his father, but not his attendants; besides the reports he has heard of their disruptive behavior, he argues that his father, having given up power, has no need of an escort. Hidetora replies, 'The Great Lord goes nowhere alone! ... Only birds and beasts live in solitude.' As Taro is swayed by Kaedi, Jiro is swayed by his counselors. That left on his own he might behave more naturally is suggested when Hidetora, now mad, walks alone out of the Third Castle and Jiro tries to go after him. One of his followers dissuades him. The paradox of the rebellious sons who turn against their father is that they are not asserting their strength but showing their weakness.

Taro is led by his wife, Jiro by his followers. But the effect they have on their father is closely equivalent to the effect Goneril and Regan have on Lear.

After his second encounter with his daughters, Lear goes into the storm. In *Ran* the storm is reduced to a powerful wind: though it was provided by a typhoon that obligingly struck during the shooting, it lacks the spectacular thunder and lightning specified in the screenplay (Hapgood 1992, p. 38). Like Kozintsev's storm, it is scaled down so that war can take over as the key image of chaos. But while in Kozintsev the war has to wait for its turn in the original story, Kurosawa again moves the image of chaos forward: the seige of the Third Castle is his equivalent for Shakespeare's storm (Parker 1986, p. 419). It takes place where the storm does, at roughly the half-way point; and like the storm it triggers Hidetora's madness. As stage and film directors have taken the storm as a technical challenge requiring an imaginative use of the medium, Kurosawa makes this battle the centrepiece of the film by cutting out the sound and replacing it with music. It is not violent music, reflecting the action, but mournful, throbbing music. Kurosawa took Mahler's First Symphony as his model (Richie, p. 218). The screenplay describes the music as 'like the Buddha's heart, measured in beats of profound anguish, the chanting of a melody full of sorrow that begins like sobbing and rises gradually as it is repeated, like karmic cycles, then finally sounds like the wailing of countless Buddhas' (Kurosawa *et al.*, p. 46). While the Shostakovich music for the Kozintsev *Lear* was the voice of human suffering (Parker 1991, p. 85) this is the voice of divine suffering at human madness. The effect of the tension between the violence of the images and the mournful music derives from Kurosawa's 'pet theory', stated years earlier, that 'cinematic strength derives from the multiplier effect of sound and visual image being brought together' and his discovery of the effectiveness of music and action working not in obvious correspondence but in counterpoint (Kurosawa, pp. 107, 197). The action itself is generalized, in that we have no sense of a battle in which we can follow the moves and see what is happening, and who is winning. Instead we have chaos: image after image of carnage, one image flowing into another as the music flows. A body stuck full of arrows hangs out of a tower. A man holds his severed arm. A man with an arrow through his eye staggers and falls leaning over a rail. Hidetora's concubines are mowed down by unheard gunfire. Bodies are piled everywhere. Buildings burn and smoke drifts through the air; the sun appears through dark clouds. Some of the images may have a personal root: Kurosawa confessed to a phobia about fire, and one of his most searing childhood memories was the sight of corpses piled up in silent streets after the great earthquake of 1923, a sight his brother insisted he confront to teach him that horror is best looked at straight on (Kurosawa, pp. 33–4, 52–4). He also made a study of thirteenth-century scrolls, particularly the scroll of 'The Burning of the Sanjo Palace' (Parker 1986, p. 420). The screenplay calls the battle a 'terrible scroll of Hell' (Kurosawa *et al.*, p. 46). The Western viewer is likely to think of the doom paintings of Hieronimus Bosch and Goya's *Disasters of War*.

Taro rides in triumph into the castle; we see him from behind. Then a shot rings out, breaking into the music, and the soundtrack is suddenly full of shouts and gunfire, the actual noise of the battle heard for the first time. The shot seems to come from nowhere, like the shot that kills Saburo near the end of the film; but the ensuing dialogue makes clear that Jiro's follower Kurosane has fired it, seemingly on his own initiative; Jiro, once again, is being led. What resumes with the gunshot, then, is not just the soundtrack but the story. Up to this point we have had a generalized image of chaos, any battle, any violence, a vision of human madness and suffering that makes a statement as universal as Kyoami's bitter wisdom. This has been achieved by a conscious manipulation of the medium of the sort that we see in the storm of Brook's film; but while the effect in Brook was fussy and diffuse, the simplicity of Kurosawa's means produces both an artifice that establishes the battle as a generalization and an emotional power that holds the viewer in a relentless grip. With the gunshot, the particular action of this particular story resumes.

The battle is the turning point for Hidetora. The screenplay comments that he 'has fought hard' (Kurosawa *et al.*, p. 50). The film tells a different story. He descends the stairs from the room in which he has been sleeping, ready to fight, but his sword snaps at the first blow. Two of his concubines kill each other, in an act to which the screenplay attributes a beauty and decorum that 'touches the heart' (Kurosawa *et al.*, p. 50). In the film the scene is too quick to establish itself that strongly, but the courage of the women following their code still plays off against the surrounding carnage. Hidetora himself cannot commit hara-kiri; he has no weapon. He is reduced to sitting in his room, staring sightlessly ahead as flaming arrows land all around him. Then he gets up and walks through the fire, his empty scabbard trailing behind him. Lear in Shakespeare's middle scenes is raging and active. Hidetora – who in the opening sequence falls asleep – tends to go into a catatonic stillness. Having left the Second Castle, and learning that there is no food in the countryside, he sits on the rocky ground, sagging in the heat, in a silence broken only by the noise of insects. This is when Tango comes to him, and in stark contrast to the brisk exchange between Lear and the disguised Kent, Hidetora's first response to Tango's greeting is continued silence. Where Lear's madness is as wild as the storm – as Gielgud put it, he *is* the storm – the madness that overtakes Hidetora in this climactic battle is catatonic. He walks steadily out of the castle, silent, staring blankly ahead, 'a man with whom communication is no longer possible' (Holland, p. 63). Appearing at the entrance to the castle, in a long shot that shows the huge scale of the burning building, he looks briefly like Kozintsev's Lear about to address his people from the top of the great wall. But he has nothing to say. He descends the stairs, reminding Brian Parker of Richard II descending to the base court (Parker 1986, p. 416). As he continues to walk, the armies part before him like the Red Sea; he takes no notice. The wind gets up, blowing his sleeping robe open to reveal, indecorously, one white leg. (Victorian engravings of the mad Lear often show him with one bare arm; Ian Holm's nude Lear would have been unimaginable.) The man who declared 'The Great Lord goes nowhere alone' walks alone into the wilderness.

Kyoami and Tango find him in a field of waving grasses – another Kozintsev echo (Parker 1991, p. 82) – smiling happily as he gathers wild flowers. His happiness is short-lived. Kyoami sings of an army of all those Hidetora killed, spreading over the plain; Hidetora flees in terror, as though the grass waving in the storm wind is that army. Later, as Kozintsev's Lear returns to the ruins of the castle where his folly began, Hidetora finds himself in the charred ruins of the castle that once belonged to Lady Sué's family, the castle he destroyed. His response to these images of his crimes is less articulate than Lear's moments of self-insight. Faced with the phantom army, he gives a stare of sheer naked terror, and runs away. In the ruins of the castle he wonders why he is there and whether he is dreaming. Lear has one running exit. Hidetora, hunted like the boar, spends a lot of time running. He hides among rocks and, when cornered, stares out like a wild animal. When he complains of being lost, he and Kyoami are standing at the edge of a cliff. Kyoami, losing patience, tells him, 'If you're tired of it, jump', and without a moment's thought Hidetora jumps. Kyoami, in a panic, finds him at the foot of the cliff, seemingly unhurt. He has had the experience Gloucester thought he had, but unlike Gloucester he has nothing to say about it. Contrary to Kyoami's lectures on the advantages of madness, Hidetora's insanity has not expanded his humanity but drained it. He is staring and inarticulate, reduced to a few basic reactions – or to none. When Kyoami puts a helmet of reeds on his head, the equivalent for a warlord of Lear's crown of flowers, he has at first no reaction, then he smiles faintly. We have no notion what if anything he is thinking. He is seen from outside, as though he were on display in a madhouse, someone we can look at in pity but find no relation to. That this madness is created by the battle in the Third Castle suggests that the violence that battle exemplifies, a violence at once reflecting the human condition and springing from the particular world Hidetora has made, is a force that wipes humanity of everything human. It will take Saburo's return to put that humanity back.

Meanwhile another force has been unleashed. It is after the battle that we see Kaedi for the first time at full strength, as she attacks and then seduces Jiro. The decorum under which she hid her earlier scheming is replaced by naked passion and violence. Structurally, this scene, coming just after the battle that stands for the storm, is the equivalent of the blinding of Gloucester, and it carries a similar charge of shock. After an image of universal chaos we are in a room, seeing people again, and what we see in that room is the violence of the human animal, one on one. Kaedi, I have suggested, is the other wild card in the deck, breaking decorum in her own way as Kyoami does in his. At first she seems offended that Jiro is wearing his dead brother's armour; he apologizes and prepares to take it off, warning her, 'Sister-in-law, I am about to be naked'. Slowly and decorously she withdraws. Later she returns, apologizes, and presents him with Taro's helmet. As he takes it she attacks him with a knife, cutting him on the neck, her movement sudden and startling after the stillness of her manner up to now. She is taking, in a very different spirit, Kyaomi's license to move freely. She seems to be avenging her husband; but when Jiro tries to put the blame for Taro's death on to Kurogani she laughs. Closing the panels of the room to create a private space of which she is in total control, she says she cares nothing for Taro's death, only for her own future. She assaults Jiro again, this time with a kiss, and as they fall together on the floor she sucks the wound on his neck. She kicks the helmet out of the way, dismissing not only her husband but the whole notion of male power. The power in this scene is hers. Through the whole sequence her changes of front are startling, her movements are sudden and violent, and her voice rises to a scream. As Lear tears at his garments, she takes the knife and rips the sleeve of her kimono.

After Kaede and Jiro have had sex they sit up together, adjusting their garments, not looking at each other. Her next demand is that she should be his wife, not his concubine, and he has to kill Sué, not just put her aside. When he seems reluctant she weeps hysterically, throwing herself on the floor. As she lies sobbing, she casually crushes a moth that is fluttering near her – as casually as Kozintsev's Goneril lacing up her boots while Gloucester's screams ring through the house. The power that has been unleashed here is a power as mad and violent as Hidetora's. But while his was expressed within the codes of a warrior world, hers is a female power that comes from outside that world. The intrusion of sex is as indecorous as the intrusion of madness; Lear's attacks on female sexuality, in the generalized idiom of his scenes with Gloucester, are here worked directly into the story. Later, when Kurogane returns with his ironic gift of the fox-head, he finds the panels of the chamber closed, as they were when Kaedi first attacked Jiro. Knowing what is happening in the room, he goes back down the stairs, loudly announces himself, then approaches again. The room opens, Kaedi adjusting her robe to receive visitors. The screenplay, less subtly, has the couple making love, in front of the Ichimonji standard and Taro's armour. Its editorial comment is worth quoting: 'Jiro and Lady Kaede are making love, in the daytime, in front of the display. All the more appealing is that she is in mourning clothes' (Kurosawa *et al.*, p. 73). (We can think back to Granville Barker's Regan, in widow's weeds, applying makeup.) The shock produced by Kaedi's first outburst has settled into fastidious distaste.

It seems high time for Saburo's return. He and his men come galloping over a river, casting up great splashes of water, an image that could be paralleled in countless Westerns. They cross the river as Cordelia crosses the sea (Parker 1991, p. 87), and the water, as in Kozintsev, is an image of salvation that counters the fire of war. Saburo's colour, from the beginning, is blue, the colour associated in the West with France, and used for that purpose in many productions of *King Lear* (including that of Robin Phillips). Now the screen fills with blue banners and Jiro's forces, in red, run away. While it is unusual for Cordelia to appear in armour (Victoria Hamilton does so briefly, then reverts to a dress) Saburo's virtues include those of a commander: the screenplay insists, over and over, that his troops are orderly and well disciplined, in contrast to the disorder of Jiro's (pp. 78, 92–3, 97), and while the contrast is not so stark in the film it is clear enough. Cordelia loses her only battle; Saburo's forces, though outnumbered, fight bravely and drive Jiro's into retreat.

Kurosawa was, we might say, a pacifist who loved a good fight. In his schooldays he was fascinated by fencing, and learned Kendo swordsmanship (Kurosawa, pp. 19–24). Films like *The Seven Samurai*, *The Hidden Fortress* and *Yojimbo* relish the skills of swordsmen who are good at their work. *Ran*, however, deals not with heroic single combat but with the horror of total war, and the last thing Saburo wants when he comes to rescue his father is a battle. Fujimaki's presence on the hills, ready to give military support, disturbs him. He has inculcated the same values in his troops: when Taro's forces come to take over the Third Castle, Saburo's followers leave without a struggle. They are going to join their exiled leader; compared with him the castle is nothing, and there would be no point in fighting. Saburo's peacefulness is not Sué's Buddhist detachment; he makes it clear that he will fight if he has to, and his army, though small, is unbeatable. It is the peacefulness of a strong man: Taro and Jiro, we have seen, are the weaklings. In a moment that does not appear in the film but survives in the screenplay as a final comment on Saburo, Fujimaki offers to attack the First Castle to avenge Saburo's death, but Tango dissuades him: 'Master Saburo had no ambition. He wanted to avoid war.' The best way to honour him is to withdraw (Kurosawa *et al.*, p. 106). In this way Saburo brings from within the military world an answer to that world's violence, of which his father used to be the chief exponent.

We have seen Hidetora's mind deadened, wiped clean of its humanity, by the horror at the Third Castle. His reunion with Saburo makes him human again. Significantly, the dialogue follows closely the dialogue of the Lear–Cordelia reunion. The

[191]

chief difference between Lear's madness and Hidetora's, as we have seen, is that Hidetora is inarticulate. Some of Lear's most important insights are transferred to Kyoami. Now Hidetora finds his voice again, and in the process he as it were picks up signals from Lear. Lear thinks he is being taken out of the grave; literalizing Lear's fantasy, Hidetora hides in a grave-like depression in the ground, and when he rises up he looks like a man rising from the dead in a Western doomsday painting. Looking at the sky he asks, 'Am I in the other world? Is this paradise?' He tries to get back into his hole: 'Why are you so cruel? Why pull me from my grave?' Recognizing Saburo he gives a cry of excitement, then tries to run away, then asks, 'Give me poison to drink.' Finally, he acknowledges, 'I am a stupid old fool.' In all of this he is close to Lear, though in keeping with *Ran*'s tendency to work through externals, he makes some of Lear's hallucinations literal, acting out in reality things that pass through Lear's mind.

But Hidetora's starting point, unlike Lear's, was the violence of his career as the great warlord. If we are to see him as having regained humanity, this needs to be dealt with. It is; and again there is a parallel with Lear, though the language is not so close. Lear loses interest in the world of power; questions like 'Who's in, who's out', which once meant so much to him, he now views with amused detachment. All he wants is time alone with Cordelia. After Jiro's troops are driven off, we see Hidetora and Saburo on the same horse, laughing and chatting happily. Hidetora is riding behind, clinging on like Kyoami when he rode with Taro. We may think of Dogberry's definition of hierarchy: 'When two men ride on a horse, one must ride behind.' Hidetora is riding behind, taking the position occupied by his fool (as Ian Holm in the Dover scene wears his fool's hat). His urge for dominance is dead. He tells Saburo, 'I have so much to say. When we're alone and quiet, we will talk, father to son. That's all I want. Nothing else.' We have never seen them alone and quiet, and when they last talked as father and son it was an angry public confrontation. 'That's all I want. Nothing else' is a surrender of the drive to power that has led to the horror of the middle scenes, and in that surrender Hidetora seems for the first time simply human – and articulate as he has never been since the fight at the Third Castle.

But the film is still following *King Lear*. A shot rings out, and Saburo falls dead. Like the dialogue of their reunion, Hidetora's final moments with his dead son are full of Shakespearian echoes:

'I know when one is dead'; 'Are you gone forever?' He calls Saburo's name repeatedly, as Lear calls Cordelia's. He clutches his throat as though choking ('Pray you, undo this button'). When Tango tries to help him, Hidetora pushes him away, the effort of doing so leads him to fall backward, and moments later he dies. As Kyoami holds him, weeping, Tango orders, 'Do not call back his spirit'. Going beyond Lear (who is intently focused on Cordelia) Hidetora just before he died asked the question his child's death provokes –'Is this justice?' – taking on something like Kyoami's role of commentator. But while in Shakespeare there is now nothing to do, and nothing to say, and the play ends quickly, Tango and Kyoami (in a passage to which we shall return) take up Hidetora's question; and after that the military action of *Ran* continues. Hidetora has, we might say, gained humanity, in love and in grief, by moving into *King Lear*. In the end we go back to *Ran*, chaos, another battle, as at the end of Peter Brook's stage production we heard the storm again. Even the battle in which Saburo's forces routed Jiro's was accompanied by slow drumbeats, mournful music, and a droning sound like the hum of an airplane, all of this recalling the siege of the Third Castle. A battle fought by a hero for a cause we can sympathize with is still a battle; it still embodies the violence against which the whole film has protested. (At the end of *The Seven Samurai* the message is that the samurai, even when they win, always lose.) In the final battle, the forces of Jiro and Ayabe fight over the First Castle, where the film's conflicts began, and where they now end – except that the ending is confusion. The screenplay's account of the battle includes directions like 'bullets shower on the soldiers, killing them at random' and 'Samurai and soldiers are running in all directions not knowing what to do' (Kurosawa *et al.*, p. 105). There is no decisive ending for the battle: Kurogane tells Jiro to prepare for death and promises to follow him. But we never see their deaths, nor do we see Ayabe's victory. What does it matter who loses, and who wins? There is only carnage. There is one decisive event: Kurogane, shocked when a samurai presents him with Sué's severed head, disgusted that Kaede's order, which he tried to frustrate, has been obeyed after all, storms into her chamber and beheads her. The splash of blood covers the wall where the family insignia once stood, and the visual effect takes us back to the screen-filling red characters of the title, *Ran*, at the film's opening (Parker 1986, p. 420; Crowl, p. 115). If we were to ask Hidetora's question – 'Is this justice?'– the answer would be, 'No; only chaos.'

That the film takes us away from Hidetora's grief and the small party who mourn over him and Saburo, and back to the violent, pointless final battle is characteristic of its wide focus throughout. This is a wide-screen film, and not just in the literal sense. It is a story of a society, and of the principle that animates that society, in which individual lives seem dwarfed. Its title is not *Hidetora* but *Ran*. This leads us to the most characteristic (and controversial) aspect of its technique, Kurosawa's avoidance of close-ups and his preference for long shots. There are exceptions. We sometimes get close enough to Kaede to see that her face is drawn and tense, as though she never sleeps. When Tango tells Hidetora that he has returned to serve him on Saburo's orders, we see a look on Hidetora's face that the screenplay, for once, describes accurately: 'Torn between joy and shame, the stern face of a great general disappears, giving way to the face of a frail old father' (Kurosawa *et al.*, p. 43). The old debate between king and father in the playing of Lear is acted out on Hidetora's face. Even these moments, however, are nothing like Peter Brook's screen-filling close-ups, and unlike Kozintsev Kurosawa does not want to look into the actor's eyes. (Kozintsev, by the same token, was not interested in filling the screen with horses; Kurosawa is.) We are close enough to read the face; that is all. Though early in his career, Kurosawa used close-ups eloquently in films such as *No Regrets for our Youth* and *Ikiru*, he came to dislike them. He wanted a certain objectivity, and he did not like his actors to be too conscious of the camera (Parker 1991, pp. 76–7; Kurosawa, p. 195). I have noted a moment when the screenplay describes a character's facial expression, and the film confirms the description. It is more characteristic for the screenplay to describe an expression that the viewer never really sees. Kaede recalls her mother's death, 'Her glance frozen, her eyes shining strangely'; Hidetora looks at Sué 'tenderly as if at his own child' (Kurosawa *et al.*, pp. 29, 34). Neither effect makes it from the page to the screen; we are too far away. At moments when we might expect a close-up the camera stays well back. In the scene in which Hidetora announces his surrender of power, we see nothing like Richard Eyre's close-ups of anxious glances around the table. The camera keeps its distance, objectively recording the whole situation. As David Denby puts it, 'These are affairs of state', not of individual psychology (*New York*, 6 January

1986). What matters is the situation, not the individual feelings of the participants. When Kaedi recounts her grievances she is seen in long shot, sitting on the left of the screen with Taro beside her, on the right; and in the middle, in the foreground, the empty mat where Hidetora was sitting moments ago. We are as far away as we would be in the theatre, and since as filmgoers we are used to respecting the camera's decisions (we have no choice), we stay back, while in the theatre we might focus our attention on Kaede. This is a moment of general, not just private significance, not one person's story but the story of a group, three of whom are represented. In Lear's reunion with Cordelia, and in his grieving over her body, other screen versions move in for close-ups; Kurosawa's camera rigorously maintains its distance. In the moment of Hidetora's death he is lying on Saburo's chest, not cradling him so that the camera can move in and catch their faces together. There is no need for Tango and Kyoami to crowd in close to keep in the shot as Kent and the Doctor do in Miller's version. That is the self-consciousness Kurosawa wanted to avoid. They can simply express their grief as the camera, keeping well back, observes.

For some viewers this is a problem. Reviewing the film on its release, Derek Elley complained of its 'clinical air: we watch, we observe, but we are not moved' (*Films and Filming*, February 1986). Darrell William Davis calls *Ran* 'a great film, but not a very human one' (Davis, p. 237). For Mitsuhiro Yoshimoto, our inability to see faces means that the characters become 'mere types' (Yoshimoto, p. 357). Stephen Prince claims that in *Ran* Kurosawa has abandoned 'social and cultural analysis' in favour of 'metaphysics' (Prince, p. 289); hence the distance. For Yoshio Arai, that is just the point: the action of *Ran* is observed 'from the eye of Heaven, that is to say, from the eye of Buddha'. This means detachment (Arai, p. 8) – a detachment like that of Sué – and up to a point we may agree. But it is worth recalling the screenplay's description of the music of the third battle as the sound of Buddha's heart beating in anguish, of countless Buddhas wailing. The long shots mean not just detachment but a full view of the scale of human suffering.

If the camera is observing from the eye of heaven, it is still observing social and natural worlds, and it does so in vivid detail. Of all the screen versions discussed here, *Ran* makes the boldest use of colour. Brook and Kozintsev film in black and white; Miller and Eyre drain the colour; Elliott's colours are pastel. Kurosawa uses a full, vivid palette, for social and natural scenes alike. On the surface the decorum of traditional Japanese culture is still, more or less, observed (Guntner, p. 131; Parker 1986, p. 420). The effect is generally ironic. Kaede's long robes whisper along the floor as she walks; but then so do the robes of the Lady Macbeth character in *Throne of Blood*, and the soft, delicate sound only sets up the moments when Kaede cuts loose and screams like a banshee. As Jiro dismisses the traitors who have served him they encounter Kaedi mounting the stairs that lead to the chamber. Still carrying their parting gifts, their final payoff, they kneel and bow to her. Then she enters the room, and all hell breaks loose. Social display includes power as well as decorum. The castles – the first two being actual historic sites where Kurosawa was allowed to film (Rothwell, p. 197) – are not just imposing but monstrous, with great creaking gates that shut Hidetora in or out, suggesting the sheer weight of the history in which the protagonists are trapped (Davis, p. 242).

Outside the gates is the natural world, and in a way this too is part of Japanese culture. The appreciation of natural beauty runs strong in this culture, and that beauty is on display here – often, like the decorum, with ironic effect. The beautiful green hill country of the opening scenes sets off by contrast the power plays that Hidetora initiates, dwarfing the human action and making it seem trivial. Amid the angry, anxious voices we hear the twitter of birds. As Saburo and his generals sit awaiting a possible battle with Jiro, we hear the cuckoo. Saburo at least is aware of it, and lifts his face to feel the warmth of the sun. As the armies mass, we hear the cuckoo again. Nature goes about its business, indifferent to the madness of humanity (Parker 1991, p. 87). Nature, here as in *King Lear*, can give comfort. We go from Kaedi's chaotic outburst to Hidetora and Kyoami lying side by side amid grass and flowers, their white and pink costumes echoing each other. But we are never far from irony: later we will see the murdered bodies of Sué and her maid lying together, in much the same way, amid grass and flowers. And (as in Kozintsev with his blasted Russian landscapes) the pathetic fallacy can be grim. Leaving the Second Castle, Hidetora finds himself without food in a hot, stony wasteland whose sound is not the twittering of birds but the scratching of insects. Later he flees across sand – the ashen slopes of Mount Fuji (Arai, p. 3) – and hides among rocks. In *Ran* as in Kozintsev's *Lear* we see one of the advantages of cross-cultural work on Shakespeare: as Samuel Crowl observes, 'England lacks a landscape consonant with the terror, brutality, and naked appetite released in Shakspeare's tragic worlds' (Crowl, p. 112). Brook went to Jutland; Kurosawa and Kozintsev found what they needed in their own countries.

The distance imposed by the camera, the wide panoramas of castles and landscapes, even the generality of the title – all these create an angle from which we observe not just individual stories but nature, society and humanity. Is it a Buddha's eye view? Over the bodies of Saburo and Hidetora, Kyoami and Tango debate. Kyoami, echoing Gloucester, and echoing many of *King Lear*'s critics, asks, 'Are there no gods … no Buddha?' and cries out in anguish: 'If you exist, hear me! You are mischievous and cruel! Are you so bored up there you must crush us like ants?' Tango tells him not to blaspheme: 'It is the gods who weep. They see us killing each other … they can't save us from ourselves … It's how the world is made'. The music under his speech is the throbbing, mournful music of the battle at the Third Castle, the sound of Buddha's grief. The fatalism recalls that of Sué, who thinks it was all decided in our past lives; and the cynical pseudo-fatalism of Jiro who, having decided to break his word and kill Saburo, declares 'It was inevitable'. Hidetora was right about one thing: he told Sué we cannot count on Buddha's mercy. Whether the gods play cruelly with humanity, or mourn over it, or simply do not exist, the responsibility finally rests with us. In Kurosawa's own words, 'What I wanted to say in the last scene is that we should stop thinking we can count on God or Buddha. We should make an effort to accept responsibility for our own lives' (Parker 1991, p. 90). But there is no final image of positive action arising from that sense of responsibility, nothing like Kozintsev's peasants beginning the work of reconstruction, or the Lear of Edward Bond's *Lear* taking a spade to the wall he himself built, the wall that is that play's image of the madness of power. There is just one more battle over one more castle; the madness goes on. 'It's how the world is made'.

Some productions of *King Lear* have tried to find a kind of consolation in the sense of order provided by formal closure, like the circle of attendants around the Lears of Irving and Olivier, or the lowering of the flags in the Phillips production. The equivalent here is the funeral procession of Hidetora and Saburo, carried on stretchers like the bodies in the Kozintsev film, not heaped together like the bodies in the Eyre production. The dignity he surrendered restored, Hidetora goes first, Kyoami walking beside him with a bouquet of flowers, recalling the meadow in which they lay side by side. While Kozintsev shoots from above, letting us see the faces of the dead, Kurosawa shoots from the side, and the main impression, characteristically, is of the whole occasion, embodied in the solemn music and the long line of soldiers. It is the equivalent of the Folio's final stage direction, '*Exeunt with a dead march*'. It is not the ending of the film.

Warned of the threats against her, Sué flees, with her maid and Tsurumaru. Tsurumaru has forgotten his flute; Sue sends the maid back for it. When the maid does not return, Sué goes back herself, leaving Tsurumaru with the scroll of the Amitabha which, she tells him, will keep him safe. We next see Sué and her maid lying dead in the grass. Cordelia dies twice in *Ran*, once as Saburo and once as Sué (Hoile, pp. 32–3). The film ends with Tsurumaru groping forward with his cane at the brink of a precipice. As he moves the storm forward to the opening scene, Kurosawa moves Dover Cliff to the end of the film. Once before we saw human figures at a precipice. Riding away from Fujimaki, Saburo and Tango found themselves at the edge of a steep drop, and turned to confront him; they found he was a friend. Tsurumaru is on foot, blind and alone. His cane taps along the ground, and suddenly encounters nothing. The sharp wail of a flute registers his shock. The flute is no longer his: like Kyoami's opening music, it belongs to the soundtrack. Tsurumaru stumbles backward and drops the scroll, which falls over the edge and lies on the ground far below, as useless to him as the divinity it represents. The film ends by insisting relentlessly on the distance it has maintained throughout. Brook ends with a close-up, then a blank screen; Kozintsev with a close-up, looking into Edgar's eyes. Kurosawa goes in the opposite direction. In a series of increasingly distant shots, we see Tsurumaru at the edge of the precipice, which gets more formidable as the camera retreats and the human figure gets smaller. It is the rampart of his family castle, which Hidetora destroyed; as the angle gets more distant, we see its charred ruins. They look small but the human figure is even smaller. And with the increasing distance the man-made ruin looks more like a cliff, a human structure becoming a natural one. The long shots have shown us nature, and the works of humanity; at this final distance we can no longer tell them apart. The scene has an eerie, inhuman beauty: it happens against a darkening pink sunset that recalls our first sight of Sué. But against her piety and trust it registers despair. The published screenplay ends with a single word: in Japanese, 'San!', variously translated as 'Disaster!' and 'Wretchedness!' (Arai, p. 3; Kurosawa *et al.*, p. 106). Lear, looking at Tom, called him essential humanity, 'The thing itself'. Tsurumaru, who appears both male and female, both old and young, is a similarly essential figure. In the final battle, as in the battles throughout, we have seen human power at work – its violence, absurdity and essential emptiness. We end with an image of human helplessness, an image that gets more piercing the more distant it becomes.

CHAPTER XII

Conclusion

Since productions depend on choices, no production will catch all the possibilities latent in a dramatic text. In that sense there will never be an ideal production of *King Lear* – or, for that matter, of *The Mousetrap*. But the range of choices offered by *King Lear* is so wide as to constitute a set of radical contradictions. Think of Lear's opening entrance: we have seen everything from barbaric pageantry with courtiers falling on their faces to a few people walking casually into a room. Is there any other Shakespearian tragedy in which the range of options for staging the hero's first appearance is so wide? The society of the play can be a primitive world on the edge of pre-history, or a modern and civilized one on the edge of decadence, or a timeless abstraction. The storm can be an explosion of the universe in which cosmic forces are unleashed and perception itself breaks down, or it can be a spell of unusually nasty weather. The battle can be a few offstage noises or the climax of the story. Central to all this is the contradiction within the hero himself, indicated in our opening quotations: titanic and frail, magnificent and silly. There is an equally radical split in the moral behaviour of the other characters, in whom the extremes of good and evil go as far as Shakespeare ever takes them. It is as though Shakespeare set out to explore human nature and human relations in the most fundamental way – parents and children, kings and subjects, cruelty and kindness, man, nature and the gods – and found at the heart of his subject a set of contradictions.

There are other Shakespeare plays in which the range of per-formance choices is comparably wide – *Henry V* and *Measure for Measure* come to mind – but none, I think, in which the issues are so fundamental. Those issues include the medium itself. It may be no coincidence that productions of *King Lear* raise basic questions not just about how the play has been approached but about how the medium has been used. The three television productions we examined handle their medium in essentially different ways, and

Peter Brook's stage production was the occasion for a fundamental re-thinking about the way Shakespeare could be presented to a modern audience. Often we are aware of the medium as we watch, as in the overt theatricality of Adrian Noble's production, or the storm in Peter Brook's film. Even in a production that is not so self-conscious, fundamental choices have to be made. A director's handling of the storm, symbolic or realistic, will imply something not just about his view of the play but about his philosophy of theatre. The storm is the most conspicuous point of decision; and this includes the decisions of Kozintsev and Kurosawa that the storm is less important than the war. But there are other questions just as fundamental, such as the relation of the supporting figures to the main ones. Are they part of the group, lending support as in the Barker and Phillips productions? Do they sink into the background, leaving the main figures isolated as in Brook's stage and screen versions? The small screen of television forces a more awkward choice, between reaction shots, breaking up the scene, and Miller's device of crowding three or four people into the picture. The purity of the division between good and evil, with a corresponding risk of stereotype, poses questions about characterization. Do the actors work against that division, as Brook encouraged them to do, or do they fill out the portraits of good and evil with humanizing detail that keeps the moral division intact – the route taken by Phillips, Eyre and Kozintsev? And speaking of filling out, what should be done with the gaps and silences in the play? The Fool's absence in the first scene and the last two acts, Lear's surprising ability to get away from the people who are looking after him, the absence from the stage of the poor who (at times) are so much in the minds of Lear and Gloucester – in each case there is an obvious temptation to round out what Shakespeare, by accident or design, left incomplete. Again questions about the medium are raised: such filling out seems obtrusive in the theatre, which is more bound to the text, but natural enough in the more open and fluid medium of film, where liberties are not just permitted but required.

That last sentence went from setting out choices to declaring a bias; and readers will by now have detected other biases in my account of these productions. Between the magnificent portent and the man, the actor needs first to give us the man. If he can also give us the portent, so much the better, but the man is essential. At the start of the story there is a titanic figure carving up a map, and an old man on the edge of death asking his daughters to say how much they love him. The play's exploration of cruelty and kindness, pain and wonder, springs more from the second than from the first. The issues, again, are fundamental: death and love. These are also the issues of the last scene, where Lear, who has endured so much, is finally torn apart and killed by his love for Cordelia and the inescapable fact of her death. At that point nobody cares about the kingdom. Yet the play has also created a society, giving us a sense of why human history has been what it is: it is 'about us'. It deals with the most basic personal fears and desires: it is 'about me'. In his volume on *All's Well That Ends Well* for this series (1984) J. L. Styan made a point of not disclosing which of the productions he discussed he had actually seen (p. viii). I have gone in the other direction, being frankly personal. There are other plays about which I might preserve a proper scholarly detachment, but not this one. It is not that one is looking for a production whose interpretive choices one agrees with. The Brook production was one of the most exciting evenings I have spent in the theatre, and I found myself constantly arguing with it. It was fundamentally weak in the family dimension I have just said is so important. I have sat through other productions, nameless in this volume, that left me little to disagree with and little to remember. Rather, there needs to be some contact, of whatever kind, between the play and the world we live in. If the awareness of the medium the play tends to create leads to the medium's self-conscious absorption with its own devices – as in the Noguchi designs, or the storm in Brook's film – the play loses power. But when the European audiences for Brook's stage production heard in Lear's howls not the lament of a father but the ruin of their own world, or when Olivier cheated time by putting on film his own struggle with mortality, the power at work was not just that of the artists; it was the power – a power, we have seen, that can break the barriers of time and culture – of the play itself.

APPENDIX

A Some significant twentieth-century productions of *King Lear*

1931	Harcourt Williams	Old Vic
1936	Theodore Komisarjevsky	Stratford-upon-Avon
1940	Lewis Casson, Harley Granville Barker	Old Vic*
1944	Donald Wolfit	Scala Theatre, London
1946	Laurence Olivier	New Theatre, London
1950	John Gielgud, Antony Quayle	Stratford-upon-Avon
1953	George Devine	Stratford-upon-Avon
1955	George Devine	Palace Theatre, London
1959	Glen Byam Shaw	Stratford-upon-Avon
1962	Peter Brook	Stratford-upon-Avon*
1963	Allen Fletcher	Stratford, Connecticut
1964	Michael Langham	Stratford, Ontario
1968	Trevor Nunn	Stratford-upon-Avon
1970	Grigori Kozintsev	Lenfilm*
1971	Peter Brook	Athena-Laterna films*
1976	Trevor Nunn, John Barton, Barry Kyle	Stratford-upon-Avon
1979	Robin Phillips	Stratford, Ontario*
1982	Adrian Noble	Stratford-upon-Avon*
1982	Jonathan Miller	BBC Television*
1983	Michael Elliott	Granada Television*
1988	Robin Phillips	Stratford, Ontario
1990	Deborah Warner	National Theatre (Lyttleton)
1993	Adrian Noble	Stratford-upon-Avon
1996	Richard Monette	Stratford, Ontario
1997	Richard Eyre	Royal National Theatre (Cottesloe)
1998	Richard Eyre	BBC Television*
1999	Gregory Hersov	Royal Exchange Theatre, Manchester
2002	Jonathan Miller	Stratford, Ontario

(Note: Donald Wolfit included *King Lear* in his touring repertory of classical plays between 1942 and 1950, reviving it in 1953. I have listed above the London run in which he achieved his major breakthrough in the part.)

B Major actors and staff in the twentieth-century productions discussed

London, Old Vic 1940 (15 April)

Directors: Lewis Casson and Harley Granville Barker
Designer: Roger Furse   Music: Herbert Menges

Lear	John Gielgud	*Edmund*	Jack Hawkins
Goneril	Cathleen Nesbitt	*Fool*	Stephen Haggard
Regan	Fay Compton	*Kent*	Lewis Casson
Cordelia	Jessica Tandy	*Cornwall*	Andrew Cruikshank
Gloucester	Nicholas Hannen	*Albany*	Harcourt Williams
Edgar	Robert Harris	*Oswald*	Julian Somers

Stratford-upon-Avon 1962 (6 November)

Director and Designer: Peter Brook

Lear	Paul Scofield	*Edmund*	James Booth
Goneril	Irene Worth		(Ian Richardson)
Regan	Patience Collier	*Fool*	Alec McCowen
	(Pauline Jameson)	*Kent*	Tom Fleming
Cordelia	Diana Rigg	*Cornwall*	Tony Church
Gloucester	Alan Webb	*Albany*	Peter Jeffrey
	(John Laurie)		(Clifford Rose)
Edgar	Brian Murray	*Oswald*	Clive Swift
			(Michael Williams)

(Note: Names in brackets indicate cast changes for the 1964 tour.)

Stratford, Ontario 1979 (5 October)

Director: Robin Phillips   Designer: Daphne Dare
Music: Berthold Carrière

Lear	Peter Ustinov	*Edgar*	Rodger Barton
Goneril	Donna Goodhand	*Edmund*	Richard Monette
	(Martha Henry)	*Fool*	William Hutt
Regan	Marti Maraden	*Kent*	Jim McQueen
	(Patricia Conolly)	*Cornwall*	William Webster
Cordelia	Ingrid Blekys	*Albany*	Frank Maraden
	(Lynne Griffin)		(Nicholas Pennell)
Gloucester	Douglas Rain	*Oswald*	Tom Wood
			(Richard McMillan)

(Note: Names in brackets indicate cast changes for the 1980 revival.)

Stratford-upon-Avon 1982 (10 June)

Director: Adrian Noble   Designer: Bob Crowley
Music: Ilona Sekacz

Lear	Michael Gambon	*Edmund*	Clive Wood
Goneril	Sara Kestelman	*Fool*	Antony Sher
Regan	Jenny Agutter	*Kent*	Malcolm Storry
Cordelia	Alice Krige	*Cornwall*	Pete Postlethwaite
Gloucester	David Waller	*Albany*	David Bradley
Edgar	Jonathan Hyde	*Oswald*	Chris Hunter

1970 film

Director: Grigori Kozintsev
Designers: Eugene Ene, S. Virsaladze
Camera: Ionas Gritsus   Music: Dmitri Shostakovich

Lear	Yuri Yarvet	*Edmund*	Regimastas Adomaitis
Goneril	Elza Radzin	*Fool*	Oleg Dal
Regan	Galina Volchek	*Kent*	Vladimir Emelianov
Cordelia	Valentina Chendrikova	*Cornwall*	A. A. Vokach
Gloucester	Karl Sebris	*Albany*	Banionis
Edgar	Leonard Merzin	*Oswald*	A. V. Petrenko

1971 film

Director: Peter Brook
Designers: Georges Wakhevitch, Adele Anggård
Camera: Henning Kristiansen

Lear	Paul Scofield	*Edmund*	Ian Hogg
Goneril	Irene Worth	*Fool*	Jack MacGowran
Regan	Susan Engel	*Kent*	Tom Fleming
Cordelia	Anne-Lise Gabold	*Cornwall*	Patrick Magee
Gloucester	Alan Webb	*Albany*	Cyril Cusak
Edgar	Robert Lloyd	*Oswald*	Barry Stanton

1982 television

Director: Jonathan Miller
Designers: Colin Lowrey, Raymond Hughes

Lear	Michael Hordern	*Edmund*	Michael Kitchen
Goneril	Gillian Barge	*Fool*	Frank Middlemass
Regan	Penelope Wilton	*Kent*	John Shrapnel
Cordelia	Brenda Blethyn	*Cornwall*	Julian Curry
Gloucester	Norman Rodway	*Albany*	John Bird
Edgar	Anton Lesser	*Oswald*	John Grillo

1983 television

Director: Michael Elliott
Designers: Roy Stonehouse, Tanya Moiseivitsch

Lear	Laurence Olivier	*Edmund*	Robert Lindsay
Goneril	Dorothy Tutin	*Fool*	John Hurt
Regan	Diana Rigg	*Kent*	Colin Blakely
Cordelia	Anna Calder-Marshall	*Cornwall*	Jeremy Kemp
Gloucester	Leo McKern	*Albany*	Robert Lang
Edgar	David Threlfall	*Oswald*	Geoffrey Bateman

1998 television

Director: Richard Eyre
Designer: Bob Crowley
Director of Photography: Roger Pratt

Lear	Ian Holm	*Edmund*	Finbar Lynch
Goneril	Barbara Flynn	*Fool*	Michael Bryant
Regan	Amanda Redman	*Kent*	David Burke
Cordelia	Victoria Hamilton	*Cornwall*	Michael Simkins
Gloucester	Timothy West	*Albany*	David Lyon
Edgar	Paul Rhys	*Oswald*	William Osborne

C. *Ran* (1985)

Director: Akira Kurosawa
Screenplay: Akira Kurosawa, Hideo Oguni and Masato Ide
Designer: Yoshiro Muraki
Director of Photography: Takao Saito

Hidetora	Tatsuya Nakadi	*Lady Kaedi*	Mieko Harada
Taro	Akira Terao	*Lady Sué*	Yoshiko Miyazaki
Jiro	Jinpachi Nezu	*Tsurumaru*	Takeshi Nomura
Saburo	Daisuki Ryu	*Ikoma*	Kazu Kato
Tango	Masayuki Yui	*Kurogane*	Hisashi Igawa
Kyoami	Peter		

BIBLIOGRAPHY

Acker, Paul, 1980. 'Conventions for Dialogue in Peter Brook's *King Lear*', *Literature/Film Quarterly*, VIII, 219–24.

Agate, James, 1943. *Brief Chronicles*, London.

Arai, Yoshio, 1989. '*Ran* and *King Lear*', *Shakespeare Worldwide: Translation and Adaptation*, XII, 1–13.

Awasthi, Suresh, 1993. 'The International Experience and the Kathakali 'King Lear', *New Theatre Quarterly*, IX, 172–8.

Berkowitz, Joel, 2002. *Shakespeare on the American Yiddish Stage*, Iowa City.

Berry, Ralph, 1977. *On Directing Shakespeare: Interviews with Contemporary Directors*, London and New York.

Bratton, J. S., ed., 1987. *Plays in Performance: King Lear*, Bristol.

Brook, Peter, 1968. *The Empty Space*, London.

——, 1987. *The Shifting Point*, New York.

Burnim, Kalman A., 1973. *David Garrick, Director*, Carbondale, Edwardsville, London and Amsterdam, reprint.

Burton, Hal, ed., 1967. *Great Acting*, London.

Byrne, M. St. Clare, 1960. '*King Lear* at Stratford-on-Avon, 1959', *Shakespeare Quarterly*, XI, 189–206.

Carlisle, Carol Jones, 1969. *Shakespeare from the Greenroom: Actors' Criticisms of Four Major Tragedies*, Chapel Hill.

Carnovsky, Morris, and Paul Barry, 'On Kozintsev's *King Lear*', *Literary Review*, XXII, 179, 408–32.

Cook, Hardy M., 1986. 'Two *Lear*s for Television: An Exploration of Televisual Strategies', *Literature/Film Quarterly*, XIV, 179–86.

Cowie, Peter, 1983. 'The Olivier Lear', *Sight and Sound*, LII, 78.

Crowl, Samuel, 1994. 'The Bow is Bent and Drawn: Kurosawa's *Ran* and the Shakespearean Arrow of Desire', *Literature/Film Quarterly*, XXII, 109–16.

David, Richard, 1978. *Shakespeare in the Theatre*, Cambridge.

Davies, Anthony, 1997. '*King Lear* on Film', in James Ogden and Arthur H. Scouten, eds. *Lear from Study to Stage*, Madison, Teaneck, and London, 247–66.

Davies, Robertson, Tyrone Guthrie, Boyd Neel and Tanya Moisei-witsch, 1955. *Thrice the Brinded Cat Hath Mew'd*, Toronto.

Davis, Darrell William, 1996. *Picturing Japaneseness: Monumental Style, National Identity, Japanese Film*, New York.

Dukes, Ashley, 1940. 'The English Scene', *Theatre Arts*, XXIV, 467–70.

Dymkowski, Christine, 1986. *Harley Granville-Barker: A Preface to Modern Shakespeare*, Washington, London and Toronto.

Fenwick, Harry, 1983. 'The Production', in *King Lear*, the BBC TV Shakespeare, London, 19–34.

Fordham, Hallam, 'Player in Action: John Gielgud as "King Lear"', Folger ms T.b.17. (Note: references to this manuscript are to scene numbers, since it is keyed to scenes rather than consecutively paginated.)

Funke, Lewis, and John E. Booth, 1967. *Actors Talk About Acting*, New York, reprint.

Fuzier, Jean and Jean-Marie Maguin, 1982. '*King Lear* ... ', *Cahiers Élisabéthains*, XXII, 117–18.

Gielgud, John, 1981. *An Actor and his Time*, Harmondsworth, reprint.

——, 1953. *Early Stages*, London.

——, 1963. *Stage Directions*, London.

Giroux, Robert, 1984. 'Laurence Olivier's Lear', *Films in Review*, XXXV, 98–100.

Good, Maurice, 1982. *Every Inch a Lear*, Victoria, BC.

Goodwin, James, 1994. *Akira Kurosawa and Intertextual Cinema*, Baltimore and London.

Granville-Barker, Harley, 1952. *Prefaces to Shakespeare*, I, Princeton, reprint.

Guntner, J. Lawrence, 2000. '*Hamlet, Macbeth* and *King Lear* on film', in Russell Jackson, ed., *The Cambridge Companion to Shakespeare on Film*, Cambridge, 117–34.

Hallinan, Tim, 1981. 'Jonathan Miller on the Shakespeare Plays', *Shakespeare Quarterly*, XXXII, 134–45.

Hapgood, Robert, 1994. 'Kurosawa's Shakespeare films: *Throne of Blood, The Bad Sleep Well*, and *Ran*', in Anthony Davies and Stanley Wells, eds, *Shakespeare and the Moving Image*, Cambridge, 234–49.

——, 1992. '*Ran* from Screenplay to Film', *Shakespeare Bulletin*, X, 37–8.

Harwood, Ronald, 1971. *Sir Donald Wolfit, C.B.E.*, London.

Hattaway, Michael, 1982. 'Shakespeare's *King Lear*... and Edward Bond's *Lear*...', *Cahiers Élisabéthains*, XXII, 119–20.

Hayman, Ronald, 1971. *John Gielgud*, New York.

Hodgdon, Barbara, 1977. 'Kozintsev's *King Lear*: Filming a Tragic Poem', *Literature/Film Quarterly*, V, 291–8.

——, 1983. 'Two *King Lears*: Uncovering the Filmtext', *Literature/Film Quarterly*, XI, 143–51.

Hoile, Christopher, 1987. '*King Lear* and Kurosawa's *Ran*: Splitting, Doubling, Distancing', *Pacific Coast Philology*, XXII, 29–34.

Holland, Peter, 1994. 'Two-dimensional Shakespeare: "King Lear" on film', in Anthony Davies and Stanley Wells, eds, *Shakespeare and the Moving Image*, Cambridge, 50–68.

Howlett, Kathy, 1996. 'Are You Trying to Make Me Commit Suicide? Gender, Identity, and Spatial Arrangements in Kurosawa's *Ran*', *Literature/Film Quarterly*, XXIV, 360–6.

Hughes, Alan, 1977. '"A Poor, Infirm, Weak and Despis'd Old Man": Henry Irving's *King Lear*', *Wascana Review*, XII, 49–64.

Jackson, Esther Merle, 1966. '*King Lear*: The Grammar of Tragedy', *Shakespeare Quarterly*, XVII, 25–40.

Johnson, William, 1972. Review of *King Lear* (Brook) and *Macbeth* (Polanski), *Film Quarterly*, XXV.3, 41–8.

Jones, Edward Trostle, 1985. *Following Directions: A Study of Peter Brook*, New York.

Jorgens, Jack J., 1977. *Shakespeare on Film*, Bloomington and London.

Kane, Julia, 1997. 'From Baroque to *Wabi*: Translating Animal Imagery from Shakespeare's *King Lear* to Kurosawa's *Ran*', *Literature/Film Quarterly*, XXV, 146–51.

Kehr, David, 1985. 'Samurai *Lear*', *American Film*, X.x, 20–6.

Knight, G. Wilson, 1949. *Principles of Shakespearean Production*, Harmondsworth, revised edn.

Knowles, Richard Paul, 1985. 'History as Metaphor: Daphne Dare's Late 19th- and Early 20th-Century Settings for Shakespeare at Stratford, Ontario 1975–1980', *Theatre History Studies*, V, 20–40.

——, 1987. 'Robin Phillips: Text and Context', *Canadian Theatre Review*, LII, 50–7.

——, 1993. 'Speaking the Verse: Robin Phillips Directs Shakespeare', A. L. Magnusson and C. E. McGee, eds, *Elizabethan Theatre*, XII, Toronto, pp. 61–76.

Kozintsev, Grigori, 1972. '"Hamlet" and "King Lear": Stage and Film', in Clifford Leech and J. M. R. Margeson, eds, *Shakespeare 1971*, Toronto and Buffalo, 190–9.

——, 1977. *Shakespeare: the Space of Tragedy*, tr. Mary Mackintosh, London.

——, 1966. *Shakespeare: Time and Conscience*, tr. Joyce Vining, New York.

——, 1973. 'Talking about his "Lear" and "Hamlet" Films with Ronald Hayman', *Transatlantic Review*, XLVI and XLVII, 10–15.

Kurosawa, Akira, 1982. *Something Like an Autobiography*, tr. Audie E. Bock, New York.

Kurosawa, Akira, Hideo Oguni and Ide Masato, 1986. *Ran* [screenplay], Boston and London.

Labeille, Daniel, 1980. '"The Formless Hunch": An Interview with Peter Brook', *Modern Drama*, XXIII, 219–26.

Leech, Clifford, 1969. *Tragedy*, London.

Lusardi, James P. and June Schlueter, eds, 1991. *Reading Shakespeare in Performance: King Lear*, Rutherford, Madison, Teaneck, London, and Toronto.

Mack, Maynard, 1972. *King Lear in our Time*, Berkeley and Los Angeles.

Manvell, Roger, 1979. *Shakespeare and the Film*, South Brunswick and New York, 2nd edn.

Marowitz, Charles, 1963. 'Lear Log', *Encore*, X, 20–33.

Mullin, Michael, 1983. 'Peter Brook's *King Lear*: Stage and Screen', *Literature/Film Quarterly*, XI, 190–6.

Nesbitt, Cathleen, 1975. *A Little Love and Good Company*, London.

O'Dell, George C. D., 1966. *Shakespeare from Betterton to Irving*, New York, 2 vols, reprint.

Olivier, Laurence, 1986. *On Acting*, New York.

Parker, Brian, 1986. '*Ran* and the Tragedy of History', *University of Toronto Quarterly*, LV, 412–13.

Parker, R. B., 1991. 'The Use of *Mise-en-Scène* in Three Films of *King Lear*', *Shakespeare Quarterly*, XLII, 75–90.

Pearce, Jill, 1997. '*King Lear* ....', *Cahiers Élisabéthains*, LII, 121–2.

Poel, William, 1913. *Shakespeare in the Theatre*, London and Toronto.

Phillips, Stephen J., 1997. 'Akira Kurosawa's *Ran*', in James Ogden and Arthur H. Scouten, eds, *Lear from Study to Stage*, Madison, Teaneck, and London, 267–77.

Prince, Stephen, 1991. *The Warrior's Camera*, revised edn, Princeton, NJ.

Reddington, John, 1973. 'Film, Play and Idea', *Literature/Film Quarterly*, I, 367–71.

Reeves, Geoffrey, 1972. 'Finding Shakespeare on Film: From an Interview with Peter Brook', in Charles W. Eckert, ed., *Focus on Shakespearean Films*, Englewood Cliffs, 37–41.

Richie, Donald, 1996. *The Films of Akira Kurosawa*, 3rd edn, Berkeley, Los Angeles and London.

Rosenberg, Marvin, 1972. *The Masks of King Lear*, Berkeley, Los Angeles and London.

Rothwell, Kenneth, 1999. *A History of Shakespeare on Screen*, Cambridge.

Salgādo, Gāmini, 1975. *Eyewitnesses of Shakesepare*, New York.

——, 1984. *King Lear: Text and Performance*, London.

Schmaltz, Wayne, 1985. 'Pictorial Imagery in Kozintsev's *King Lear*', *Literature/Film Quarterly*, XIII, 85–94.

Shattuck, Charles H., 1976. *Shakespeare on the American Stage: From the Hallams to Edwin Booth*, Washington.

Shaw, William P., 1986. 'Violence and Vision in Polanski's *Macbeth* and Brook's *Lear*', *Literature/Film Quarterly*, XIV, 211–13.

Sher, Antony, 1988. 'The Fool in *King Lear*', in Russell Jackson and Robert Smallwood, eds, *Players of Shakespeare 2*, Cambridge, 151–65.

Simon, John, 1964. 'Theatre Chronicle', *Hudson Review*, XVII, 421–30.

Sinfield, Alan, 1982. '*King Lear* versus *Lear* at Stratford', *Critical Quarterly*, XXIV.4, 5–14.

Smallwood, Robert, 1998. 'Shakespeare Performances in England [1997]', *Shakespeare Survey*, LI, 219–55.

Sokolyansky, Mark, 2000. 'Grigori Kozintsev's *Hamlet* and *King Lear*', in Russell Jackson, ed., *The Cambridge Companion to Shakespeare on Film*, Cambridge, 199–211.

Speaight, Robert, 1962. 'The Actability of *King Lear*', *Drama Survey*, II, 49–55.

——, 1963. 'Shakespeare in Britain', *Shakespeare Quarterly*, XIV, 419–32.

——, 1971. 'Shakespeare in Britain', *Shakespeare Quarterly*, XXII, 359–64.

Sprague, Arthur Colby, 1944. *Shakespeare and the Actors: The Stage Business in his Plays (1660–1905)*, Cambridge, MA.

——, 1953. *Shakespearean Players and Performances*, Cambridge, MA.

Sternfeld, F. W., 1963. 'Music in *King Lear* at the Royal Shakespeare Theatre', *Shakespeare Quarterly*, XIV, 486–7.

Stone, George Winchester, Jr, 1948. 'Garrick's Production of *King Lear*: A Study in the Temper of the Eighteenth Century Mind', *Studies in Philology*, XLV, 89–103.

Styan, J. L., 1977. *The Shakespeare Revolution*, Cambridge.

Trewin, J. C., 1971. *Peter Brook: A Biography*, London.

——, 1964. *Shakespeare on the English Stage 1900–1964*, London.

Tynan, Kenneth, 1994. *Letters*, ed. Kathleen Tynan, London.

Venezky, Alice, 1951. 'The 1950 Season at Stratford-upon-Avon – A Memorable Achievement in Stage History', *Shakespeare Quarterly*, II, 73–7.

Welsh, James M., 1976. 'To See It Feelingly: *King Lear* through Russian Eyes', *Literature/Film Quarterly*, IV, 153–8.

Wilds, Lillian, 1976. 'One King Lear for our Time: A Bleak Film Version by Peter Brook', *Literature/Film Quarterly*, IV, 159–64.

Williams, Harcourt, 1949. *Old Vic Saga*, London.

Williamson, Audrey, 1948. *Old Vic Drama*, London.

Worthen, William B., 1984. 'The Player's Eye: Shakespeare on Television', *Comparative Drama*, XVIII,193–202.

Yoshimoto, Mitsuhiro, 2000. *Kurosawa: Film Studies and Japanese Cinema*, n.p.

Yutkevich, Sergei, 1971. 'The Conscience of the King', *Sight and Sound*, XL, 192–6.

Zarrilli, Phillip, 1992. 'For Whom is the King a King? Issues of Intercultural Production, Perception, and Reception in a *Kathakali King Lear*', in Janelle G. Reinelt and Joseph R. Roach, eds, *Critical Theory and Performance*, Ann Arbor, 16–40.

INDEX